FRANS BLOM, MAYA EXPLORER

Frans Blom in his workroom, Uxmal, 1930. *Courtesy Middle American Research Institute, Tulane University*

FRANS BLOM, MAYA EXPLORER

Robert L. Brunhouse

UNIVERSITY OF NEW MEXICO PRESS

Albuquerque

Library of Congress Cataloging in Publication Data

Brunhouse, Robert Levere, 1908-
Frans Blom, Maya explorer.

Bibliography: p. 265
1. Blom, Frans Ferdinand, 1893-1963. I. Title.
F1435.B63B78   972   [B]   75-40833
ISBN 0-8263-0408-7

© 1976 by the University of New Mexico Press. All rights reserved.
Manufactured in the United States of America
Library of Congress Catalog Card Number 75-40833
International Standard Book Number 0-8263-0408-7
First edition

CONTENTS

Lists of Maps and Illustrations   vi

Acknowledgments   vii

Preface   ix

1   Frans Blom the Man   1

2   Apprenticeship   18

3   Launching a Career   40

4   The Department of
Middle American Research   68

5   The Expedition of 1928   88

6   From Success to Failure   114

7   The Uphill Climb   146

8   Interests and Activities   171

9   San Cristóbal—Home   200

Epilogue   237

Appendixes   241

   1   *Tata, a Prince of an Indian,*
by Frans Blom   243

   2   Louis Bristow, Jr.,
to his mother, May 6, 1928   251

   3   Don Carlos B.   255

Notes   259

Sources   265

Chronological Bibliography of Frans Blom   273

Index   285

ILLUSTRATIONS

Following page 82

1. Frans Blom, 1922
2. Temple of the Inscriptions, Palenque
3. Expedition of 1925
4. Stucco figure from Comalcalco
5. William E. Gates
6. Maya marble bowl
7. Louis Bristow, Frans Blom, and F. Webster McBryde
8. Members of the John Geddings Gray Memorial Expedition
9. Frans Blom, 1928
10. F. Webster McBryde
11. Louis Bristow
12. The Nunnery, Uxmal
13. Frans Blom, 1937
14. Museum, Department of Middle American Research
15. Frans Blom and friend, 1938

Following page 178

16. Frans Blom and an assistant, 1948
17. Frans Blom, 1948
18. Temple 33, Yaxchilán
19. Group at Na Bolom, early 1950s
20. Frans Blom in Lacandón jungle, 1951
21. Lacandón Indians
22. Zinacantán Indians
23. Chamula Indians
24. A Lacandón Indian
25. Frans Blom excavating, 1951
26. Frans Blom, Chiapas, 1948
27. San Cristóbal de las Casas
28. Na Bolom
29. Gertrude Duby Blom
30. Library, Na Bolom

Maps, following page xi

1. Route of the Tulane University Expedition of 1925
2. Area of the Tulane University Expeditions of 1928
3. Frans Blom's Explorations in Chiapas, 1943-63

ACKNOWLEDGMENTS

I am happy to acknowledge the kindness and cooperation of numerous persons who aided me in my research. Gertrude Duby Blom generously gave unrestricted access to the correspondence and diaries of Frans Blom at Na Bolom and also loaned numerous photographs. At Tulane University Robert Wauchope, until recently director of the Middle American Research Institute, and his assistant, Gertrude P. Brown, likewise opened the files of correspondence and photographs for my use, also without restriction of any kind.

I cannot detail the aid of many other persons, and I trust that they will understand my gratitude in listing their names: C. Prestiss Andrews, E. Wyllys Andrews V, Doris Antin, Anita Bayles, Alice Blengsli, Kathryn Davis, Gordon F. Ekholm, Arthur E. Gropp, Esther and Jorgen Kiaer, Gerhardt Kramer, Helge Larsen, Marjorie LeDoux, F. Webster McBryde, Vera Morel, Lillie Olsen, Ross Parmenter, Maurice Ries, Martha Robertson, Michael Thomason, Clarence W. Weiant, Doris Watt, Lee Woodward, and Sue Woodward.

I also made use of the resources of the following libraries: Brigham Young University, Free Library of Philadelphia, New York Public Library, Tulane University, University of Pennsylvania, University of South Alabama, and University of Texas.

PREFACE

The roster of Maya studies contains many fascinating personalities, ranging from Jean Frédéric Waldeck and Augustus Le Plongeon to Teobert Maler, Sylvanus Morley, and Herbert Spinden, to mention only some of the striking individuals who devoted themselves to the search for an understanding of the ancient Maya. In that roster one of the least known persons is Frans Blom (pronounced "Blahm," to rhyme with "calm"). Perhaps one should say that he is not completely known, because too many of his associates remembered only that he fell on evil days, and they dismissed him as a failure. The more remarkable part of the story, that is, what he did after he recovered from apparent failure, remains unknown or only dimly realized, and hence the full stature of the man has not been understood.

The sweep of his life, from birth in a wealthy home in Denmark to death in the highlands of Chiapas seventy years later, reveals an individual who tasted success, suffered from despair and degradation, and at the age of fifty began a second career from scratch. In that later period he came to grips with himself, attained maturity, and found satisfaction and fulfillment. The young people of today who believe in living one's own life according to the inner urges, striving for simplicity, escaping from the banalities of civilization, and coming closer to nature might well find a kindred spirit in Frans Blom, who followed a similar credo during the last decades of his life in a little-known region of Mexico.

His story provides a fascinating study in personality. Although he possessed marked natural gifts, he had to struggle endlessly, both when he followed his profession in the United States or while he carried on a freer, more congenial life among the fog-capped mountains of San Cristóbal at the entrance to the jungles of Chiapas,

Mexico. Although his life could be portrayed as an endless series of defeats, his eternal optimism carried him forward. As an archaeologist, he could not ignore the fact that only one of his numerous expeditions was ever fully reported in print. As the owner of Na Bolom, the unusual home he and his wife created for themselves, he could not deny that project after project to make it self-sustaining failed. Fortunately for his peace of mind, he was able to forget the disappointments and dwell on the satisfactions he enjoyed. He learned that every day brought its problems, even though he had achieved an existence close to utopian, according to his standards.

We cannot forget that Blom had to pass through several years of personal humiliation and emotional and physical suffering before he could achieve the clear perception of a proper goal, before he could attain a healthy attitude toward life and toward other people. Alcoholism dragged him into the depths for several years before he arose a new man. For the rest of his life he had to fight off the attractions of the bottle, and occasionally he succumbed.

Finally, it is interesting to realize that he revised his values after he moved to Mexico in 1943. Interest in nature and concern for people took first place. Although he continued to work in archaeology and built a research library, he put aside many of the values esteemed so highly in contemporary culture, including acclaim in his profession. Of course, he liked recognition for the work he did, but that took on incidental, not primary, significance. His manuscripts still lie unpublished on the shelves of his library at Na Bolom. Laborious projects like the elaborate map of Chiapas he prepared from firsthand experience in the region were never recognized, and his last book, *La selva lacandona*, written in collaboration with his wife, enjoyed only limited circulation. But if he grumbled a bit to friends about his disappointments, he was more interested in the natural beauty of his surroundings and in the welfare of the Indians he came to know so well. Frans Blom had found himself.

In indicating the sources I used in the preparation of this book, I have departed from general practice in several ways. To save embarrassment to living persons, I have not identified quotations from Blom's correspondence. Some of Frans's friends who provided confidential information wished to remain anonymous. When quoting from Frans's unpublished writings, I have occasionally added punctuation for clarity, though never sacrificing the spontaneity of his style.

I emphasize Blom's personality and character, and I attempt to present a fair picture of him, including human weaknesses as well as admirable characteristics. He did not excel in all directions, as we shall see, and those failures are duly noted. The various facets of his nature, however, make him an intriguing man.

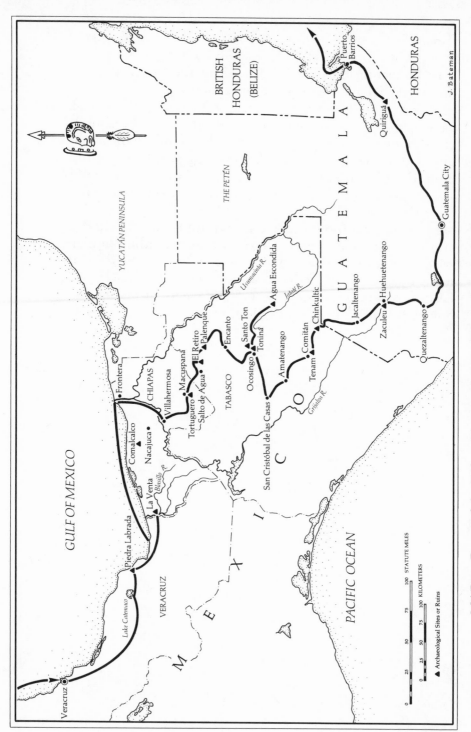

MAP 1 Route of the Tulane University Expedition of 1925 (adapted from Blom and La Farge, Tribes and Temples)

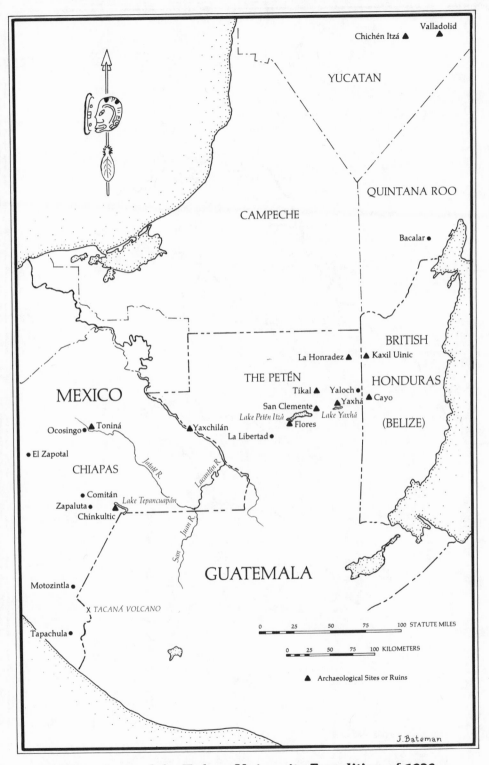

MAP 2 Area of the Tulane University Expedition of 1928

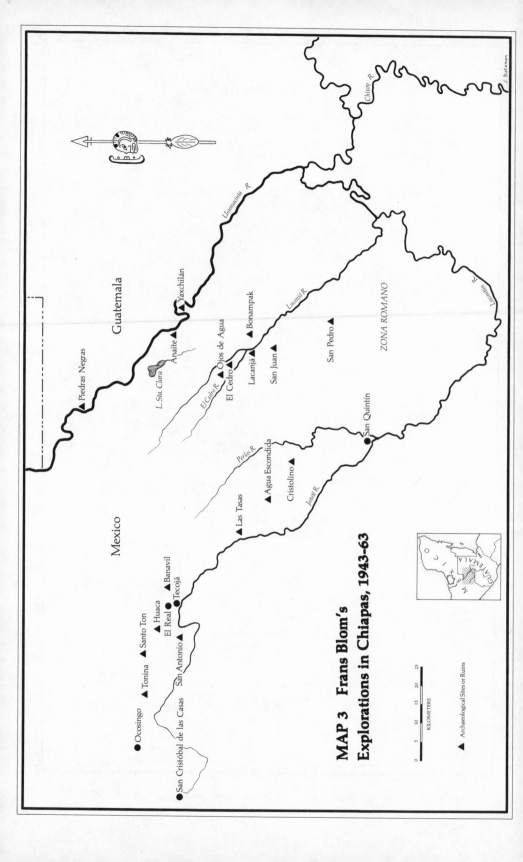

**MAP 3   Frans Blom's
Explorations in Chiapas, 1943–63**

Mexico

Guatemala

ZONA ROMANO

● Ocosingo
▲ Tonina
▲ Santo Ton
▲ Huaca
● El Real
▲ Banavil
▲ Tecojá
▲ San Antonio
● San Cristóbal de las Casas

Piedras Negras ▲

L. Sta. Clara
Anaite ▲
Yaxchilán ▲

El Cedro R.
El Cedro ▲
Ojos de Agua ▲
Bonampak ▲
Lacanjá ▲
San Juan ▲
San Pedro ▲

Perlas R.
▲ Las Tasas
▲ Agua Escondida
Cristolino ▲
San Quintín ●

Jataté R.

Usumacinta R.
Lacanjá R.
Lacantún R.
Chixoy R.

J. Bateman

0   5   10   15   20   25
KILOMETERS

▲ Archaeological Sites or Ruins

MEXICO
GUATEMALA

1

Frans Blom the Man

Frans Blom's personality was too varied and vibrant, his character too complex and dynamic to be summarized in a phrase or a sentence. Although he had many traits in common with other men, there was something unusual, distinctive, impressive about him. Although Blom was known as an archaeologist, explorer, author, and administrator, the most interesting aspects of the man were his personal traits. To add to the problem of characterization, he changed some of his views and attitudes in his later years. We can approach him only by describing the various facets of his nature.

Blom was a strikingly handsome man. Blond hair, sometimes flowing back over his head, and penetrating blue eyes reflected his Nordic origin. The attractive face became engaging when he smiled, and he retained a youthful appearance well into middle age. Although he was only five feet nine, most persons testify that he was tall; something about his presence seemed to add to his stature. Lean in build, he weighed 150 pounds, though he grew a bit heavier in later years. He gave the impression of being wiry and athletic, which suggested his remarkable physical endurance.

During the years he worked at Tulane University he was a dashing young man about town, already bearing the reputation of a romantic Viking explorer as a result of the expedition of 1925, which was widely reported in the newspapers. In social circles he conformed to current conventional styles in clothing, appearing not only neat but a bit dapper and modish. He displayed a different outfit, however, at the Department of Middle American Research at Tulane, where he was director for sixteen years. He seemed to fit into the atmosphere of the Central American exhibits, for he appeared in the garb of a Mexican peasant—a simple white cotton shirt and trousers, with a red sash about the waist.[1] In conformity with the custom of the day, he was clean shaven, though he usually grew a beard when out of the country on field expeditions. He slipped easily into casual informality if the opportunity appeared. When a newspaper artist accompanied him to his living quarters in 1929, Frans removed his gloves and jacket, pulled down his tie, opened his collar, rolled up his sleeves, and sat for the sketch.

Until he married, he lived in an apartment with relatively simple appointments. At first he resided at 1314 Audubon Street near the Tulane campus; in 1927 he moved to a larger apartment in the heart of the French Quarter, at 511 St. Ann Street, in the Pontalba row on Jackson Square. During his bachelor years the living room, where he entertained guests, displayed evidences of his profession—Maya decorations, pottery, textiles, photographs of Indians, and shelves of books and manuscripts. He admitted that he liked his apartment so much that he spent most of his evenings there in company with his library. After Frans had married, a reporter still found the living room overflowing with books in Spanish and English.

As a young man in the late 1920s and the 1930s, he cut a colorful figure in New Orleans. Many a young woman fluttered at the sight of him and hoped to attract his attention. He had an active social life, though only occasional glimpses of it have survived. Friends included faculty men as well as artists and writers from the French Quarter. In the late 1920s Sherwood Anderson, William Faulkner, William Spratling, who taught architecture at Tulane, and Lyle Saxon, a writer for a local newspaper at the time, were among the better-known denizens of the Quarter. At one dinner party Blom attended, Anderson and Spratling were guests. Later the group adjourned to Saxon's apartment and enjoyed "good talk and claret." On another occasion Saxon entertained Frans and a few other guests, and years later Frans recalled the occasion as "one of those rare evenings which are not forgotten." Sometimes Frans was a weekend guest at a friend's plantation or on a yacht. When he joined a dozen writers and artists for an excursion on Lake Pontchartrain, however, rain, mosquitoes, and engine trouble with the boat spoiled the fun.

Shortly after he came to New Orleans, he gained notice in a small book that originated in the Quarter. Faulkner and Spratling drew up a group of caricatures of interesting people in the city. Blom appeared in the third sketch, which showed him looking on from above, with a magnifying glass nearby, as he raised the thatched roof of a hut and a native girl fled from the scene. It bore the caption "Frans Blom the Tulane Champollion" (a reference to the decipherer of the Rosetta stone), suggesting that the searcher for glyphs also examined other things in Central America.[2]

With ease and confidence he associated with all kinds of people. He had friends in the New York social set, and he was equally at home with the Indians of Mexico and Guatemala. Although he appreciated the wealth and importance of certain persons, especially those who might become benefactors of the department at Tulane, he kowtowed to no one; in fact, a strong streak of independence ran through his character. There is no doubt that he was quick to detect human weaknesses, and sometimes he catered to those foibles. Once he bluntly advised an associate that the only approach to a certain wealthy woman was through the use of excessive attention and unabashed flattery.

Gallantry was second nature to him. At one social occasion he made a noble gesture to spare the feelings of a lady. On entering the room of his host, he placed his hat on a chair. Soon a young woman came into the room, sat on the hat, and crushed it. While she poured out apologies in embarrassment, he assured her that nothing was amiss; he crushed the hat in his hands, stuffed it into his pocket, and remarked, "It's that kind of a hat." She was immensely relieved.

A more striking example of gallantry occurred in 1927. Zelia Nuttall, the aging archaeologist who had befriended Frans when he arrived in Mexico in 1919, had fallen on hard times. Accustomed to wealth, she lived in the baronial Casa Alvarado in Coyoacán and had entertained leaders of social and political life. Blom helped her without embarrassing her. He invited her to New Orleans, installed her in the city's best hotel, and placed a chauffered car at her disposal. He arranged a lecture which brought her $100, and bought her copy of the Dresden Codex for Tulane. The following year he arranged another lecture, which produced a tidy honorarium, and he paid her $250 for the Breton reproduction of murals in the Temple of the Jaguars at Chichén Itzá. He knew how to aid the proud lady without compromising her dignity.[3]

The classic anecdote of his gallant thoughtfulness comes from his later life, when he and Trudi, his second wife, traversed the jungles of Chiapas. Following the trail in continual rain one afternoon, they paused on a riverbank. Everything was wet, and Trudi feared the ruin of their cameras, film, and notebooks. With tears coming to her eyes, she sat in despair at the foot of a tree. Suddenly Frans jumped into the river, swam to the far side, and returned to offer her a beautiful orchid. "My fair lady, this flower would cost many dollars in New York." "I gave a great laugh and felt much happiness," Trudi remembered. The muleteers brought up the cargo, the rain stopped, they made camp and refreshed themselves with hot coffee.

He could also be the perfect host. Friends have testified to the good times they enjoyed when visiting him. He quickly put the guest at ease and gave him considerate attention. He could adapt himself to the academics from the campus as well as to the less conventional friends from the Quarter. When he invited Hermann Beyer, a scholar in the department, for lunch, he told the cook to prepare for three, knowing that Beyer ate double portions of each dish.

He could exhibit an all-embracing spirit of generosity and goodwill. An employee of the department recalls his first interview. He found Frans "a youngish, pleasant, and vibrant individual, who extended me a pleasant welcome." He "put me at ease immediately, and after a short conversation took me around his beloved museum and library," and presented him with a copy of the two-volume *Tribes and Temples.* Blom whisked the young man off to his apartment and then to the famous Antoine's restaurant for an exotic meal. As they parted, Frans remarked casually, "I'll see you in September," which was more than an idle pleasantry, for the applicant soon received confirmation of his appointment. Juan Martínez Hernández, of Mérida, always remembered Blom's generous spirit in loaning him a rare book from the department and asking Hermann Beyer to make translations of German works to forward the Mexican scholar's research.

Although Frans liked certain persons and had a circle of friends, he showed only moderate interest in social and professional clubs. At times he attended luncheon meetings of the Harvard Club of New Orleans, and served as its vice-president and president. He was proud to be a member of the Explorers Club of New York and flew its pennant at every camp he set up during the expedition of 1928. A few years later, however, one of its policies disenchanted him, and he sent in a curt letter of resignation. A few years later he paid a sizable fee (for

that day) to become a member of the Century Club of
New York.

Good health and a strong physique were among his
assets. Like anyone, he had minor ailments to contend
with. Several times he contracted malaria in the Mexican
hinterland. While attending graduate school he suffered
a slight injury to his leg and then to his foot. The most
serious ailment, however, was sinus trouble, for which
he underwent several operations; he suffered from the
affliction at intervals in New Orleans and less frequently
in his later life. His physical condition was excellent. He
bounded up the sixty-nine steps to the fourth floor of the
building where the department was located, a climb
which evokes complaints of exhaustion from many
persons today. Expeditions in the field put his stamina to
the test. He shared the work of clearing the trail, guiding
the mules when it was necessary, and negotiating
difficult passages the entire day. One college boy who
accompanied him in 1928 devoutly wished that Frans
had not been so active. When Blom reached his fifties, as
we shall see, he continued to display remarkable endurance on the trail.

He liked cigarettes and liquor. He always smoked,
apparently rather heavily. A caller at his apartment in the
1930s found him "smoking Turkish cigarettes in rapid
succession and drinking cups of coffee." He continued to
smoke right up to his last illness, and was prevented
from indulging his habit then only because he was in an
oxygen tent. He engaged modestly in social drinking and
used liquor as a stimulant on expeditions. F. Webster
McBryde, one of his companions on the long, arduous
journey of 1928, testifies that "Blom always relished his
slug of aguardiente ('Comiteco' was the local name of our
'white-lightning' rum). But so did we all" at the end of a
hard day's work on the trail. "The Comiteco was a
life-saver; and the two little two-gallon kegs were our
most prized *subornal,* or top cargo. I would never say
that Blom was an alcoholic then, much as he liked his
several daily drinks." In fact he celebrated the last day of

that expedition in Mérida by buying one bottle of wine to be shared by the whole team at dinner.

In the late 1930s, however, he succumbed to alcoholism and suffered from its effects for several years. His strong-willed second wife helped him to curb the problem and fight the continuing temptation during the last decades of his life. There is a rumor that at one time he asked a donor not to advance all the money for an expedition at once, because he would be tempted to spend some of it on liquor.

At the age of thirty-nine, seven years after he came to Tulane, Blom married for the first time. In 1932 he escorted a group of society people on an excursion to Mexico. The party included three married couples and a number of unmarried women, including Matilda Gray, Mary S. Thomas, and Dorothy Dix, the well-known lovelorn columnist, whose real name was Mrs. E. M. Gilmor. Soon after Frans came to Tulane, he struck up an acquaintance with Miss Dix, sixty-six years old at the time, and described her as "a sweet old lady and very enthusiastic about our work" in the department.

As the best-known person in the party, Dorothy Dix gained the headlines in the newspapers. When the departure of the group was announced, New Orleans papers featured her and only listed the other members. In Mexico City Frans introduced her to a reporter, and in the resulting story she received almost as much attention as Blom. When the group returned to New Orleans, again she dominated the news story. "Going to Mexico with Frans Blom is like being shown over heaven by an archangel," she exclaimed, and then she reeled off all of the interesting things she had learned about the Maya. There was one item, however, which she did not tell.

On that trip Frans fell in love with nineteen-year-old Mary Thomas. Rumor has it that Dorothy Dix brought the two together. Mary came from a wealthy New York family that owned the Harriet Hubbard Ayers cosmetics company. She had acquired her education in the United

States and Europe, and was accustomed to an active
social life. Six weeks after she and Blom returned from
the trip, the engagement was announced. In the middle
of June they were married at Sefton Manor, the family
home on Long Island, with an Episcopal bishop presid-
ing at the garden ceremony and Archie Roosevelt, a
friend of Frans, as best man.

Mary came to live in New Orleans. An accomplished
pianist, she installed a grand piano in Frans's apartment
and redecorated those quarters in more feminine, formal
style. She also brought a maroon Isotta Frachini sports
car, which attracted attention. For some years it appears
that Mary and Frans were happy. She made some effort
to fit into the life of the city by seeking advice on social
practices from some of the staff members' wives. She
allowed her collection of original music scores by famous
composers to be exhibited at Tulane, and in time she
acquired a few pieces of Maya art. It seems, however,
that she did not understand her husband's friends,
especially the less conventional compatriots of the
French Quarter. Some persons considered her shy and
ungregarious in contrast with Frans. Although she was
absent for periods of time in the North and abroad, she
and Frans got along together remarkably well. He visited
her homes in New York and on Long Island, thoughtfully
ordered flowers for her and her mother on anniversaries,
and shared her interest in purchasing a house on St.
Peter Street in New Orleans (she left him before the
actual purchase took place).

During the marriage Frans became accustomed to a
more expensive style of life. Although he earned only a
modest salary, he enjoyed things associated with a much
larger income. He bought his calling cards at Cartier's in
New York, purchased expensive dishes in a fashionable
New York store, and joined his wife in giving an
anonymous gift of $1,000 to the department. He and
Mary enjoyed an extended stay in Europe in the summer
of 1933.

The foreign sports car was the talk of the town. When

it arrived by boat from New York two weeks after the wedding, a reporter described a policeman in Jackson Square showing it off to the local population "before it was locked up beside the owner's spouse's modest Chevrolet." The reporter could have added that Frans was paying for his own car in monthly installments. McBryde, who sometimes accompanied Blom in the Isotta, remembers the silver-inlaid running boards and "that radiator ornament that looked like a silver monument a block away." When Mary and Frans went to Europe in the summer of 1935, the car accompanied them at a cost of over three hundred dollars so that they could make long motor tours through the northern part of the continent.

The marriage failed in 1938. In May, Frans made reservations for Mary and him to go to Copenhagen two months later. In June something happened. Mary left him and in August secured a divorce in Reno on the grounds of cruelty. Friends gave various explanations for the separation. Frans's version appeared this way: "She wanted to live in New York in order to develop her voice and I had to stay with my job in New Orleans; so, as our interests were divergent, we felt it best to part." He vacated the third floor of the apartment on Jackson Square and, once more a bachelor, confined himself to the first and second floors.

It appears that an unfortunate aftermath of the divorce was Frans's inability to adjust to his modest income. It should be noted that in the early 1930s he voluntarily reduced his salary from $5,000 to $3,600 a year "to help our limited funds" in the department. After Mary left, friends believed that he could not retain money, that it slipped too easily through his fingers. If he had a spendthrift streak in his nature, it is unfortunate that the trait was encouraged during the few years of his first marriage.

The marital adventure had little apparent influence on Blom's work in the Middle American Research

Department. He had the ability to get the most from his staff. His enthusiasm—"This is the most fascinating job in the world"—infused those who worked for him. When he was out of the city on business, he received detailed reports of everything that occurred. If a deadline had to be met, one or more workers willingly labored at night to complete the job. By accident or design he allowed each individual as much latitude as possible in carrying out assigned tasks. It should be added that he defended his workers and gave them strong recommendations when they decided to leave.

His authority in the department showed itself in small ways. Although he was on a first-name basis with friends, he insisted that his workers address him as Don Pancho, a Mexican abbreviation of Francisco, the nearest approximation to his name of Frans. The only exception was Mrs. Doris Stone, daughter of Samuel Zemurray, who endowed the department; he and she used first names. When an assistant wrote to Frans and signed himself "your subordinate," Blom replied, "I don't like the idea of 'subordinates.' 'Associates' suits me much better. We are mules pulling the same cart. I'm just the lead-mule."

The members of the several expeditions sent out by Tulane were also "mules pulling the same cart," and Blom found a way to give them a feeling of identity with a common project. In 1931 he had a number of small emblems made, each one bearing the letters "TUX" (Tulane University Expedition). To every participant in those journeys he presented the emblem, with the man's name and year of the venture engraved under the letters.

He himself was a hard worker. At least during the first year at Tulane he sometimes labored at night in the department and occasionally four or five hours on Sundays. He drew up endless reports to secure grants from foundations. Trips to northern cities to continue good relations with other museums and to give illustrated lectures to potential donors were run-of-the-mill duties which he assumed. If he ever complained about overwork, it did not creep into his writings. His correspondence as director—and it is voluminous—always reflects the confidence of an administrator in command of the situation.

His sense of humor sometimes had a peculiar twist, if the few examples that have come to light are typical. He christened his bachelor apartment "Bumbay" because of the bums its sheltered—actually a reference to respectable friends who found hospitality there when they stopped over in the city. The title page of his diary of the 1925 expedition bears the legend, "Five Months in Hell, or with Blom in the Maya Area." In fact, he relished the difficulties and enjoyed every moment of the journey. He probably had a hand in the joke his men played on Sylvanus Morley in 1930. Morley headed the archaeological project at Chichén Itzá sponsored by the Carnegie Institution of Washington and had money available for some civilized amenities. When Frans's team from Uxmal visited Chichén for dinner, the men noted that the linen napkins bore the insignia of the Carnegie Institution. When the Tulane men returned the favor and had Morley and his men to Uxmal for dinner, Blom's assistants made a point of displaying toilet-paper napkins bearing the initials "TUX" for Tulane University Expedition.

In expressing anger or disgust, Frans could use the stiletto phrase. When he failed to receive an item requested from Washington, he wrote: "I must express my admiration for the lack of efficiency with which the Government Printing Office handles the orders it receives. . . ." He resigned from the Recess Club in New Orleans because the food dispensed at the St. Charles Hotel, a well-known hostelry of the city, "is worse than what is served at a thirty-five-cent hash-house." On several occasions when an editor of a journal mislaid a review Blom had written, he indicated that he would have nothing to do with the magazine in the future.

There was also a moody side to Blom that friends sometimes found difficult to understand. In his relations

with Oliver La Farge, as we shall see, he alternated
between appreciation and sharp criticism. At Uaxactún in
1924 Oliver Ricketson and A. Monroe Amsden found him
unpleasant during the hours after work. Several of the
book reviews he wrote were unnecessarily biting, even
after Professor Tozzer showed him how to tone down the
language. Although Sylvanus Morley had generously
helped him to get a start in archaeology, Frans became
critical of his mentor, and once wrote him a letter of
unmerited abuse. Blom had strong likes and dislikes, as
do most men; it appears, however, that he did not make
an effort to suppress his feelings.

There was another side of the coin, for Blom made it a
point to encourage certain promising young men. From
the time he took on Arthur Gropp, then in his mid
twenties, as librarian of the department, he put him on
his own initiative and gave him tasks to carry out in his
own way. In later years Frans secured a grant which sent
Gropp to Central America for seventeen months to
survey the library and archival resources of those
countries.

Frans also encouraged F. Webster McBryde and
Gerhardt Kramer, both Tulane students when he first
employed them. He chose McBryde as photographer on
the expedition of 1928. After the young man
demonstrated that he could take good pictures, Blom
gained respect for him, later employed him for a year at
the department, and then strongly recommended him for
a better job. Kramer, an outstanding student at the
Tulane School of Architecture, joined the expedition to
Uxmal in 1930. Frans thought so highly of him that he
kept him on at the department for years, making models
of the Nunnery and then of the Castillo. When the
Oberlaender Trust (Carl Schurz Foundation) invited
Frans to study museums in Europe in 1936, he
generously had Kramer sent in his place, raised his
salary twenty-five dollars a month, and had him
entertained at his wife's home at Sefton Manor, Long
Island, while Kramer waited for the boat. When the

young man poured out his appreciation of the favors, Blom stopped him with, "Now, don't you thank me for the Germany trip. You know that I always consider you fellows as sort of children of mine, and spend more time than any of you know thinking of ways to make things go well for all of us."[4]

There were times when Frans stood on formality and protocol, usually as a form of self-defense. When he left Mexico for Guatemala in 1925, he insisted on receiving a document which declared that he took no artifacts with him. Sometimes he turned to immediate action. New Orleans authorities sent him a bill for a license to operate a horse and cart; asserting that he had never owned a horse and cart, he ordered the police department to find and prosecute the impostor who used his name. A young woman whose attentions he rebuffed charged him with being a drug addict. At once he warned her to desist, threatening that he would have a doctor examine him so that he could prosecute her for a false statement. When he worked in Mexico for an oil company, he was given the job of paymaster for a large number of men. According to one story, bandits held him up and demanded the money he carried. With no choice, he countered: "All right, I'll give it to you, but you give me a receipt." And they did!

Blom's natural gifts did not include the ability to speak effectively to large audiences. Although he could be loquacious and entertaining in a small circle of friends, he froze up on the public platform. In New Orleans he appeared before small groups, but not as often as one might expect for a man with the reputation of an explorer. Sometimes he attempted to couch his theme in a striking title, such as "History in the Garbage Can." For professional groups, he prepared the text of his remarks and carefully chose topics suitable to the interest of the audience. Unlike Sylvanus Morley, who gained wide popularity for the entertaining way he could present a complex subject like Maya glyphs, Blom was uncomfortable on the public platform.

He had no standard fee for a lecture. In 1931 he charged $175 to speak in Shreveport, Louisiana, and $50 for each additional lecture. In the following year he quoted $500 as his price to speak outside of New Orleans, which can be interpreted as a device to discourage invitations. By 1938 he was willing to accept $30 at Brookhaven, Mississippi, and explained that the fee depended on the size of the audience and the relative wealth of the community. Had he possessed the gift of entertaining and effective public speaking, his entire future might have been different.

Blom spoke a number of languages. English, French, German, and Danish he acquired in his youth. On going to Mexico in 1919, he quickly picked up Spanish, though there were serious flaws in the vocabulary he learned. In 1924, when he addressed a letter to "Señora Marguerite," he observed, "that's about as far as I dare write in Spanish. I can speak it, but as I have learned the most of it from muleteers, I am always afraid that some bits of profanity should creep in." When he held a minor governmental job in Mexico, he had all of his written Spanish reviewed by a native. In time, however, he mastered the language. "His Spanish was perfect, colloquial," McBryde remembers, "and he loved to tell jokes in the most idiomatic Spanish, often the double-meaning, sometimes off-color variety." He could, moreover, move easily from Spanish to English, German, French, or Danish, "two or three smoothly going at once."

If he had the choice of languages, he preferred to use English, which he also spoke without an accent. Two decades of residence in the United States equipped him with a perfect understanding of all levels of the language from profanity to formal usage. In fact, for some years after he moved to Mexico in 1943, he continued to use English in the records of his expeditions. He began the diary of a 1948 journey in Spanish, but after some sixty pages reverted to English.

When he wrote English, he tended to reproduce the

conversational aspects of the language. Occasional errors in grammar and sentence structure led some friends to believe that he lacked a college education. It is more likely that he had little interest in academic formality. Although he read books, it was the content, not the style, that he sought. He seemed to be on guard when he wrote for publication, and the result was a loss of spontaneity. It would be unfair to belittle his style, for some of his articles are models of simplicity. He was at his best, however, in letters and diaries not written for publication, which sometimes display unusual force and pungency.

One of the traits that gave Frans the power to push ahead in the face of obstacles was the combination of self-confidence and optimism. His early life from the time he went to Mexico in 1919 until he assumed charge of the department at Tulane in 1926 gave him good reason for strong confidence in himself, for he succeeded in every task he undertook. That success in turn supported his natural optimism that everything would turn out right.

On rare occasions he stretched his confidence too far. During the expedition of 1928, when he had two college boys with him, the exploring team ran into a mountain barrier in Chiapas. Blom refused to retreat, and only by good luck did the men finally find a way around the barrier. Later Blom confessed his foolhardiness. "I really think I was darned glad to be out with the boys safe; that is between us, though," he reminded a friend; "it was more serious in there in the forest than the boys will ever realize, and than I will want to tell about. I got a severe course in responsibility, which I hope has done me some good." His confidence and optimism played him false during the unfortunate period from 1940 to 1943, when he succumbed to alcoholism. He told himself that he could conquer the problem, and he was incorrect.

In the long run, however, confidence and optimism helped rather than hindered him. Those traits carried him over many disappointments, kept his outlook bright, and put the best face upon unpleasant situations. One cannot imagine Blom without those qualities, for they were an integral part of his nature.

Equally a part of his nature was a strong aesthetic appreciation, which found outlets in his love of natural beauty and the art of the Maya. If his early study of European art was a tentative attempt to satisfy that inward feeling, it failed. From his first travels in Mexico, however, he could not forget the grandeur of the landscape and the peace and consolation he experienced as he moved along the trail, surrounded by the wonderful creations of nature. As the years passed, the records of his expeditions contained an increasing amount of natural description. In Chiapas he considered the ruins of the ancient Maya and the presence of contemporary Indians a part of the landscape. McBryde recalls Frans's reactions: "The way he would suck in his breath, the ohs and ahs in response to the beauty of Maya art, of a sunrise on a volcano, his deep feeling for the Indians, his great love of the land, of living off the land, were all the feelings of a true artist." Blom expressed his feeling succinctly when a journalist asked him if he was lonely in the jungle. "Lonely!" he exclaimed. "The day I start off on my expedition is the happiest day in my life. After that there is no time to be lonely."

Not only was he at home in the forests of Mexico, but he preferred life there to the hectic pace of urban civilization. He carried no firearms unless he had to hunt for food. As far as he was concerned, the forests were not only beautiful, they were safe. When an insurance company asked him about dangers of travel in the backcountry, he replied that he could not understand why explorers were unable to secure insurance, "as I must admit that I feel myself safer when I am traveling through the jungles of Central America, days away from cities and people, than when I have to cross one of our ordinary streets. . . ."

The highlands of Chiapas attracted Blom from the first

time he visited the region in 1922. Later trips to the area refreshed his spirits and confirmed his love for the area. He "was a creature of the jungle," according to his friend McBryde; "only there or dreaming and talking of those spellbinding lands was he really ecstatic." When events prevented him from returning to Mexico in the 1930s, his spirits slumped. He must return to Chiapas—the mist-covered mountain tops, the untamed country, and the Indians, patient in their work and colorful in their costumes. He longed to live there, an aim which he fulfilled only in 1950.

Blom's personal traits explain much of his success. They also explain in part how he rose from failure at the age of fifty and proceeded to build a second career. The explanation is not quite that simple, however, for he also reacted to his environment—to people, places, and situations. We shall now follow the story of Frans and his environment and learn how he eventually achieved a satisfying life.

2

Apprenticeship

Two of Blom's personal traits were important in shaping his apprenticeship, which began in Mexico, in 1919. Artistic urges and self-confidence guided him from youthful adventure to professional commitment. In the forests of Mexico he found natural beauty to satisfy his soul; in the art of the ancient Maya he discovered man-made aesthetic expression to arouse his amazement; and strong self-confidence led him into the study of archaeology and introduced him to leaders in the field. One might easily conclude that the choice he made was foreordained, because professional archaeology combined love of nature and curiosity about the Maya. Blom's career, however, was not a simple product of determinism. He had the ability and aspiration to make contributions to knowledge, and so he submitted to the discipline required to enter the profession of archaeology.

Frans enjoyed far more than ordinary advantages in the affluent home in which he was reared in Denmark. His father, Albert, had graduated in law from the national university, married Dora Petersen, daughter of the director of H.C. Petersen and Company, and soon became a member of the firm. The company imported and sold machinery for International Harvester. Frans was born in 1893, and was reared, along with his two sisters, Esther and Vera, in a wealthy home where proper breeding and good taste were the rule. The children learned English, French, and German; one language was spoken exclusively for two days each week, with native Danish allowed only on Sunday. Frans earned high grades at Rungsted preparatory school, on the coast north of Copenhagen, and went on to the liberal arts college of the University of Copenhagen, where he received the degree of bachelor of philosophy. In later years he liked to boast that he had studied under Harald Höffding, noted Danish philosopher.

Sometime during the First World War Blom fulfilled his compulsory military service in the Danish navy. His reason for choosing this branch of the service is not clear. The only known result of the experience was his lifelong habit of tying ropes with the peculiar knot he learned on shipboard. A later archaeologist testified that it was "a good safe hitch" for a hammock.[1]

An interest in art directed him to courses in the Museum of Arts and Crafts in Copenhagen, where he cultivated his ability to draw. Later on, he sometimes remarked that he had been a student under Emil Hanover, director of the Art Gallery in Copenhagen.

The chronological order of Frans's activities during the early period of his life is confused, so that it is impossible to determine the exact sequence of events. His father made strong efforts to train him for the family business by requiring him to undertake commercial education and to work for a time in the firm. But all to no avail, for the young man showed a strong distaste for the daily routine of costs, sales, and profits.

Unable to interest him in the family business which he was expected to join, his father gave him the opportunity to find a congenial vocation. Frans traveled through Belgium, Germany, France, and Italy, reading in libraries

and studying art in the famous galleries. He explained in
later years that he "dedicated considerable time to the
study of European art. . . ." It may be unfair to question
the value of his peregrinations in search of an understanding of the history of art, but his efforts left no dis-
cernible effects in later life. Perhaps he developed a
sharper artistic awareness, which led him to appreciate
the aesthetic achievement of Maya art. Although he assembled a small collection of colonial Mexican religious
paintings near the end of his life, that form of art did not
greatly appeal to him. If he possessed inherent artistic
ability, he expressed it almost entirely in sketching artifacts and inscriptions on Maya monuments. Those performances are good, serviceable, and pleasant to look at,
but hardly outstanding. The only artwork he seems to
have produced for the sheer joy of it are several small
watercolors he made in the Southwest in the summer of
1924. We may surmise that his wanderings from city to
city in northern Europe appealed to youthful wanderlust
as much as to the search for knowledge.

On his return to Copenhagen he failed to solve the
problem of choosing a career. For a short time he bought
and sold antiquities, a venture in which he lost money
and had to be bailed out by his father. He is said to have
associated with young blades of the city in regular
meetings in the garden of the Hôtel d'Angleterre and
engaged in youthful pranks and escapades. From what
we know of Frans, he was certainly capable of those
activities, but the report comes from only one
secondhand source and has been repeated without
confirmation.

After he reached the age of twenty-five, some crisis
changed the course of his life. According to family
tradition, he left the country because he was unable to
find a suitable position in Denmark.[2] It is said that his
parents gave him sufficient money to return home in the
event that he failed to find a job to support himself.
Perhaps his father, seeing his son in his mid twenties
without a job and refusing to enter the family business,

told him to make his own way. Whatever his reasons for leaving home, he maintained friendly relations with his parents. A lengthy diary that he kept in Mexico was designed to tell the family of his adventures. When a friend of Frans visited the Bloms in Denmark in 1924, he found the father proud of his son's achievements.

There is evidence of a strong attachment between Frans and his mother. In the fall of 1925 Mrs. Blom came to the United States to visit her son. Unfortunately, she was ill on shipboard and during her stay here. Frans brought her from New York to New Orleans and installed her in his apartment. She found the Negroes a strange part of the population and considered Frans's friends in the French Quarter unconventional. It seems that she was not quite certain that he was headed in the right direction. When she left, she pled with a young woman who worked for Frans to "take care of my son." In 1930, when she became seriously ill, Frans traveled all the way to Denmark to get to her bedside. She recovered and lived until 1933. She left him a small bequest, which he did not receive until 1950.

Blom's relations with his father are more difficult to estimate. After the death of Mrs. Blom, Frans visited his father a number of times, and planned to have him journey to the United States and Mexico. There were, however, signs of irritation on Frans's part. Several years after the young man left home and was desperately short of money, he blurted out to a friend, "I would rather go brick laying than ask for money from my family." In the 1950s, after his father had died, Frans remarked that the family company had been reorganized and that the 400 kroner he held in it had been wiped out. "That's nice," he remarked sarcastically. "I don't argue, but such things sort of put the family bonds at a distance." Perhaps his failure to share in the family fortune created some resentment.

The years of carefree life ended when he went to Mexico to find himself and to make his own way. At first, his travels appeared to be a continuation of wanderlust.

As we shall see, however, he emerged from the Mexican experience with two major interests that guided him through his later years.

In Mexico Frans started at the bottom and moved up without the aid of his family name. On arriving in the capital, he made friends easily and looked for a job, hoping to find one that would take him into the backcountry. While he waited for the right opportunity, he made the most of his leisure time. A few days after arriving, he bought a copy of T. A. Joyce's *Mexican Archaeology,* the earliest indication of his interest in the ancient civilizations of that country. With some boldness he wrote a note to Mrs. Zelia Nuttall, the well-known archaeologist, who lived in a suburb of the capital, and she responded with an invitation to tea. Early in 1919, however, archaeology was a luxury Frans could not afford, for he had to find a job.

He worked at temporary assignments for several months. He and an American spent a brief period in the mountains, supervising Indians and mules in transporting machinery to a silver mine. Another temporary job took him to the country east of Mexico City, where he supervised natives in reclaiming abandoned railroad track. He learned to eat tortillas and beans, work in the scorching sun, and sleep at night in frost-tinged forests. He learned also to beware of the raiding bands of rebels that infested parts of the country; once he refused to carry on a job because insurgents were too close for comfort.

On these early ventures he became acquainted with the Indians firsthand and admired their sterling qualities. Each native cargador, or carrier, bore a load on his back, supported by a strong band around the forehead. Because of the weight he bent his body a bit forward and traveled at a trot hour after hour with little rest. Each man received fifty centavos a day. Frans found the natives well behaved and polite; they made no demands and exhibited unbelievable physical endurance.

After completing a number of temporary tasks, he

secured a permanent job in the fall of 1919 with the Eagle Oil Company at Minatitlán in southern Veracruz on the Coatzacoalcos River. The place bristled with oil tanks, pipes running in all directions, boiler houses, and pumping stations. Some distance away on higher ground stood the company town of one-story brick houses, where he had a comfortable room and bath, with cross ventilation. He became paymaster for 3,000 native workers and 200 engineers and office employees. After several months the routine office work bored him, and he asked for an outside job. Perhaps his superior smiled when he assigned him to travel through the hinterland, which entailed more trouble, inconvenience, and danger than work in the paymaster's office.

Frans considered it an answer to a prayer to be able to travel through the wild country. He was assigned to locate abandoned oil wells and to place them on the map for possible development after the country achieved internal stability. One trip took him up the Uspanapa River to a region no foreigner had visited for eleven years. Did he fear those journeys into the unknown? Never! The experiences provided the adventure he sought. As time passed, he was detailed to more distant areas, some of them unknown even to the oil company men. Once he stayed at Tecuanapa in a palm hut for several months. He tamed some squirrels from the forest, spent days alone traveling through the woods and nights in the hut, pondering on what he had seen. The luxuriant exuberance of the forest, with its birds and animals, directed his thought to the perfect arrangement of self-perpetuating nature; he admitted that concern over the petty details of his own life or that of any other individual appeared insignificant in view of the grand design of nature. The new way of life agreed with him, for he enjoyed good health and a good disposition.

By 1922 the oil company sent him to more distant parts of the country. The first journey of that year took him through the western area of Tabasco with a Filipino assistant. They scaled mountains, gazed down on the

ocean of forest below, camped in the open, drank hot
cocoa under the stars, and then wrapped themselves in
raincoats and slept soundly. Traversing a -circular route,
they returned to the Gulf Coast.

The second expedition of 1922, and the last one Blom
made for the oil company, led him directly into his profession. He accompanied a party of geologists who
worked for the oil company. They left Frontera on the
Gulf Coast, struck south into the Tenosique-Ocosingo region, and then cut through the middle of the state of
Chiapas to the Pacific Coast.

After the party sailed from Frontera to Tenosique,
where the land expedition would begin, Blom had the
opportunity to demonstrate his ability at organization. A
local representative of the oil company in Tenosique had
two weeks' advance notice to assemble horses and
supplies. Frans, however, found everything amiss. The
horses were six miles out in the country and the saddles
were in tatters. He got things moving fast. When the
animals were brought to town, eight had to be sold
because they were sick, and new mounts had to be
bought at high prices. He put natives to work mending
the saddles. He packed provisions for six weeks of travel.
Within two days he had everything in readiness. After
the chief of the local garrison insisted on giving a
farewell party for the visitors, the expedition got off.

Blom was alive to everything in sight. One afternoon
the party arrived at the hacienda of Santa Margarita; a
heavy-set, jovial lady invited them in for refreshments.
In a formal living room they received a sickly sweet
drink, watched a child drive a flock of geese through the
room, and observed three shy daughters peek from
behind doors at the visitors. After they left, Frans
learned that the lady was not married, and he remarked
that it did not matter, for she had beautiful daughters.
The travelers entered Ocosingo on Good Friday. A
stuffed figure of Judas hung outside the church, to be
burned on Easter Sunday, and Indians prayed in the
dark interior of the building in a blue haze of burning

incense. Later in the day Frans spent some time in the plaza, observing the Indians—tall, strongly built men with dull expressions, and women, small but strong, each mother carrying a child held by a shawl over her back. A German in town insisted on housing the visitors, a friendly invitation which Blom later regretted accepting because the man talked so much.

Frans's spirits increased as the party proceeded over mist-capped mountains and precipitous trails toward Palenque, fabulous city of the ancient Maya. At last he saw the ruins at a distance, with forest-covered mountains on one side and on the other flat lands sprinkled with lagoons that appeared like patches of silver in the forest. Already well read in Maya archaeology, he spent an exciting day at the site, examining the old structures at first hand. In the Palace he admired the stucco reliefs and praised the architectural perfection of the building. The Temples of the Sun, the Cross, and the Foliated Cross also elicited his admiration, as did the aqueduct, which led a stream away from the foundations of the structures. One glorious day at Palenque—what better introduction to the ancient Maya!

For Frans, Palenque was the highlight of the entire expedition. From there he and the oil men traveled north to Macuspana and then turned south, passing through Tila, Simojovel, and Tuxtla Gutiérrez to Arriaga, near the Pacific Coast. There they took a train for the return trip to Puerto México on the Gulf Coast.[3] After some ten days Blom fell sick with malaria. Despite doses of quinine, he failed to recover, so he went to Mexico City for medical treatment, and voluntarily ended his employment with the oil company.

The forty months Blom spent in Mexico from 1919 to the middle of 1922 appear at first glance to be no more than a period of adventure in an exotic land. That is the picture he chose to present in the book *I de Skore Stove*, which he wrote to appeal to young men. Those years can be viewed as a continuation of the wanderlust he apparently indulged in Europe. If so, wanderlust paid off, for he discovered the interest he wished to follow and soon found his way into archaeology as a profession.

As he recovered from malaria in Mexico City, he made the most of the metropolis. Manuel Gamio, the head of the Dirección de Antropología, was a scholar of repute who had just gained his doctorate from Columbia University with an outstanding study of the Valley of Teotihuacán. He could recognize scholarly attributes in others, and was eager to advance scientific studies in his native land. Blom sought him out and placed his notebooks and photographs in his hands. The neat sketches and careful observations impressed Gamio, and the pictures created interest among other members of the department. Remarking that Frans was worth more to archaeology than to the oil business, Gamio offered him a job in the Dirección, though at a lower salary than he had received from the oil company. Soon he was assigned to go to Palenque to investigate the preservation of the monuments.

Before undertaking the new task, Frans made good use of the several months he remained in the capital. Back in May 1922 he had visited Tortuguero and copied glyphs he found there on a stela. In Mexico City he looked through the journal *Ethnos* and discovered that an article on Tortuguero by Ramírez Garrido, who had visited the site seven years earlier, made no mention of the stela. So Blom wrote to Sylvanus Morley, enclosing a copy of the inscription and asking for his interpretation of it. That action demonstrated that Frans knew exactly what he was doing. Morley, thirty-nine years old at the time, was emerging as the leading scholar of Maya hieroglyphs. He had trained at Harvard, secured a post with the Carnegie Institution of Washington, and had spent a decade collecting date glyphs in annual expeditions to the Petén and Yucatán. In a few months he would be negotiating a contract between Mexico and the C.I.W. to create a vast archaeological project at Chichén Itzá. Morley was astonished at the accuracy of the transcription by an unknown amateur. He read the date as A.D. 386; and he found the glyphs interesting enough to pass on to Professor Alfred M. Tozzer of Harvard, academic high priest of Maya studies in the United States. Frans also renewed his acquaintance with Zelia Nuttall and brought his sketch of the glyphs to her attention; she sent the drawing on to the American Anthropological Society. She also made her excellent library· available for his use. Later on, Frans looked back on her as the one who "first encouraged me to study Middle American archaeology."

At this time he also prepared his earliest articles for publication. Perhaps with the encouragement of Gamio, who served as editor of *Ethnos,* Blom wrote a short account of the stela at Tortuguero. Although he condemned Garrido in private for a poor job of investigation, he refrained from criticism in the article.[4] This was Blom's first publication on Maya archaeology. He also prepared a brief paper on a detail of folklore in Tecuanapa which appeared a few months later in the *Journal of American Folk-Lore.*

Morley was excited over the young man who, though only an amateur, appeared to know his way around Maya archaeology. Frans provided him with a modest account of his years with the oil company. He had been á "sort of . . . handyman attached to geological parties. . . . But my heart is with the archaeology, and every moment I can spare I have been nosing after ruins, etc." Traveling through the forest "day after day I noted down what I saw, be it the customs of the Indians, myths, or archaeological remains. Often I was sent out alone to collect information of oil seepages. The life in those parts charmed me, took more and more hold of me, and finally the [tropical] fever got me. I went to this town [Mexico City] to get fixed up, and have now left the famous oil game to be able to give all my time to the study of the secrets of southern Mexico and its Indians."

Morley was eager to meet the Dane, but months passed before the two men could find a time when both

were in Mexico City. Morley was dashing about, negotiating the contract with the Mexican government, and the
Dirección sent Blom to Palenque on special assignment.

Frans was thrilled with his first job as an archaeologist.
The day's visit to Palenque in April 1922 had provided
no more than an overall view of the site. Now, beginning
in December 1922, he spent over three months there to
find ways to preserve the structures. "The first visit to
Palenque is immensely impressive," he observed.
"When one has lived there for some time this ruined city
becomes an obsession."

Although the Palace intrigued him again, this time he
was aware of details. He found the main court enclosed
by buildings, "with their roofs covered with clusters of
wild pink begonias. From in among the shrubbery,
which covers the floor of the court, stare faces of crudely
carved gods, and right in front lies a stairway with
excellently carved hieroglyphs on its steps. It is a fairy
tale palace beyond description." On wandering through
the structure, he discovered that "water drips from the
roofs, and clouds of bats flash by as my echoing steps
disturb them. Stairways and dark passages lead to
subterranean galleries."

Although he had been sent to find ways to preserve
the buildings, curiosity led him to examine every part of
the site. On some structures he found traces of original
paint, preserved in protected spots. "The Maya temples,
like the Greek," he concluded, "were painted in many
colors, among which deep red was predominant." He
excavated every burial that had been disturbed by nature
or by fortune seekers. In following the aqueduct, he
found an elaborate drainage system and evidences of
bridge constructions over creeks.

In several instances he made interesting judgments.
The stucco tablet of the Beau Relief, made famous by
Jean Frédéric Waldeck's drawing in the 1830s, had
disappeared except for a small portion at the bottom.
Despite the criticism that the French artist read too
much of his own feeling into the picture, Blom studied
the remains carefully, and was "inclined to believe that

Waldeck's drawing is essentially correct." Two carved stone tablets had been taken from the site and placed in the wall of the church in the village, and archaeologists disagreed as to which temple they had come from. By measuring the tablets and the empty panels on the front walls of the three major temples, Frans determined that the tablets belonged to the Temple of the Cross.

In another instance, however, he failed to follow a lead, one that explorers before him had also ignored. In the Temple of the Inscriptions, he found the floor "made of huge stone slabs, of which one has two rows of perforations, which used to be closed with stone plugs." Unable to imagine what these holes were intended for, he passed on to other things. A quarter of a century later Alberto Ruz Lhuillier saw the same curious slab, raised it, discovered a subterranean stairway filled with rubble, and eventually uncovered sixty feet below the temple floor the finest Maya tomb in Middle America.

Blom also spent much time in preserving the structures. In the beginning he "found the ruins in a bad state, all covered with dense bush, the so-called caretaker and his peons living a lazy life in the village." After two weeks of work, "the buildings start to show up. . . . But how to protect them? I think the only thing to do will be to clear the roofs, and cover them with a coating of mortar, so that rain and roots will not be able to enter from above. Moisture is doing more damage than anything else."

The task of preservation required nice judgment. When he discovered that the mortar of a temple was of poor grade and the glyphs were falling, he removed the inscription and placed it on a table in a makeshift museum he had set up near the Palace. At the Temple of the Inscriptions, where deterioration had already begun, he took no action. "During the visit of a former Mexican Government Inspector of Monuments, these tablets were washed with an acid, with the fatal result that the inscriptions are now peeling off. I did not touch these tablets for fear of furthering their destruction."

After carrying on some repairs, he began to appreciate

how much manpower had gone into the original construction of the edifices. When he needed lime to reinforce the roof combs of two temples, he had natives build kilns to burn wood and stone. The operation revealed that "though we laboured hard for about a week, only a comparatively small amount of lime was produced. This made me realize what an enormous amount of labour it must have required to produce sufficient mortar for all the great buildings of this city."

Under his guidance, restoration assumed several meanings. When reinforcing the roof combs, he was careful not to engage in restoration, that is, he did not supply missing parts of the structures. Loose and fallen stones were put into place and fastened, but no additions were made. In quite a different way, however, he "restored" a number of objects to the site. On learning that a former caretaker, then living in the village, had appropriated objects from the ruins and secreted them in his house, Frans seized them. "I had quite a time making the old man deliver the different objects he was holding. I wonder how much he sold to visitors. It took seven men, well loaded, to carry away the items I took from him."

On his return from Palenque, Blom had his first meeting with Morley on Friday, April 6, 1923 in the lobby of the St. Regis Hotel in Mexico City. In retrospect, it was a historic occasion in Frans's life. Morley had already questioned Gamio about the young man and received a favorable report, especially about Frans's enthusiasm for his work. When Morley walked into the hotel lobby, he had no trouble recognizing Blom. He saw a blond young man with a longish face, blue eyes, a lean body, and an elegant appearance.

They hit it off from the start. Morley, an enthusiast for things Maya, could not help but respond to Frans's zealous interest in his archaeological work. After lunch they visited the National Museum, where Blom pointed out some carved stones from Ocosingo. Morley was delighted, for in his widespread search for date glyphs he had missed the Chiapas region. Then they went to Blom's room, where Morley marveled at the notebooks—the sketches were neatly drawn and the descriptive text concise—and listened as Frans described the two new temples he had found at Palenque. In the days that followed, the men met a number of times, despite the fact that Frans was suffering periodically from malaria.

Morley decided to add Blom to his staff of field workers, who would begin excavations at Chichén Itzá and Uaxactún in the following year. Blom had the major requirements which Morley sought, ability and enthusiasm. One qualification which he lacked, academic training in archaeology, could be easily acquired. Morley had an arrangement with Professor Tozzer at Harvard to have a promising man take courses during the fall semester and be free to work in the field after the middle of January. In two semesters the candidate could fulfill the requirements for the master's degree.

Almost before Frans knew it, he was signed up to attend Harvard in the fall. Although he had some savings, he did not have sufficient money to meet the total expenses of tuition, room, and board. Ten days after the first meeting, Morley wrote to Tozzer, asking him to find a tuition scholarship for Blom. It seems that Zelia Nuttall also wrote for the same purpose. Near the end of May the matter was settled. Frans received the help he needed and could draw on his reserves at the rate of $100 a month for living expenses at Harvard.

Blom worked at an office job for Gamio during part of the summer of 1923. He described his frustrations: "Oh, what a life this is! Here I am working like a slave, and running my head against one thousand walls." His secretary altered what he dictated. The man who corrected flaws in his written Spanish was a Yucatecan Maya specialist who had never visited the famous ruins of his native region. Frans complained that money was lacking to print photographs. At his desk he concentrated on Maya inscriptions by studying the great collection of

Maudslay's drawings. "Have you ever had the feeling," he asked a friend, referring to the problem of decipherment, "that the whole thing is so very near our reach, just like a dog that looks at you and wants to tell you something, but can only speak with its eyes? That's how I have often felt these days, when staring, my eyes tired, on Maudslay's drawings and photographs.

Because he had to subsist entirely on the small salary he received, he lived in a modest room in the old part of the city. A friend who visited him described the location of his room in a colonial building at the corner of Tacuba and Isabella la Católica. One entered a large public hall with cigarette and bootblack stands, passed by a billiard parlor, and in the rear mounted a narrow, winding staircase leading to a dance parlor on the second floor. A narrow passageway led to more stairs. On reaching the roof, the visitor found Frans's room in a corner of the third-story level. It was a pleasant place, with two low casement windows, old beams, plastered walls, and simple furniture.

Late in the summer he gave up his job with Gamio in order to make a trip abroad before enrolling at Harvard. He took with him a motion picture film of Maya ruins, prepared in Gamio's department. He made a quick trip to Denmark to visit his parents. In Copenhagen he set up an exhibition of Maya archaeology with objects Gamio had given him and items he had collected in his travels. He attended the exhibition frequently and lectured on Mexican antiquities. After the exhibit closed, he turned over all the objects to the Danish National Museum.

No opportunity, it seems, escaped him. On leaving Denmark, he stopped off in England. At the British Museum he admired the splendid Maya collection recently assembled in honor of Alfred P. Maudslay, and that experience moved him to visit Maudslay at Morney Cross, his home. The aging gentleman, who was the acknowledged dean of Maya studies, was revered for his precise photographs and superb line drawings of Maya monuments and their inscriptions, which appeared in *Biologia Centrali-Americana* and provided the best collection of source material on the subject.

Frans hastened back to the United States. He stopped off in New York, met the archaeologist Marshall H. Saville, and gave a private showing of the film at the Heye Museum. The audience included Saville, Thomas A. Joyce, archaeologist of the British Museum then visiting in this country, William Gates, scholar of Maya languages, and the philanthropist Archer M. Huntington. During the fall and early winter Blom showed the film before the American Folk-Lore Society, the Explorers Club, and the Harvard Club of Boston. Allison Armour, the philanthropist who had helped Edward Thompson and financed an expedition to Yucatán in 1894, received a private showing of the film. During the Christmas holidays Frans went to Washington, D.C., and entertained the trustees of the Carnegie Institution with the pictures; he said that the film was so successful on that occasion that he had to show it three times. He was also scheduled for performances before the Maya Society and the American Anthropological Society. It is evident that he lost no time in meeting the people who counted for something in the field of Maya archaeology. Blom was making progress. Two years earlier, in December 1921, he was traveling through the forests of Tabasco and Chiapas escorting geologists for an oil company; now he was associating with the prominent men in the archaeo-logical profession.

The fall semester at Harvard was largely a chore, for it provided few pleasures and scant satisfactions for Blom. There were some inspiring moments and a few teachers whom he respected, but all in all the routine of daily study, examinations, and term papers had little appeal. He wrote, half humorously, "I feel like one of halach uinic's [the chief's] hardest working slaves, and about examination time I will be ready to be sacrificed. . . ." What did books have to offer to a man who had wandered over the crumbled temples, climbed the pyramids, copied glyphs, and studied the details of Palenque? His courses, moreover, dealt with the general fields of ethnology and archaeology; his exclusive interest, of course, was the Maya.

The lack of money restricted his social life in Cambridge. He lived in a room in a cousin's house, allowing himself only $100 a month for expenses. One day on the front steps of the Peabody Museum he met Oliver Ricketson, Jr. Twenty-nine years old and a great-nephew of Andrew Carnegie, Ricketson received his A.B. from Harvard, and began and deserted the study of medicine after joining archaeological expeditions in southwestern United States. Three trips with C.I.W. teams to the Maya area launched him on his career. Because he had already visited Uaxactún, Morley chose him to lead the expedition to that site in 1924, with Blom as second in command. Frans and Oliver had one common bond at Harvard, for Tozzer had them work on a joint project of listing all Maya ruins and preparing a map of those sites for their master's theses. Morley wrote to Blom to secure tickets for the Harvard-Yale game and overnight quarters. He suggested that he, Frans, and Ricketson might have dates after the game, but Frans had to confess that "as I do not know very much of what is going on in Boston, and know no girls, I am at a loss as to how I can amuse you." There was also joking about the use of liquor in that era of prohibition. "Who said that the U.S. was dry?" quipped Blom. "I believe that it was some reporter in Europe who wanted to cause a sensation; in Europe they speak of how many glasses they have had; here they speak of how many gallons they have mopped up. . . ." If Blom had a roaring good time in Cambridge, as is sometimes rumored, he did it on a shoestring.

There is no doubt that his major passions at Harvard were archaeology and expeditions. "Man, I want to talk with you. Thousand and one things," he wrote to Morley. When Thomas Gann visited Cambridge in the early part of October, Blom had the opportunity to speak with a veteran of many years of field experience. Irish-born and trained as a physician, Gann had served for almost three decades as medical officer for British Honduras; his work did not prevent him from trekking all over the colony to examine Maya sites. Frans's enjoyment of the skinny, somewhat cantankerous man was marred by news of an act that embarrassed all archaeologists. When Gann visited Mexico, he bought an attractive, carved Maya jade, sewed it into the cloth of his jacket, and passed undetected into the United States. He then boasted of his feat, and Mexican authorities became furious over his blatant disregard for their law against the export of antiquities. Morley, who had accompanied him on the trip, wanted to employ him as physician on the Chichén Itzá project. But C.I.W. officials refused to consider him unless the jade was restored to Mexico. Gann had a great fondness for jades—he later gave a collection of them to the British Museum—and forfeited the appointment.

Blom endured the academic work only because of the prospect of a C.I.W. expedition in February. Although he was scheduled to go to Uaxactún, he made a bid for a trip through Chiapas. He told Morley late in October that he had set his heart on Chiapas. Two months later he informed Gamio that the plans called for Chichén, Belize, the Petén, Ocosingo, Palenque, and Tortuguero; and a few weeks after that he asked Gamio for a permit to travel through those areas in Mexico. Morley, however, stuck to his own plan: Blom and Ricketson would spend several months at Uaxactún in the upper Petén to prepare the site for excavation. In the last months of 1923 Ricketson wavered as to whether he would go into the field at all. The problem of his uncertainty was minor compared with news from two other fronts. In Guatemala, William Gates, director of archaeology in that nation, determined to cancel C.I.W.'s contract to excavate Uaxactún. And in Yucatán revolutionaries overthrew Governor Felipe Carrillo and closed the ports of the peninsula, an action that threatened the beginning of the project at Chichén Itzá.

Through December and January Frans spent day after
day on tenterhooks. Would the expedition ever leave the
United States? At first Morley attempted to solace him
by saying that he would transfer him to the project at
Chichén. Then the revolution in Yucatán appeared to
jeopardize that prospect. When an official of the C.I.W.
informed Blom that it was doubtful that either expedition
would leave, he was downcast. What did academic
studies amount to if he could not get a job? "This
university makes me so damned blue," he sighed to
Morley on New Year's Day, 1924, "so write and cheer
me up." In letter after letter he asked about the
prospects of both expeditions. Once in desperation he
begged for "some news, even if it is bad. That's better
than none. . . ." The man's tension was rising. "Even a
girl most madly in love cannot be awaiting a letter from
you more eagerly than I am at present. What is going to
be done?" Morley had heard that question from all of his
staff members, and he rebuked Frans, explaining that
nothing certain was known at the moment. Blom replied
in a passage that expressed his inmost emotion:

> You are right in calling me down, but I was
> feeling like a race horse ready for the start. My plans
> for equipment were laid and I was longing to see
> the things come in, and smell the leather and other
> nice smells that foretold a new expedition to start.
> Studying is all right, but, man, the sweetest music I
> know is the sound of the bell-mule at the head of
> the packtrain and the singing of the insects in the
> tropical night. . . . That is how I feel, the young colt
> in the corral, eager to get out in the great open for a
> canter. And you bet your soul I will be standing at
> the gate, waiting for you to open.

In addition to the uncertainty, Blom suffered from a
dwindling supply of money. By the end of January he
would not have a cent left. Would the C.I.W. pay him if
the expedition failed to set out? In case he did not leave
the United States, he proposed preparing a bibliography

of Chichén Itzá. In that event he would have to receive $200 a month instead of half that amount, which he received when he was in the field. He was promised the higher salary for six months if the expedition did not get under way.

Suddenly the air cleared. Gates resigned his post in Guatemala. The revolutionists opened the ports of Yucatán. On January 26 Blom received notice to report to New York as soon as possible to begin the expedition with Ricketson to Uaxactún.

Although Frans spent less than two months at Uaxactún, he demonstrated the ability to get things done. Ricketson, Blom, and A. Monroe Amsden, as assistant, crossed British Honduras from Belize to El Cayo, where they bought mules and hired a gang of laborers, and arrived at Uaxactún by the end of February. Ricketson, who was familiar with the site, introduced Blom to the job to be done and then left for an excavation in British Honduras. After a time, Amsden fell sick and was sent to Chichén Itzá to recuperate. Thus most of the work fell on Blom. He had vegetation cut down, erected palm-roof houses for staff and workers, cut trails to the major ruins, had a reservoir dug to supply water, began a survey of the site, copied the inscriptions, found the quarry, and cleared out one temple to serve as staff headquarters.

In the middle of the season he gave a semihumorous description of the conditions at Uaxactún: "We have plenty of everything here except water and excavations. Plenty of heat, ticks, game, ruins both known and newly found ones, stelae with and without inscriptions, lazy niggers and mules that run away." Among the workers was an excellent cook, who had already been a Spanish soldier in Cuba, a Mexican political spy, and a rumrunner. The blacks, doubtless from British Honduras, amused him: "They fall into trance and cramps when they get bawled out, turn the whites out of their eyes when they have to go into ruined temples . . . and are as lazy as possible." Although Frans could not claim the discovery of new stelae, he boasted of "some new

readings" and predicted that when he showed the results
to Morley there would be a wonderful time "fighting
about who is right." The tone of his letter indicated that
he was satisfied and confident in what he was doing.

He closed down the work near the end of April. On
the return to Belize, however, he visited fourteen other
Maya sites in the Petén. After boarding a boat at Belize,
he discovered that it was a rumrunner, and when he
landed at Progreso he was arrested. How he extricated
himself from that situation is not known. When he
arrived in Chichén, Morley reported that he looked thin.

If the preparation of Uaxactún for future excavation
might be considered a routine matter, requiring only the
ability to direct natives, Frans also displayed other
qualities. In addition to new readings of inscriptions, he
made an interesting discovery, the kind that occurs to an
inquiring mind. He found that a pyramid and three
temples had been arranged to form an observatory of the
movements of the sun. As he sat on the steps of the
pyramid and looked ahead, he saw three in a row. He
was able to determine that the sun rose over one temple
on the longest day of the year, over another temple on
the shortest day, and over the middle temple twice a
year during the equinoxes. Although this was not a
brilliant discovery, it added one more proof of Maya
knowledge of the movements of the sun by A.D. 235
(Morley correlation).

When we remember that in April 1922 Blom was a
cruiser for an oil company, using his spare time to make
a first examination of Palenque, his performance at
Uaxactún was remarkable. He showed that he could
manage an expedition and he displayed the earmarks of a
professional archaeologist. Unfortunately, his personal
experiences during the season's work at Uaxactún were
never described in print.

In July and August he worked under Neil Judd of the
Smithsonian Institution in the southwestern part of the
United States. Judd carried on annual excavations at
Pueblo Bonito, New Mexico, under the joint auspices of

the Smithsonian Institution and the National Geographic Society. There is no doubt that Frans took the job solely to make money during two summer months. He found the work "interesting, though I must say it is no pleasure to live in a constant sand storm when one is used to the wonderful forests of Chiapas and the Petén." It was during that expedition that he produced the several small watercolors that were his only attempt at creative art.

Blom was ready to do things on his own. During the years from 1919 through 1924, he had discovered a profession for himself and had mastered the knowledge necessary to take his place in that fraternity of scholars. Perhaps it was fortunate that he reversed the general order of things by acquiring his knowledge from first-hand experience in the field before entering upon academic work, for the forest meant more to him than cold theories from books. By the end of 1924 he was eager to find a full-time job. The period of apprenticeship had ended, and the job was waiting for him.

3

Launching a Career

The way Blom launched his career within a period of little over a year is one of the most curious episodes in the story of Maya archaeology. It involved three personalities—William Gates, Albert Dinwiddie, and Blom—and the newly created department of Middle American Research at Tulane University. The event underscores Frans's confidence in his own actions and his ability to judge men shrewdly. The story begins with his discontent over his job with the Carnegie Institution of Washington.

As soon as Blom returned to Harvard in the fall of 1924 to complete the requirements for the master's degree, he felt pressure on all sides. He attended classes and worked on the list of ruins and map of the Maya area that served as his thesis. In addition, his personal finances were low; he had only $240 to see him through the next four months in Cambridge. He also had to prepare a number of maps for some unexplained project. Then Morley kept after him to draw up the report of his work at Uaxactún, but Frans refused to do a hasty job, and he expressed his anger to Morley over the many tasks he was expected to accomplish, seemingly at once.

Irritation and frustration increased when Morley explained that the coming field season was in doubt. There was trouble again over the contract in Guatemala, and the completion of the C.I.W. budget had been delayed. Morley had to admit that he could make no commitment for the coming season until later. Once more Blom's job, a part-time job at that, was in jeopardy. He was ripe for an offer of full-time employment at a regular salary. In the early part of October William Gates began to talk with him about a new appointment.

Gates is an odd figure in the story of Central American archaeology. At that time sixty-one years old, he appeared to be entering the most productive period of his life. As a young man he had made sufficient money in the printing business to provide an independent income so that he could indulge his desire to collect the best library of original sources on the linguistics and prehistory of Mexico and the Maya area. Lacking formal training in archaeology, he devised his own approach to the decipherment of glyphs. At times a convincing speaker, in 1921 he secured the post of director of archaeology in Guatemala, where he hoped to exert rigid control over excavations by foreign organizations. He had fallen out with the C.I.W. and hoped to exclude Morley from working at Uaxactún. As it turned out, Morley had more influence with high officials in Guatemala than Gates had, and Gates angrily resigned his post in protest against a contract granted to the C.I.W. Within a few weeks Gates sought revenge by attempting to have Morley expelled from membership in the Maya Society, which Gates headed. That action destroyed the organization.

Angry over his defeat in Guatemala and the dissolution of the Maya Society, Gates hoped for some new position to reestablish his prestige. An unusual combination of events thrust an attractive appointment upon him. He offered a portion of his library for sale in New York. Marshall Ballard, editor of the New Orleans *Item*, learned of the forthcoming sale and induced Samuel Zemurray, president of the Cuyamel Fruit Company, to buy the collection for Tulane University, provide an endowment of $300,000 to support a new Department of Middle American Research in the university, and supply money for an archaeological expedition. On acquiring the library, the university insisted that Gates must head the department. Gates was only too willing to be of service.

In 1924 Gates was building a small staff and looking for a staff archaeologist. As he himself was aware, members of that profession considered him a difficult man to work with. Several scholars turned down the post, and he knew that he must convince Frans Blom of the wisdom of joining his staff.

A hardheaded, practical man, Blom had a difficult choice before him—uncertain part-time employment with the C.I.W. or a full-time position with the cantankerous Gates in a new department with limited resources. Gates made the most of the young man's dilemma. He visited the Peabody Museum and cornered Frans twice for long conversations. He was a persuasive talker, pointing out, among other things, that much more money would be coming to the department at Tulane.

Frans asked professional friends for advice. Morley told him to decide the matter for himself and not to allow their friendship to interfere with the decision, because his feelings for Frans would remain unchanged. "Thank you so much for your letter," Blom replied. "It felt good to hear you say it . . . it warmed." "Send me a nice letter, so that I can get my mind made up," he pled during a fit of indecision. Tozzer gave little help; he advised that if it were anyone but Gates he had to work under, Frans should take the job. He added a prophetic note, however: Tulane might tire of Gates and then Frans would be ready to move into his post. At this time, Blom concluded that he knew how to get along with Gates. "I think that if one pats G.'s back, and gets him in the front page of the newspaper about once a week, you can run him fairly well," he observed. "If I join him I am going to organize a press bureau for this particular purpose." Sometime during the negotiations Frans learned that he would lead the new department's first expedition. The prospect of a journey into the Mexican hinterland under his own direction must have influenced his decision to join Gates.

By the end of October Frans believed that he had solved the problem. "Now that I have gotten over the first excitement, I take the Gates matter very cold blooded," he explained. "I will simply not go to him if I do not get a legally formed contract with careful stipulation of salary and other conditions." If trouble comes, "it will then be up to him to break it, and for me to make a little on the side." When President Dinwiddie wired acceptance of the terms at the end of October, Blom was satisfied: "Better salary, and as this work will sort of be under the president of the university, I do not think it will be so bad." Even after Blom expressed to the president his "feeling of uncertainty as regards Mr. G.'s somewhat unstable temperament, and a consequent wish to have all terms on a clear and unmistakable base," it appears that the only terms he received in written form were a salary of $3,000 a year and a contract for three years.

After Frans accepted the job, Gates invited him to Auburn Hill, his home in the Virginia countryside. "The old man fell all over me at once," Frans explained, "and we did not leave each other for three solid days." Gates showed off his books and manuscripts and explained his research on the Dresden Codex. But sooner or later he would fall into a rage, usually against Morley and President Merriam of the C.I.W. "We cannot get away from his explosive temperament," admitted Frans, "but behind this he is a dear, kindhearted old man. Very enthusiastic, very keen. I am glad that I have joined him." In addition, Blom believed that he would receive good scholarly criticism of his work from the older man.

Gates crowed over his new acquisition. He declared that Frans was "ten times Morley's superior. Morley never sees anything but 'dates'; Blom sees everything, topographic and cultural." When New Orleans newspapers announced the appointment in mid December, the director boasted that "Frans Blom possesses the most remarkable technic I have ever seen in a man of his age."

High praise, indeed, but exactly what did Gates mean?

Later in the same month Blom had a long talk with Gates, who became ecstatic over his young assistant. "The Blom matter was delightful," the director reported to Dinwiddie. "Once settled, he knows he did right, and can't wait to get to work—with us—even with me. Not a bit of friction, and won't be. His reactions suit me just right." He was impressed with Frans's background. "He is a gentleman born. Old Danish family; five languages; King's messenger in the war; was slated for high position in Denmark; left against father's opposition (did not want to sit at a desk and run a factory); had all sorts of rough times; sold gasoline at a street stand in Mexico, etc.—all to get into Middle American archaeology. Now has made good and has it on his father. . . . Blom counts his friends in the Legations crowd; always stays with Archie Roosevelt at Oyster Bay. Knows young Frick[1] well, and reports him as getting very keen on our subjects."

At the time of the meeting Blom had an unfavorable impression of Merriam of the C.I.W., and Morley's pressure to receive the report on Uaxactún still rankled. Gates believed that the young man had turned against his former employer. "Points came out, of Merriam's dictatorial pettiness; also Morley wrote him he was sacrificing his whole future if he came to Tulane. Now Blom laughs, and sees the whole problem, and coming C.I. troubles, just as we see it. Says work at Chichén is impossible—too much 'bridge playing' " (a reference to one of Morley's hobbies). "And Blom is back at Cambridge rubbing it in."

Apparently Frans was playing an astute game. He still had sufficient regard for Morley to make a trip to Washington, D.C., at the end of December to say good-bye. "It will mean that I will have to cut short on other things" to find the money for the trip, he told Morley, "but I do want to shake your fist before you go" to Yucatán.

Blom looked forward to the expedition he would soon undertake. Although his employment at Tulane officially began January 1, 1925, he stayed on at Harvard to complete his graduate study, collected library materials for the department at Tulane, and gathered equipment for the coming expedition. He arrived in New Orleans on February 9, made a few public appearances before local audiences, and then set off for Mexico. He had already hired Oliver La Farge as his assistant on that first expedition sent out under the auspices of the new department at Tulane. La Farge joined him in Mexico City.

The expedition of 1925 became an important landmark in Blom's career. Everything he had done since 1919 prepared him for the experience; now he gained recognition as an explorer in strange lands and found unknown Maya ruins. The journey, moreover, took him into the highlands of Chiapas and strengthened his attraction for that region. Fortunately, the record of the expedition appeared in print as *Tribes and Temples,* the only published report of his many expeditions.

The route the expedition would follow and the assemblage of baggage received careful consideration. Acting on suggestions of people and books, Frans laid out an itinerary to include numerous ancient remains that he wanted to examine. Also for months in advance of departure he consulted the accounts of former travelers and copied passages from their publications about the places he intended to visit, and he took that condensed "library" with him. He chose equipment judiciously, with a view to carrying as little as possible. Hammocks took the place of more unwieldy camp cots, and only a small quantity of canned goods was included for use in an emergency, because he planned to buy staples along the way and to live off the land by hunting. All supplies were placed in kayaks, light fiber containers of a standard size which he had selected for the purpose. Each box held about one hundred pounds; two boxes could be carried by a pack animal and, when necessary, one box by an Indian carrier.

The route, which he was able to follow almost exactly according to schedule, emphasized the less well-known archaeological areas of Mexico. From Veracruz he skirted along the coastal region of the Gulf, and at Frontera struck south into the hinterland of Tabasco and Chiapas. He announced the aim of the expedition as the study of archaeological remains and the examination of the customs and languages of the Indians. He intended to do no more than explore ancient ruins and to make known the sites he found. In fact, he considered himself a pathfinder, searching out unknown remains for later investigators to examine in detail.

The archaeological results of the expedition provided a list of over one hundred sites in Veracruz, Tabasco, and Chiapas. In some cases in which earlier explorers had recorded ruins, Frans added more information. In other instances, that is, for almost half the sites in the list, he described the finds in his published report. It is certainly more than coincidence that fifty percent of the ruins listed are in Chiapas, which had already become his favorite hunting ground for archaeology.

The first significant area that he examined lay in the Olmec region. Using a sloop to navigate the Blasillo River, he made his way to the ruins of La Venta and found a colossal head and a number of stelae, which he illustrated in his report. The style of those works, he believed, showed a strong Maya influence. Fifteen years later Matthew W. Stirling included La Venta in his itinerary because of the information in Blom's report. Stirling found all of the carvings mentioned and eventually unearthed striking remains of Olmec culture, which he dated much earlier than that of the Maya, thereby adding a new dimension to the prehistory of Mexico. This was precisely the way Blom hoped that his reports would be used by future explorers.

After sailing to Frontera, Frans moved south into the Maya territory. At Villahermosa he bought animals for a journey to Comalcalco, where he planned to reexamine a site that Désiré Charnay had explored in 1880. Blom's action amply confirmed the value of reexamining ruins already reported. Grateful as he was for the map of the site in Charnay's account, he found that the structures were not as large or imposing as his predecessor had described them. That, however, was a minor matter compared with what happened on the day he thought would be the last at that site.

Frans was about to close his work in the late afternoon. He had mapped the site, drawn plans of the temples, and made archaeological notes. A small ruined room, hidden by the undergrowth, remained to be placed on the map. He had already made a record of it, which ended with "nothing much to note."

Then something happened. The rays of the low afternoon sun cast a light on the inner wall of the room. Frans looked, and then looked again. "What was that on the walls—some stucco ornaments?" He and the native assistants cleared away the debris. "The feathered ornaments of a helmet appeared, all modeled in stucco low relief. More feathers and part of another face. . . . Here before me was a buried chamber with delicately modeled figures on the walls." He would not be leaving next day, after all.

In the morning, with the help of five Indians, he learned the full extent of the discovery. There were nine full-length stucco figures in the chamber, "some of the finest pieces of art as yet found in the Maya area." His diary expressed his enthusiasm in the vernacular: "They are beauties. . . ." At once he informed Manuel Gamio, archaeological official in Mexico City, of the find.

After the chamber had been cleared down to the polished red cement floor, little could be learned of the dignitary honored by the artistic setting. Moisture had seeped into the room and destroyed the physical remains except for a few fragmentary bones and a collection of clam shells, each one pierced for a necklace. Apparently the body of the man had been placed on a wooden slab slightly raised above the floor; the supports were there, though the slab had crumbled to dust.

After the stucco figures had been revealed, the next task called for was preservation. Blom and his associates spent a day cleaning the stucco reliefs and filling the cracks with cement to prevent further deterioration. Fortunately don David Bosada, municipal head of the near-by town, appreciated the discovery and ordered a roof built over the chamber to protect it from tropical rains.[2]

Blom was not always as fortunate as he had been at Comalcalco. On another venture for ruins he came away disappointed. At Finca Iowa he heard the rumor that a mysterious Maya ruin was hidden in the forest. Explorers had been hearing about this site for many years, but one could not dismiss the rumor for fear of losing a promising lead. Frans was intrigued with the story that a stone with glyphs was on the wall of one of the rooms. He secured a local guide who knew the location of the site. "Hopes therefore ran high," Blom wrote, "when we got up the next morning about 5 A.M., hurriedly swallowed our breakfast and jumped in the saddle." The party traveled by horse, canoe, and on foot. "It was a tough climb up to the hut of an Indian. . . . It was a moment of high tension—the temple was there. Now, what about the tablet?" They were too late. Some months earlier a large cedar tree had fallen on the temple, crushing the center of the building, and the tablet lay buried under tons of debris. Disappointed as he was, he measured and noted the features of the ruins of El Retiro.

Blom attempted to reconnoiter every ruin on the route and also to inspect privately owned artifacts. All told, he mapped and described dozens of sites—Tortuguero, Agua Escondida, Chinkultic, Hun Chabín, Finca Encanto, Santo Ton, Tenam, and many others, which are described in *Tribes and Temples*. Although he examined local collections of artifacts, public and private, hoping to piece together evidence of the prehistoric style in each region, he received little help from these sources.

The site that attracted him most, of course, was Palenque. "Both of us were full of expectation," he wrote on arriving at the place. "To the writer it was the joy of returning to a place that had become dear to him

through previous visits; to La Farge it was the thrill of
going for the first time to this famous and beautiful
ruined city, of which he had read and heard so much."
Oliver gave a different version of his introduction to
Palenque. When Frans took him to the Temple of the
Cross, he awaited exclamations of praise. It was "a
marvellously encouraging sight," La Farge explained,
"but I was humorous about it and he misunderstood—a
pity." By the next day, however, the younger man
considered the place "stupendous," and pleased Frans
by copying some stelae for him. At the main plaza Blom
surveyed the changes which had occurred during the two
years since his last visit. The palm-roof museum he had
constructed was falling, and his own palm shack had disappeared. Leandro Alvírez, the old caretaker, came forth
to greet him and proudly showed three slabs he had
found and preserved; Frans examined them carefully.

Blom fumed over the run-down condition of the site.
With indignation he wrote at once to the proper Mexican
official and complained of the lack of care of the place.
Leandro had not been paid for six months, though he had
faithfully carried out all the instructions Frans had given
him two years earlier. It was unfortunate, Blom wrote, that
"the government maintains only one man to look after one
of the most remarkable ruined sites on this continent."

Palenque stirred visions in Frans's imagination:

> We see all the great buildings around us and
> marvel at their size. They appear to us as if grown
> up overnight a thousand years ago. But look!—there
> at the entrance to the aqueduct many slaves are
> hauling a large stone block and trying to put it in
> place; stout vines are tied around the block; a
> foreman directs them with loud cries; all the slaves
> lay their strength to the ropes, and the block moves
> a few feet. Over on the main plaza a large lime kiln
> is burning. Hundred of trees, cut by burning and
> with stone tools, are stacked up around blocks of
> limestone quarried with stone hammers. Long lines
> of workmen carry stones and baskets of lime and dirt

to build the pyramid of the Sun Temple. From the hills we hear the songs of the workmen in the quarries, cutting tablets by the slow process of chipping stone against stone.

He continued his musings: "High above the palm-roofed town the holy city would be hidden behind the fogs of early morning, and as the sun climbed higher the mist would rise like a curtain disclosing the mountainside, where rows of temples painted in many colors shone in the sun against a background of green forests." It is necessary to note that these were rare statements of his imagination, but they indicate that archaeology meant more to him than artifacts, maps, and the decipherment of glyphs.

The theoretical aspects of archaeology elicited little in print from him. When he reported on the expedition of 1925, he made a few remarks typical of the thought of his day. What was the story of the Maya before they built the elaborate structures? Although the buildings displayed a sophisticated level of artistic achievement, no stratification of Maya sites had been found to indicate a progressive development from an earlier, simpler stage. He made a few other comments about the Maya. Where had the people come from? He suggested an Asiatic origin; in the next sentence, however, he indicated that Maya culture was indigenous to Central America. Perhaps it had its first growth in the Petén. Like other scholars, he assumed that a large population and an adequate supply of food provided labor which could be employed to raise striking temples and devise an intricate calendar.

Such speculation paled in comparison with the news he and La Farge picked up accidentally in Comitán near the end of the expedition. It was more exciting than the report of an unknown site. Don Gregorio de la Vega, leading citizen of Comitán, in a leisurely conversation with the Americans in the main plaza of the town, mentioned casually that the Indians of Jacaltenango in nearby Guatemala held an annual celebration for the

year bearer. That was exciting news, indeed, for the year
bearer went back directly to ancient Maya civilization.
Was the celebration a vestige of the old worship which
had come down to the Indians of today? When Frans and
Oliver reached Jacaltenango ten days later, they learned
that every spring men secretly acted as priests of the
ancient cult and announced the year bearer and the
prophecies for the new year. The practice was worth
investigating, and in 1927 La Farge and Douglas Byers
spent several months in Guatemala documenting the
curious survival.

Despite the satisfactions derived from archaeology and
ethnology, Blom's interests also embraced the world of
humanity. He liked people if they were sociable and
intelligent. He was not quite prepared for a most unusual
person, a simple, old Indian, who became a permanent
member of the expeditionary team. Lázaro joined the
party in an unpretentious way.

At Macuspana Frans bought saddle and pack animals,
mainly horses because mules were scarce, for the
remainder of the journey through Chiapas. He needed a
man to care for the animals and equipment. On inquiring
for a muleteer, he received a high recommendation for
Lázaro Hernández Guillermo. And so he sent for him.

The interview barely suggested the outstanding
qualities of the man. He appeared in the usual local
dress—blue cotton trousers, a white cotton shirt, a
sombrero, and sandals. Frans told him of the projected
journey, which might extend from three to five months.
He offered to take Lázaro on trial as far as Palenque and
pay him fifty dollars a month. The Indian remarked
simply that he liked to travel, and asked only when they
would leave. He would go home to say good-bye to his
wife and two children and report for work in the
morning. With his meager traveling equipment rolled in
a small mat, he joined the expedition the next day.

Little time passed before Blom and La Farge began to
appreciate the humane character of Lázaro. Although he
was considered an old man, he was probably no more

than forty, and he demonstrated far greater physical stamina than the younger Americans. An able and conscientious worker, he quickly learned the desires and habits of the gringos. Frans and Oliver, accustomed to crude, profane muleteers, looked on with amazement as Lázaro urged on the animals gently and called them *niños,* his children. After the day's journey, he washed and fed his charges before caring for himself. With this example before them, the Americans began to treat their own mounts well, lest they receive a reproachful glance from Lázaro. Soon they began to address him as Tata, a term of respect Indians applied to their elders.

As the days passed, the unsuspected qualities of the man unfolded. When he heard his employers asking local Indians about their customs and beliefs, he suggested that "he could tell them a thing or two in that line himself." And so La Farge drew from him valuable ethnological information and compiled a brief vocabulary of his Yocotán, a dialect of the Chontol language. He never complained, though as a lowland Indian he suffered from the cold when they reached the mountains of Chiapas and Guatemala. On the grueling night ride over the savanna, noted later in this chapter, it was Tata who bolstered the morale of the weary men and urged on the animals. Generous in spirit, kind to man and beast, wise in his outlook on life, he deeply impressed Blom and La Farge with the sterling attributes that could be found in the natives of Central America.[3]

If archaeology gave Frans a professional reason to carry on an expedition, there was a deeper, personal reason, which he did not openly admit in those early years. He enjoyed the varied experiences of travel, the thrill of meeting new people, seeing strange sights, and reveling in the beauty of nature.

On several occasions he found ranch owners sociable and hospitable. Don Aureo Cruz, whose lands contained the ruins of Toniná, graciously led Frans to the site and then entertained him at his home. Although it was a simple two-room thatched-roof building with adobe walls and a hut nearby for a kitchen, Frans could not forget the evening he spent there. They "sat outside the hut and listened to Don Aureo's tales of the Indians, while his pretty daughters were busy flirting with our guides, and with us, too. A pine stick fire lit up the walls of the houses and flickered over the brown faces of our hosts and our Indian laborers, who sat just back of us, chatting in their own strange language and enjoying the local cigars we had given them. Out in the dark our animals could be heard grazing, and now and then a pig or a dog would approach the fire, to be driven away with shouts or sticks." Farther along the route the explorers met another ranch owner, don Enrique Bulnes, a man of surprising attainments for that region. Trained abroad, he greeted the Americans in English, and inquired about New York and Mexico City. With genuine hospitality, he installed them in a comfortable guesthouse, where fresh pine needles covered the floor.

After a side trip to Tecojá, Frans and Oliver returned to the Bulnes finca. "That evening we had a small dance," Blom explained.

> One of Don Enrique's sons and a foxy looking old muleteer (a part of the inventory of the finca) dressed in corduroy trousers, a bulky jacket and a red bandana handkerchief, played guitars and sang Mexican songs. La Farge and I were the cavaliers to Don Enrique's daughter. After we had danced, the musicians struck up one of the Indian tunes, and two of the Indian girl servants in the house came in to dance for us. Gliding noiselessly over the floor to the strains of the guitars, they would first meet, then part. In the yellow light of the oil lamp their brown faces became darker than usual, and not a smile passed over their features. Every time the music stopped, they would disappear into the dark yard, to reappear when the "orchestra" started another tune. The evening passed rapidly: to us a novel pleasure, to our hosts a rare occasion.

Frans found the Indian natives perhaps even more interesting than the local aristocracy. At Comalcalco he marveled at the spirit of the laborers who cleared away the bush. "During the day they slashed their way through the thick undergrowth which covered the ruins, all the while joking and teasing one another with much laughter. But the climax of their hilarity came when their work was over and each man passed us by, receiving his pay, a cigar and a small drink as a special reward." Weeks later in the mountains of Chiapas, the native trail cutters also enjoyed their work. "Our Indians were a cheerful crowd. All day they would walk ahead of us, cutting the trail, now and then stopping to cut the heart out of a small palm and eating it as a great delicacy, especially when fresh. At other places they would break open the huge nests of white ants and with their machetes dig for bags of honey deposited by some small bees who favor these ant nests for their hives."

Near the end of the expedition Blom employed cargadores, Indians who carried loads of baggage. A contingent of them arrived at Tenejapa "shortly after dark, still lively despite the long day and steep climb. More remarkable still, one of them had developed fever, 'so that he lost his breath,' and another had made almost the whole trip with two kayaks, over 200 lbs., on his back. They camped on the town hall porch, where we with our beds on piles of grass in a room . . . heard them, as we fell asleep, still chattering over a friendly bottle." On another stage of the journey he used two cargadores who showed their pleasure "because we looked a little after them. Usually the Germans here treat them roughly, but I don't like that." The natives "are helpful; and if you are a little kind to them, quite cheerful."

There were other experiences along the route, ranging from the solemn to the ludicrous. On the Grijalva River Blom passed the launch of the governor of Tabasco, with an orchestra on the roof of the cabin, turkeys and chickens tied to the railing of the stern, and heavily armed natives guarding his excellency. "It looked like a circus," Frans observed. At Comalcalco he and La Farge tasted "foaming chocolate," which reminded Blom of the ancients' high regard for that beverage. When a friend in the oil town of La Crusada made company quarters available, "a bath in a bathroom was a luxury after swimming in dirty rivers." And that night they slept in beds covered with sheets, another unexpected luxury. At Ocosingo they found the children engaged in a baseball game on the town plaza. "A quaint phraseology, a mixture of American baseball words and Spanish cussing, cheered the play." One night the travelers slept in a way station for muleteers where the furniture was made of solid mahogany. In Nacajuca the town jail bore a large sign reading "Sal si puedes" ("get out if you can"). Perhaps the most ludicrous incident occurred in a settlement in Chiapas, where Blom and La Farge were identified as "strangers who were following the footsteps of Jesus Christ," because of muleteer in another town had heard Frans describe a glyph date as "422 after the birth of Christ."

Sometimes an incident impressed Blom as sharply as an etching. After a night ride on the way from Villahermosa toward Comalcalco, his party entered a settlement and sought lodgings. "On and on we rode, until after 11 o'clock we clattered in on the cobblestone pavement of the village Nacajuca. A nice, small town it was, with red tiled roofs and colonnades in front of the houses. Here and there hung a kerosene lamp. Dogs barked at the intrusion." On the main plaza Frans found "two heavily armed policemen and the local inebriate, celebrating with a phonograph." When the strangers inquired for overnight quarters, the unstable citizen took them to the house of Doña Teresa and called for her. A light flickered through a crack in the door and voices whispered inside. "Two women were discussing whether or not it would be safe to open the doors at that time of night; it might be bandits or rebels." Then the door opened slightly and one of the inmates saw Frans's blond hair. "Strange as it sounds, that sight induced her to open the door, and we were admitted. . . . We unloaded our animals outside the house, and led them right through the parlor out into the back yard. While we were hanging up our hammocks, the old lady produced a good meal."

Despite the hardships of travel along the trail, Blom relished the challenge of getting through difficult situations. In the region of the Bascán Valley on the way to Palenque, the explorers met one of the worst passages. Although the finca owner had sent Indians ahead to clear the trail, "nonetheless we found that the hardest was yet to come. The climb up to the Mirador pass was steep, the soil slippery from the rain, and the new cutting difficult to negotiate in many places." As they ascended the path, the animals slipped and fell. Each time they had to unload the fallen creatures, get them to their feet, and then reload them. This happened time after time. On reaching the top, "we slid and rolled down until we reached a small arroyo. . . , where we made camp. . . ."

On the route from Ocosingo to San Cristóbal the party negotiated another difficult passage. At one place they had to cross a deep ravine and ascend "a palisade almost perpendicular and infinitely high. . . . The road assumed a steep grade, rising in a series of zigzags. . . . Straight up, almost like a ruled line, lay the Indian trail. . . ." The native carriers, who preceded them, ascended "that fearsome climb. We tried it, but the horses slid and fell back upon their haunches, and we ourselves could barely keep our footing." So they took the zigzag road, battled heat and dust, and climbed nineteen hundred feet in two hours.

La Farge became the victim of the last difficult passage before the expedition ended. On the way into Guatemala he had a spill. "The small town of Zapaluta lies on top of a small hill, and as we rode up an unusually vertical street La Farge's horse slipped, tumbled over backwards, and fell on top of him. It looked very bad at first, and I feared that at last our good luck had changed, but, fortunately, I was wrong. When he was extricated, he presented a badly bruised leg, a watertight metal matchbox squashed absolutely flat, and a broad grin."

Although Blom gained a sense of triumph in conquering difficulties on the trail, he was happiest when observing the passing scene and contemplating nature in its unending variety. At one place his party stopped briefly for a midday rest. As he looked at the scene before him, he could not resist noting the details: "Sitting on the bank of an arroyo, while the Indians drank posole. Water falls over stones, gurgles and sings. Green plants, small palms, broad bay leaves, spots of sun, boys squatting, mixing posole in gourd. Packs stacked up on stones. Tall, well-built Indian bathes. . . ."

When he made the passage by boat along the Gulf Coast to Frontera, he saw a vivid scene. "Toward dark the wind began to blow, the waves were crested with white, and as night fell the water was shining with a bluish green phosphorescence. It was very beautiful and strange. The moon rose fiery red, and everybody was on constant lookout for the low coast, as for a long time we could not see the lighthouse of Frontera. At last it came in sight, and about 10 P.M. we anchored, as it would be too dangerous to try to enter the river at night."

The sights and sounds of the tropical night had a peculiar fascination for him. At Villahermosa he bought horses for overland travel to Comalcalco. "The night was magnificent with millions of stars and millions of fireflies," he exclaimed. "Fortunately, we found an Indian with a lantern at the second pass and persuaded him with silver to ferry us over the river. Picturesque enough was the black water, the heads of the snorting horses alongside and an Indian at each end of the canoe balancing an 18-foot paddle."

The outstanding experience of travel by night occurred on the way to Palenque. The combination of adventure, physical endurance, and the nocturnal aspects of nature on the savanna makes it the most dramatic incident of the entire expedition. "Between Iowa and Palenque village, our next stop, are large savannas, with clusters of bush and low trees. During the dry season it is an extremely exhausting trip for men and animals across those savannas during the heat of the day: so, as there was a full moon, we decided to make the journey by night."

At first the traveling was pleasant. They began at 8:30 in the dark night. When they entered the forest, they let the animals find the trail. Then as "the moon began to climb over the horizon," they had no trouble following the way. On the sides of the path thick bush and elephant-ear plants "took the most fantastic forms in the light of the moon." Small animals wandered onto the trail, then darted into the bush. The temperature was cool, and leaves sparkled with dew.

They ran into difficulties after midnight. The guides accompanying them lost the way, and the party spent an hour in making a complete circle. "On we went. We were getting very tired, having been on the move, working and riding since 5 o'clock the previous morning. Often we dozed in the saddle, to wake with a jerk when our animals stopped to nibble the grass. We began to see strange things. Bushes took on the oddest shapes. We dismounted and walked for a time and that helped somewhat to overcome the desire for sleep."

Dawn gave the tired men hope. "Sun and warmth seemed to infuse new life into our wearied bodies and into those of our animals." The party encountered men on the way to till their fields. They entered the village of Palenque at nine o'clock. "We rode directly to Ernest Rateike's store. He came out, and we greeted him with the stiffest of bows—not that we did not like him, far from that—but we really were unable to greet him more gracefully, having been in action for twenty-eight hours. We could scarcely bend our rigid backbones." They ate a light meal and then fell asleep until the late afternoon. On awakening, they learned that while they had been lost on the savanna, bandits had robbed a merchant on the trail they had been seeking.

When Blom approached San Cristóbal, his affection for the country increased. The descriptions he wrote abound in details, especially of colors, which impressed him. He did not admit that he had fallen in love with the region, though it is evident from his account. As he passed through the Chamula country on the way to San Cristóbal, he took in every aspect of the scene:

> In the late afternoon we came up to the 2500 meter level (about 7,900 feet). The country was

pine-clad, with rolling valleys. Then we crossed a
canyon and swung around onto a great, open,
wind-swept moor, reaching away to the horizon,
with one or two oak trees beaten down by the wind,
like trees near a stormy coast. Underfoot was a vivid,
green carpet of fine, close-growing herbs dotted
with tiny, pale yellow flowers. Along the road
washouts had cut gashes of red soil, burnt orange
and sienna in color. Against the skyline a rounded
hill stood up, bearing a row of huge, towering
crosses with a wrack of clouds flying behind them.
At their feet was a maze of small crosses, a Chamula
cemetery.

Everything fascinated him. There were neat houses
with pointed thatched roofs, truck gardens, plots of
wheat and corn. "Beyond this was a succession of small,
green valleys of fine grass, each with a stream in the
center, many yellow flowers, and the ridges between
clothed in pine and live oak." As he described the
Indians from various tribes, each with distinctive
costume, he noted that the natives lacked the "fugitive or
humble appearance" common to so many Indians. All
roads, lively with traffic, led into the town. He admitted
that "the excitement of this strange country that lay
behind the Mexico of the books held us spellbound."

Then he saw the panoramic setting of the town, and
gradually entered its streets.

The road turned abruptly, bringing us around the
cliffs to a view of the valley and San Cristóbal at
last. We looked down into a little bowl ringed with
green mountains. Around the edge was a band of
meadows cut by streams with scattered white
farmhouses, a grouping of white walls, red roofs,
green trees, and the domes of twenty-two churches.
On a hill, as steep as any pyramid, just behind the
town, the little temple of San Cristóbal himself
looked down over the town.

The road became a cobbled street, the shingled,
white houses closed together and took on red roofs.

We trotted past block after block of the smallest shops in the world, mere doorways, in which hung every imaginable Indian product or thing that an Indian would buy, while natives of every village in the highlands bartered at the doors. The streets debouched into the plaza, cool with the massed green of camphor trees, beside the cathedral with its cream-colored walls and terra cotta pilasters. Around and in front of the modern and ugly Palacio Municipal, to the dark, arched doorway of the Hotel Español, we clattered into a shaded, flowery patio, and dismounted at last in San Cristóbal las Casas.

Blom and La Farge spent twelve days in the town. They wandered about the streets, visited churches, and delved into the history of the place. Frans addressed the high school students, and then looked into the private libraries of the town. Only one had survived the periodic uprisings of the past: the daughters of the deceased don Flavio Paniagua opened his collection, but they refused to unlock the bookcase filled with manuscripts; it was secured when he died and it would remain that way as long as they lived.

Although the expedition officially ended at Huehuetenango in Guatemala, where the horses and mules were sold, the team had some traveling ahead. Blom and his companions visited Zaculeu; Quezaltenango; Guatemala City, where they were received by the president of the country; Quiriguá; and finally Puerto Barrios, where they boarded the boat for New Orleans. Frans returned from the six months' jaunt with his heart set on San Cristóbal and the Chiapas highlands.

Tata accompanied the men to New Orleans in the middle of August. It appears that they wanted to give him a taste of the United States; they also wished to learn more about his tribe and language. As the boat ascended the river at night and Tata saw New Orleans, he is reported to have exclaimed, "It is the city of stars!" Unfortunately, Frans had not arranged in advance for the Indian's entry into the country, and the poor fellow was detained two days and nights in the immigration office in New Orleans until special permission could be arranged. As might be expected, Tata showed remarkable patience and understanding during his detention. After he was free, there was some difficulty in lodging him. At first Blom stayed with him at a New Orleans hotel, but "his little idiosyncracies were a matter of great concern, especially at the dinner table." So he spent the remainder of his days with La Farge and the nights with Blom in his apartment. The investigators had learned much about the culture from which he came in Chiapas, but no one, it appears, recorded Tata's views on the civilization of the United States. After two weeks in New Orleans he returned to his tribe in Mexico and vanished into oblivion.

Blom's explorations received considerable notice. This time he allowed himself to boast, a trait that rarely appeared as blatantly in the future. "When our reports are made," he asserted, "we will have many of those great scientists up in the air," as he referred to archaeologists. "We discovered twenty-four ruined cities hitherto unrecorded by scientists. . . . To sum up the matter in a few words, the work that we have begun in Central America will put Tulane University on the map as having the greatest department in the country on Maya Indian study." These words, so uncharacteristic of the man, might have been Frans's way of pleasing Gates, who planned to do great things at Tulane.

By the time Blom and La Farge returned from the expedition, Gates had already developed an ambitious and expansive program for the new department. At first he was modest, proposing only linguistic and historical studies and the support of field expeditions. A few days after his appointment he added the translation of Maya medical lore as the first project. A week passed, and he had another inspiration. He would set up a vast bibliographical project to provide an index of all data about the Central American countries, past and present, including "information useful to the Port of New

Orleans, and the business that lies behind it. . . . I want
to card index those countries." After arriving at Tulane,
he explained that expeditions sent out by the department
would serve Central American nations by helping them
to build roads and improve their public health. By the
fall of 1924 he was more specific. "Honduras has been
selected as the first of the Central American countries for
study," he announced; that study would include "the
present Indian languages, the botany of commercial
plants. . . , the medical value of herbs, . . . sanitation,
transportation problems, air and steamship mail service
and the education of the Indians." The program, he said,
would stimulate trade between Central America and
New Orleans.

In a strange remark, made just after Blom had been
appointed in the fall of 1924, Gates told President
Dinwiddie that he did not want to put archaeology in the
forefront of the work of the department. At the same time
Gates praised Blom to everyone. It seems curious that, in
view of the total program he announced, Gates added an
archaeologist to his staff. In the end, that appointment
helped to bring about his undoing.

While the director told the public about his expanding
plans, he struggled behind the scenes to finance them.
He approached Zemurray, suggesting the need for an
endowment of $2 million for the department and a
budget of $50,000 for the coming year instead of the
$15,000 on which the department operated. Gates,
however, failed to induce the philanthropist or President
Dinwiddie to add one dollar to the endowment. To make
matters worse, the university informed the director at the
end of September 1925 that he had overspent his budget
by several thousand dollars.

Gates encountered another problem after Blom and La
Farge returned from the expedition. When the two
explorers arrived in New Orleans in the middle of
August, they received much public notice. Although
Gates had sent out two other expeditions, one to Mexico
and another to Honduras to study tropical botany, those

activities received little notice in the newspapers. Despite Gates's wishes, it was archaeology that brought fame to the department.

For a time Blom and Gates got along well together. When the expedition left New Orleans in February 1925, Gates hailed it as "the beginning of Tulane's ranking on the scientific map." In April the director joined Frans and Oliver for a brief period in Mexico. "Mr. Gates is a most dear man to work for," Blom remarked to Zelia Nuttall. "Moreover, he is a great help as he criticizes the work." It appears, however, that Blom had reservations. In his diary he noted that Gates was not in good health and was resting at Comalcalco. "I am glad he has had a rest; he is usually too busy." After Gates returned to New Orleans in July, he gave a glowing report of Blom's work. He had accomplished as much, Gates boasted, as might be expected of a three-year expedition, and for good measure he added that Frans's record in Mexico "is the finding of a monument a day." The director also wrote confidential letters to his archaeologist during the remainder of the summer. Frans in turn radiated optimism, telling Tozzer as late as September 1925 that the more he worked for Gates the more he liked him. When Frans prepared articles or addresses about the 1925 expedition, he attempted to flatter the director by saying that his journey aimed to study medicinal herbs and to achieve closer ties between the businessmen of New Orleans and Central America; neither statement had any basis in fact. These favorable comments were the last Frans made about his director.

In the fall of the year Gates continued to have trouble with President Dinwiddie over the need for money for the department. "It is not my place to continue begging," he protested, "and I will not do it. I have given Tulane and New Orleans my strength without stint as all know." He resigned over a small matter, then reconsidered and withdrew the resignation. Dinwiddie, in turn, cooled toward him and insisted that he must follow university procedures in regard to spending money.

Gates became aware of another problem. He began to realize that his promising young archaeologist was taking on independent—in fact, impudent—airs. On his own Frans proposed a budget for the department that would provide only $1,500 for Gates and his plans. So the director had a meeting with the young man and could scarcely believe what he heard. Gates reported the interview this way: "He tells me that my 'botany program . . . has thrown people off the track,'. . . . That he feels 'great responsibility' for the 'big job' I have 'entrusted him with,' and that though he admires my broad plans, he is afraid they 'are running away with me,' and so I am 'endangering the Dept.'s' success, and to his mind we have to cut down right away and get on to *sound* ground before we run too far. The publicity given this year's field work should be taken advantage of." Gates could not mistake Frans's meaning: archaeology must take first place, to the exclusion of the grand plans the director had set forth.

Blom went to New York to cultivate good relations with archaeological organizations and to seek grants for an expedition. At that point Gates, to show his authority, ordered Blom to cease his activities. Blom wired Dinwiddie, "Hate walking on volcanoes, so propose definite amount set aside for my work, and I deal direct with you." The last words referred to another wound Gates felt that Blom had inflicted. The young man was in the habit of taking problems of the department directly to the president and bypassing the director. There was also the matter of writing the report of the 1925 expedition. Gates vowed that he would not allow Frans to leave on another expedition until he had completed the report of the last one. In an encounter between the two men, Gates reported Blom as declaring, ". . . I will not work with you; I am going to turn in my report and quit." A few days later Frans sent his resignation to the president, to take effect October 1, 1926. At the same time Blom noted in his diary: "It is getting unbearable to work in a mess of a library like this, and under such hopeless conditions like the ones here." He told the president that he resigned because of the disorganization of the department, the ineffective library, and "acts and accusations against me by the Director."

He elaborated his complaints in a letter to a friend. "You can imagine how I felt when I found out that my mail was censored and I was not put in communication with people who called me on the telephone." There was a more immediate reason for his action. Gates had scheduled him to go to Honduras to further the plan of aiding that nation, a project which Blom opposed. By resigning, Frans found a way to avoid the assignment. It appears that Blom was sure of his ground, for his resignation was tabled by the trustees pending a reorganization of the department.

Dinwiddie closed in on Gates early in 1926. He placed the library of the department under the control of a university committee, with a view to having the books cataloged, an action which the director had refused to take. Gates held on to his job, was careful not to resign again, and continued to complain about Blom.

During these troubles, Frans considered the alternatives of earning a doctorate or finding another job. He had already inquired about the advanced degree at Harvard. In June 1924 Tozzer urged him to seek the degree, explaining that it would take two years and require much reading in the field of anthropology. After sending in his resignation in November 1925 Frans thought about advanced study again; at that time Tozzer advised the doctorate only if Blom planned to teach. Later on Dinwiddie thought that Tulane might grant the degree based on scientific papers by Blom, to be judged by experts in the field. Nothing came of that plan. As late as 1927 Frans considered the idea of the advanced degree, but remarked that it was out of the question because he could not leave his job at Tulane; moreover, he wanted the Ph.D. only from Harvard. There was also the possibility of finding work at another institution. Early in January 1926 Clarence Hay of the American Museum of Natural History visited the department and

offered Frans a job. By this time, however, Blom insisted
that he wanted to build up the department at Tulane.

Gates refused to give up his post. When Blom went to
New York early in 1926, Gates again ordered him to
cease his activity there, and once more Blom resigned.
This time Dinwiddie took over direction of the
department and authorized Blom to hire Oliver La Farge
as his assistant. Instead of giving up, Gates sent a long
recital of his wrongs to the president and threatened
legal action against the university. The tone of the letter
was so offensive that he was dismissed, with salary until
October 1. The unpaid bills that flowed into the
department and overran the budget were generously
paid by Zemurray.

We have little of Blom's version of the trouble with
Gates. Frans told Tozzer that when he took the job he
hoped to steer "old Gates out of the turbulent waters in
which he was paddling around. . . . I have the impression
that I did not throw sufficiently large bouquets of flowers
at him when I gave my first talk at the university on the
results of the expedition. I have found that a large part of
our funds was imaginary. Gates shifted from archaeology
to tropical botany . . . people here suddenly saw the aims
of the department split and wondered." Gates's "position
as director went to his head. Many of his ideas are
excellent, but he is too erratic to carry them out on a
sound basis." On the other hand, Frans found Dinwiddie
a splendid man to work for, "and he is the chief reason
for my having stuck through the last unpleasant couple of
months."

Although Gates had been dismissed, he had the last
word. The university, reluctant to advertise its internal
troubles and perhaps embarrassed over having hired the
man in the first place, issued no public statement of his
dismissal. Despite the emotional shock Gates suffered
from his firing, he holed up at Auburn Hill, pored over
his correspondence, and wrote a seventy-page pamphlet
relating the deceit, treachery, and villainy he had
experienced at Tulane. He printed and distributed the

pamphlet at his own expense. Only in May, when the statement appeared, did Tulane release the official minutes of his dismissal.[4]

It is difficult to estimate Frans's role in the imbroglio that had developed at Tulane, since we have so little of his version of events. Certainly he was an ambitious young man who made the most of opportunities. It appears that after Gates had discredited himself, Blom used his friendship with Dinwiddie to forward archaeology as the major function of the department. Events showed that he estimated his relations with the president correctly, for the drama moved on toward the conclusion Blom expected. If we can believe Gates's stories, Frans acted unethically and impudently. Gates, on the other hand, was a vain and imperceptive man who performed ineptly from the beginning of his tenure at Tulane.[5]

Blom achieved his goal of ousting Gates and taking his place as director of the department. Not yet thirty-three, he assumed new responsibilities. The victory surely increased his self-confidence and the conviction that he could solve any problem he chose to undertake.

4

The Department of Middle
American Research

In operating and expanding the department, Blom displayed creative ability as an administrator, an achievement for which he has not received adequate credit. Although he entered the job with no administrative experience, he knew precisely what he wanted to do, and within the limits of the budget he accomplished most of his aims. He quietly dropped Gates's impractical plans, focused the activities of the department on archaeology,[1] and aimed for modest goals. His plans were original; no one directed his work, and he followed no known model, unless he drew unconsciously on his acquaintance with the Peabody Museum. In addition, he was able to inspire workers to their best performance. Fortunately, Frans also served under a sympathetic university president, who had faith in his program.

Blom considered the department an institution for research. Expeditions and the specialized library provided the raw materials from which new knowledge could be derived. The museum served a dual function:

to provide artifacts for study and to display an array of objects to interest and educate the general public. An additional duty of the department was the publication of scholarly monographs, when money became available for the purpose. Frans believed that all branches of the organization must develop simultaneously.[2]

With research as the ultimate objective, he opposed the intrusion of academic instruction into the work of the department. Teaching was a separate function that would only interfere with a program of expeditions and full-time devotion to study of the documents. One of his associates believes that Frans lacked the qualities for effective teaching. If it is difficult to assess that point, it is noteworthy that he avoided classroom instruction. Once in 1926 he casually mentioned teaching a course in anthropology, though it appears to have been no more than a passing thought. Twelve years later, when the administration called on the department to offer graduate courses, Blom was listed to teach Middle American archaeology; there is no evidence that he ever conducted the course.

Even in the matter of expeditions there was a difference of opinion between him and the administration. He believed that he should be in the field three-quarters of the year and spend the remaining months at Tulane in writing and research. The administration would have reversed the figures. In the end no great issue arose, because he got along well with President Dinwiddie and because money for expeditions failed to appear.

In the early years Frans believed that more money might be forthcoming to expand the department. One of the factors that induced him to come to Tulane was Gates's glowing intimation that increasing funds could be expected. Soon, however, he learned that this was no more than a pipe dream. With the departure of the troublesome Gates, Blom had good reason to be optimistic. He received an increase of $1,000 in his salary. Dinwiddie began talking as if a larger budget might be possible. Zemurray, after a long absence, visited the department, expressed gratification at Frans's work, and also gave the impression that more money could be expected. In view of what actually happened, perhaps the new director read more into those remarks than was justified.

As Blom contemplated new projects, he turned naturally to the administration for money to carry them out. He submitted a budget of $25,000 for operating expenses in 1927, an increase of $10,000 over the $15,000 income from the Zemurray endowment. His request was not granted. After he started on the expedition of 1928, he asked the president to raise $5,000 in additional funds for the coming year. Nothing happened. He requested a budget of $25,000 in 1929, with a proposal to publish some of the manuscripts in the department. No increase was granted. In 1930 there must have been a compelling reason for his remarkable optimism, for he asked to change the department to an institute, and submitted a budget for $201,000. Nothing came of these proposals, and salaries and operating expenses were kept within $15,000. Except for a small special appropriation for the library one year, the administration did not increase the annual budget until 1937, and then only by $2,500 from a special fund.

Unable to gain additional help from the administration, Frans looked in other directions. Among individual philanthropists, Samuel Zemurray was the most likely patron. After all, he had endowed the department and paid some of the expenses to get it off to a good start. It appears that Blom had cordial relations with Zemurray as the years passed by, but the benefactor never again made a notable gift to the department.

The only other patron who helped significantly was Matilda Gray. She and her brothers financed the expedition of 1928 and set up a modest fund to purchase occasional rare books and manuscripts. Blom made her an honorary associate of the department in 1935, and in that capacity she went to Guatemala at her own expense, collected some sixty native Indian costumes and gave them to the department; the collection remains one of the prized possessions of the department today. Her gifts were helpful and cannot be ignored, but her wealth and Frans's assiduous cultivation of her appeared to some persons to be out of proportion to the modest aid she gave.

A plan to gain numerous small donations from individuals had only limited success. Under Gates the Exploration Society came into being as a device to raise money to put expeditions in the field. The plan called for a contribution of $100 from each member annually for three years. Gates's expectation that the society would raise $20,000 a year turned out to be another miscalculation. Blom revived the plan, and worked on it intensively in 1926 and 1927. He managed to raise $2,500 to support the expedition of La Farge and Byers. Thereafter, the Exploration Society languished. By 1930-31 it provided about $1,000 a year. As small gifts came in in the 1930s, the money went into the general fund of the department and was used to defray travel expenses of staff members. Thus the society gradually lost its original purpose.

Appeals to foundations netted more money in the long run than donations from individual patrons. Frans was in New York in May 1929, presenting his case to the Rockefeller Foundation and the General Education Board, and he also planned to visit the Rosenwald Foundation. On several occasions in New York he induced a wealthy friend to hold a private party, with members of the Morgan and Lamont families as guests, so that he could show motion pictures of the Maya. At one of those gatherings he expected John D. Rockefeller, Jr.; when the philanthropist failed to appear, Frans was grateful, for that night the rented projector tore the film nineteen times. "I was frantic," he admitted, though he believed that the audience showed interest.

The money he secured from foundations over the years added materially to the growth of the department. A sizable grant in 1931 strengthened the library; other grants initiated the publication of the *Middle American Papers*, brought the index of Maya sites up to date, and started the cataloging and photographing of every object in the museum. In 1938 Frans reported that during his tenure the department had received $229,400, which amounted to more than the income from the Zemurray endowment.

More important than money was personnel, and Blom did remarkably well in assembling a group of specialists to carry out the various phases of the work. Until 1931 the entire staff consisted of five persons, including Ralph Roys in Maya language and Hermann Beyer in Mexican archaeology. During the next five years the staff increased to nine persons. Mrs. Doris Stone filled a post in ethnology, Arthur Gropp became librarian, Ernest Noyes worked in philology, Gerhardt Kramer in architecture, and Maurice Ries served as editor of publications. Thereafter the staff dropped to six persons, except for one year when a few additional aides held temporary jobs. It is not clear how Frans managed to pay his staff on the annual budget, supplemented by grants. One worker later complained that no one received raises throughout the depression years of the 1930s. We know that Blom voluntarily cut his own salary in order to help the department in that period.

There can be no doubt that he had potential contributors in mind when he introduced the practice of naming honorary associates to the staff. Beginning with the appointment in 1929 of T. A. Willard, the battery manufacturer turned amateur archaeologist, Frans eventually gave ten persons that title. He explained the practice as a way of acknowledging the interest of the recipient in the work of the department. Surely he hoped that the honorary associates would demonstrate their interest by donations of money or services. Generally, however, the plan produced no more than small contributions at most.

Blom struggled to make the library a first-rate tool for research. Gates had failed to have the books cataloged, a defect which was not remedied until a librarian began the task at the end of 1926. It became apparent that the Gates collection lacked a number of titles which had appeared in the original sale catalog. No one accused Gates of deliberately withholding the items, but somehow carelessness or oversight deprived Tulane of volumes it should have received.[3] Also, when Gates started his bibliographical project, he bought a thousand books of general interest in Mexico, which Blom considered worthless in the specialized collection of the department.

The condition of the library and the state of some of the volumes moved him to appeal for improvements. Early in 1926 he "picked out some books to show" the "sad condition" of old volumes, which required repairs. Later on, he told a friend how he dramatized the need for better shelving for the library. He placed weak boards on cinder blocks, loaded the shelves with books until they sagged under the weight, dimmed the lights, and invited the trustees to visit the department. If the dramatic scene actually took place, it does not seem to have provided results. Only in 1929 did the trustees appropriate $2,500 for the library, but the sum was designated for new books.

The small budget for the library caused trouble when desirable items suddenly became available in dealers' catalogs. Frans devised his own way to handle the problem. At times he bought books "and paid for them myself, giving them to the library when the budget was low. At times I paid personally for valuable books and held them until the budget was able to take care of them."

It should be added that President Dinwiddie was sympathetic and sometimes found money to acquire a special item. Once Blom had the opportunity to buy the manuscript of the first Spanish laws in America, the Ordenanza of 1524. After examining the ink and paper to be certain that the document was genuine, he approached the president for the necessary cash.

Dinwiddie had to admit that funds were not available. So Frans asked him for an advance on his salary to make the purchase, the amount to be returned when the money could be found. The president could not resist that kind of appeal. "Next morning Dr. Dinwiddie informed me that he found the money," Frans explained. "That's the kind of a guy he was."

The Ordenanza was significant enough to merit publication. So Frans approached lawyers in New Orleans for contributions to carry out the plan. "What the hell did they care?" was his summary of their reaction. Then he went to the dean of the law school at Tulane for the same purpose, and was also turned down.

Blom continued to add to the specialized collection of books. Arthur Gropp, librarian of the department for over a decade, testifies to Frans's deep interest in the library and to his grasp of pertinent bibliography. He "had an overall, rather definite plan for the library," reports Gropp, "and I felt the responsibility for divining it and carrying it out." In addition, Frans "frequently punctuated his comments with references from memory to the sources . . . and to well-known recent authorities. . . . He could recall data from more obscure writings, showing a broad knowledge of the field."

His desire to acquire primary materials brought some interesting items to Tulane. When Frans was in Mexico City in 1932, he visited the well-known Porrúa bookstore. On asking if they had anything interesting, he was shown several hundred bundles of manuscripts in storage. After a cursory examination, he bought them for $1,000. When the material arrived at Tulane, "they were found to cover the period 1588 through the colonial period and well into the national period of Mexico's history. Among them was a 1757 petition made for the restitution of property by the town of Tenango, to which was attached a supporting copy of a hitherto unknown letter of Hernando Cortés, originally written in 1525."

"On other occasions," continues Gropp, "he obtained such choice rarities as the Tulane Codex, a hieroglyphic manuscript of Mixtec origin, written on deerskin. There was the Cortés original letter of 1524, signed by Cortés himself; the Oroz manuscript on the lives of the Franciscan fathers, dated 1585; an early Franciscan Maya-Spanish and Spanish-Maya manuscript dictionary; and a book of original sketches by an English engineer, operating in Mexico in 1914, of Mexican and American soldiers, with numerous details of uniform and equipment. . . ."[4]

Blom's strong interest in Chiapas was also evident in some of the acquisitions. He secured early newspapers and other publications from that state. He paid David Amram, who was traveling in Chiapas, $100 a month for three months in 1934 to secure all pertinent printed and documentary material he could lay hands on for the department. One of Amram's best acquisitions was part of the Flavio Paniagua collection, which Blom had seen in San Cristóbal in 1925.

To celebrate a meeting of the American Library Association in New Orleans in 1932, Frans had Arthur Gropp prepare a pamphlet, *Rare Americana,* which described twenty-five unusual books at Tulane, most of them published in the sixteenth century. The following year Gropp issued an account of eighty-eight of the more important manuscripts in the department library. Eventually Blom managed to receive a grant from the Rockefeller Foundation to initiate a survey of the resources of libraries and archives of the entire Middle American area, a task which Gropp carried out.

The library expanded significantly over the years. In 1926 it contained 3,500 items (books, manuscripts, pamphlets, and autographs); by 1938 the number had grown to 35,500.[5] In the latter year a new administrative policy required the centralization of the library resources of the university, and Frans faced the loss of the department's specialized library. Before the actual transfer took place, he was no longer working at Tulane.

The museum, housed on the fourth floor of the Science Building (now Dinwiddie Hall) with the library, provided the most spectacular aspect of the department, for it gave the public a visual presentation of the artifacts of ancient American civilizations. Blom made the most of every opportunity to gain objects by gift or by loan for display.

Over the years he acquired many items for the museum, including some particularly choice objects. The collection of marble vessels from Honduras is outstanding. Ulúa polychrome pottery and a nephrite Olmec figure, also from Honduras, are noteworthy. There are stunning carved shell ornaments from the Huasteca and a gold pectoral ornament in Monte Albán style. The Indian costumes from Guatemala assembled by Matilda Gray constitute one of the finest collections to be found anywhere. Among the smaller plaster casts are items from Palenque, Uxmal, Chichén Itzá, and, of course, copies of sculptures which Blom discovered at Comalcalco.[6]

The largest objects that came to the museum in the 1930s were casts of monuments in the Maya area. Edward H. Thompson's reproduction of the facade of Labná, displayed at the World's Fair of 1893, was donated by the Field Museum of Chicago. Likewise, the reproduction of a portion of the Nunnery at Uxmal, erected at the World's Fair of 1933, was turned over to the department. Other casts came from the Carnegie Institution of Washington, the Peabody Museum at Harvard, and the University of Pennsylvania. Only a few pieces from those collections could be displayed in the museum. The remaining casts, which must be bulky indeed, were stored under the grandstand of the university's stadium. Only recently have some of them been removed for display at the New Orleans Museum of Art.

The museum became one of the major problems of the department, for it was difficult to bring the large collection of artifacts under control. The Rockefeller Foundation trained Ray Trahan in museum techniques in the United States and abroad, and he was named curator in 1937. The same foundation also made a small grant for a pilot project to catalog and photograph every item in the collection, but the money ran out long before the work was completed. Artifacts accumulated so fast that by 1938 the fourth floor of the Science Building was crowded. When the campaign to erect a separate structure for the department failed, the central section of the fourth floor was walled off from offices and storage rooms, modern display cases and a low ceiling were installed, the best objects were placed on view, and the remainder were stored. Blom left Tulane about the time the alterations were made.

In addition to the library and museum, Frans cultivated an interest in maps. The combined index and map of Maya sites became a permanent feature of the department. He began the project for his master's thesis at Harvard, and on coming to Tulane he planned to enlarge the project and open it to all interested scholars. He appealed to explorers to send in new information in order to make the index and map as complete as possible.

Only occasionally did he publish the map. The master's thesis was issued in an edition of thirty-five copies. By 1929 he was angry to find that Herbert J. Spinden had also prepared a map of Maya sites, which Blom termed "a pirate edition." He gave Spinden credit, nevertheless, for "some additions," and prepared a revised edition in 1929, though he had only a few copies printed. Over the years he wrote some articles about new Maya sites. In the late 1930s the Carnegie Institution of Washington gave a small grant to bring the index and map up to date, and in 1940 Tulane published the final edition of the map. Today the index cards are still available for consultation at the department.

On at least two occasions Frans tried to enlist the cooperation of the American Geographical Society. When he prepared for the expedition of 1928, he invited the society to send a cartographer as a member of the team; the organization declined on the plea that no one was available. Three years later he approached the society again, suggesting that it should take the initiative in providing good maps of Central America.

On expeditions Frans always drew small maps of sites and areas through which he traveled. The catalog of the map collection at Tulane credits Blom with several dozen maps, not counting those that appear in his original field notebooks. As we shall see, his interest in mapping increased during the later, Mexican period of his life.

Blom and the work he was doing attracted visitors to the department. When Mrs. Theodore Roosevelt stopped off in New Orleans in the mid 1930s, Blom took her in tow, reminding her that her son Archie had been best man at his wedding. In 1936 a local newspaper noted that fourteen "celebrities" visited the department within a period of six weeks. Danes coming to the city were often greeted by Blom, and if they were persons of some prominence, a notice and a photograph appeared in the newspaper. In 1938 Charles Lanthrup, Danish orchestra conductor, received this treatment, with Blom acting as host.

Frans also took note of the people who came to see the exhibits. One morning he saw a distinguished-looking man and his granddaughter intently examining the objects on display. Blom introduced himself and gave the visitors a tour of the museum. Then the man identified himself as Frederick L. Hoffman, who had traveled in South America and had collected anthropological and geographical data. When he offered to give the material to the department, Frans accepted with pleasure.

It was another story, however, when Blom dealt with Thomas Gann. The retired physician-archaeologist of British Honduras visited New Orleans twice in 1926. He proposed that Tulane join the British Museum or some other archaeological organization to excavate Copán. Frans asked his old friend Tozzer at Havard for advice on the proposition. Tozzer warned him against any joint arrangement, remarking that he did not like Gann's methods of publicity and his lack of ethics in buying and selling artifacts. Surely Frans also recollected the story of Gann and the jade he smuggled out of Mexico in 1923. Although we know nothing more about the proposed joint expedition, Blom later made Gann an honorary associate on the staff of the department. His contributions consisted of some small stucco heads from British Honduras and a gift of books from his library, which the department received after his death in 1938.

Blom also took an interest in his staff members. Oliver La Farge and Hermann Beyer became the best-known persons affiliated with the department. They could not have been more dissimilar. La Farge was a creative writer with a deep interest in Indians past and present; Beyer represented the old-fashioned scholar who engaged in minute research. Each in his own way experienced a time of troubles—about the only thing they had in common.

La Farge had benefited from a distinguished background and good training. His father was a well-known architect; his grandfather was the famous artist John La Farge. When Oliver was at Groton, he read a book on the Old Stone Age, which turned his interest to European anthropology. As an undergraduate at Harvard, he enjoyed several seasons in the field in the Southwest, which attracted him to the American aborigines, especially the Navajos and Apaches. In addition he aspired, at first rather vaguely, to become a writer, and received encouragement when some of his stories appeared in student publications at Harvard. He was elected president of the Harvard *Advocate* and was class poet in his senior year. After receiving the A.B., he continued the study of anthropology in the graduate school in the fall of 1924, where Blom met him.

Frans formed a favorable opinion of the young man. He described him as "a bright boy, with a keen mind," and hired him at $100 a month and expenses to accompany him on the expedition to Uaxactún in 1925. Before Oliver assumed the job, Blom left the Carnegie Institution of Washington and took the post at Tulane. As

soon as Frans knew that he was slated for an expedition
through Mexico, he hired La Farge to accompany him on
that venture. Oliver's qualifications look good: he had
experience in the field, knew how to handle horses and
boats, and had training in linguistics and anthropology to
supplement Blom's knowledge of archaeology. He
interrupted his graduate study to join Frans in Mexico
City, where the expedition began.

In the course of the journey Blom had moments of
doubt about his young assistant. At Comalcalco, La Farge
came to the site one morning without his digging tools.
"I sometimes do wonder what he fills his head with,"
Frans confided to his diary. "He is quick to remember
reading, but slow in movements, and impractical and
absent-minded in work. I gave him a lecture. . . ." When
Blom sent him back to the village at noon for tools, food,
and other items, Oliver returned, again having forgotten
some of the articles he was to bring. Later on during the
journey Frans was so irritated over the young fellow's
action that he wrote that he "is somewhat of a weak
sister and seems to hate hard work. Either he complains
because he has eaten too much or because he is hungry."

La Farge's temperament was not suited to the work of
the expedition, though he does not appear to have
realized the problem. His diary reveals that he held
Frans in high regard as a leader. When Blom doctored a
sick native and arranged for a physician at Puerto México
to care for the man, Oliver called the behavior "very
nice." On another occasion he noted with obvious
approval that Frans "doctored several children for fever."
One night he had a talk with Blom "on things in
general," and found the conversation "very good." In his
own record Oliver admitted that he had been inefficient
and had forgotten the important tools.

La Farge was grateful also for the older man's paternal
oversight. At a village where they stopped, Oliver "went
on a big private binge second night." He noted in his
journal that he considered the indulgence "very
satisfactory and a good value for $10.00, but that is really

more than I can afford." Frans had fallen asleep, woke up, and "was worried by my not coming home, and went to find me. . . . Darned nice of him."

Only in one minor instance did Oliver turn upon his leader. When La Farge contracted a fever, he took to his hammock. "Hoped for a quick sleep, but 148 troubles with hammock." The ropes loosened and he bumped to the ground. Blom heard "a new kind of profanity, probably 'special Harvard.'" Oliver admitted that he "swore a bit, which annoyed Frans, and then swore at him."

Was Oliver as ineffective as Frans portrayed him? In the report of the expedition we learn that La Farge found carved stones in unlikely places on several occasions. The ethnographic and linguistic data that appear in the report represented a great deal of activity on the younger man's part. And sometimes he engaged in tasks not connected with the field of his interest. At Agua Escondida "La Farge spent a great part of the day dangling from a rope on the side of the temple roof, a part of which he cleared, making studies of the roof crest."

After the two men returned to New Orleans, Blom continued to have reservations about his friend. Although Frans received the lion's share of public notice for the expedition, Oliver also gained some attention, including a lengthy account of his finds in ethnology in *The New York Times*. Some weeks later Blom feared that "social activities, artistic temperament, and fame of being a great explorer" went to the young fellow's head. He estimated Oliver's work on the expedition with mixed opinions. "Oliver made good on the trail," that is, in collecting scientific information, "but he certainly was green when he started" and is "still green." When Frans collected the manuscript reports of the journey to prepare the account for publication, "Oliver very cheerfully writes and tells me that he has lost our original field notes." When the missing papers turned up, Frans exclaimed, "How the hell did you do it?" In the next breath, however, he praised the man for the linguistic data he had assembled.

Apparently Blom did not consider Oliver's deficiencies serious, for he arranged to add him to the permanent staff of the department in 1926. "I am doing my damnedest to get a place for you, but I can only do it when I know you will stick with us for a certain length of time." Despite an unfavorable report from Tozzer about La Farge's attitude toward graduate work, Blom hired him as his assistant, with Dinwiddie's approval, before Gates left Tulane.

La Farge cut a unique figure in New Orleans. If his work for the department was routine, his residence in the French Quarter allowed him unconventional forms of self-expression, perhaps to be expected on his first complete separation from home. He associated with Faulkner and Spratling, who found him amusing when he came in late at night and revealed his newest discovery, the introduction to the mysteries of sex. Sometimes he wore an Indian band about his forehead and gave a graphic performance of Indian dances.[7] At one party, for which Spratling had borrowed a dozen expensive tumblers, Oliver found it diverting to drop the glasses, one by one, out of a third-story window, curious to hear the sound they made as they crashed on the pavement below.

Blom had some trouble with La Farge. Although he carried on his work satisfactorily at the department, one could not be certain what he might do in his free hours. Frans reported that "the young man got mixed up in a row here, and that has caused me some trouble. . . . I believe, though, that the matter is settled now, and we will at least be able to work in peace." This "row" was undoubtedly the incident that occurred at a masked ball in April 1926, when Oliver became involved in a dispute with the son and daughter of a trustee of Tulane. Although the details of the affair are not known, his action was not forgotten.

By the latter part of 1926 Frans arranged for Oliver to

1. Frans Blom at Puerto México, Mexico, 1922, when he was employed by an oil company. *Courtesy Middle American Research Institute, Tulane University*

2. The Temple of the Inscriptions, Palenque. In 1922–23 Blom noted the perforations in an interior floor slab but failed to investigate them. Years later a Mexican archaeologist, Alberto Ruz Lhuillier, lifted the slab and eventually discovered a fine tomb at the bottom of the pyramid. *Photo by Linda Schele, courtesy University of South Alabama*

3. From left: Oliver La Farge, Frans Blom, and Tata (Lázaro Hernández) at San Cristóbal de las Casas during the expedition of 1925. *Courtesy Middle American Research Institute, Tulane University*

4. One of the stucco figures found by Blom in tomb at Comalcalco, 1925. *Courtesy Middle American Research Institute, Tulane University*

5. William E. Gates. *Courtesy Middle American Research Institute, Tulane University*

6. Maya marble bowl, with double-headed handles and scroll decorations, from the Ulóa Valley, Honduras. The first gift received by the Department of Middle American Research. *Courtesy Middle American Research Institute, Tulane University*

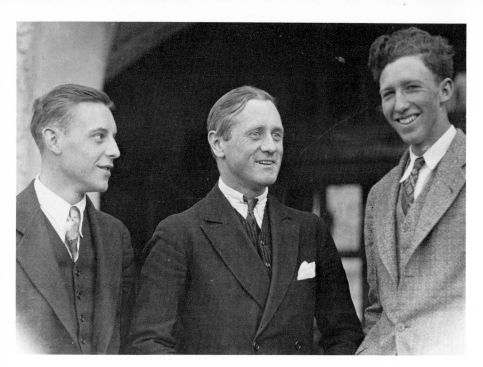

7. Tulane group before leaving on expedition of 1928. From left: Louis Bristow, Frans Blom, F. Webster McBryde. *Photo by Dan Leyrer, courtesy Middle American Research Institute, Tulane University*

8. Members of the John Geddings Gray Memorial Expedition, 1928. From left: Ciriaco Aguilar, Gustavo Kantor, Louis Bristow, F. Webster McBryde, Frans Blom, and Acting President Bechtel of Tulane. *Courtesy Archives, Special Collections Division, Tulane University Library*

9. Frans Blom on 1928 expedition. *Photo by Louis Bristow, courtesy Middle American Research Institute, Tulane University*

10. F. Webster McBryde, photographer, expedition of 1928. *Photo by Frans Blom, courtesy Middle American Research Institute, Tulane University*

11. Louis Bristow, medic, expedition of 1928. *Courtesy Middle American Research Institute, Tulane University*

12. The Nunnery, Uxmal. Blom was commissioned to reproduce the entire structure for the World's Fair of 1933, but only a small portion of the complex appeared at the fair. *Author photo*

13.   Frans Blom, Tulane University, 1937. *Courtesy Middle American Research Institute, Tulane University*

14. Part of the museum of the Department of Middle American Research, Tulane University, about 1931. *Courtesy Tulane University, Latin American Library*

15. Blom and friend, Tulane University, about 1938. *Courtesy Tulane University, Latin American Library*

make an expedition to Guatemala to investigate the survival of the old Maya calendar. As the time for departure approached, the young man got cold feet and doubted his ability to carry on the venture himself. So Blom told him to add Douglas S. Byers, another Harvard student, to accompany him, and, as Frans put it, to "stabilize" him. Despite Frans's prediction that Oliver would return with superficial data, the two investigators brought back excellent material, which appeared in *The Year Bearer's People.*

During his years at Tulane, Oliver wrote both articles and fiction in his free time. One of his short stories, "North Is Black," appeared in the *Dial* and was included in *Best American Short Stories of 1927.* His description of the native towns he had visited during the expedition of 1925 appeared in *Scribner's* magazine, and local newspapers also carried some of his writings. As part of his work at the department, he wrote sections of *Tribes and Temples* and collaborated with Byers on *The Year Bearer's People.* He did not tell friends that he was working on a novel, *Laughing Boy.* Although he began the manuscript in the fall of 1926, he made only spasmodic progress due to interruptions.

One of the interruptions occurred in the first half of 1928, when Oliver directed the department during Blom's long absence on the expedition through Chiapas, Guatemala, and Yucatán. When news from Frans failed to arrive a month after the scheduled time, La Farge had Dinwiddie wire to Chiapas inquiring about him; that afternoon a telegram from Blom arrived at Tulane. Later on, Frans expressed his appreciation of the way Oliver had handled affairs during his absence: "En fin, I want to say to you that I am very glad for your friendship. . . ." In September Oliver joined Frans and Beyer in attending the International Congress of Americanists in New York City, and then Oliver went on to Harvard to do some work for the department. Early in October he failed to receive his salary check from Tulane. Without notification he had been fired from his job.

A spiteful trustee and a forgetful university president made La Farge's separation an unforgivable event. Oliver had been put on half time from March 1928 until the end of August. Blom was so pleased with his work that he recommended him for a full-time job at an increase in salary. When the board of trustees met and Oliver's reappointment came up, the trustee whose children had had the run-in with Oliver at the ball two years earlier opposed the young man, and another trustee tended to support him. Under the circumstances Dinwiddie considered it unwise to make an issue of the matter. So La Farge was dropped. Then Dinwiddie failed to inform either La Farge or Blom of the action, and Oliver did not discover his fate until October. Dinwiddie, conscious of his failure to inform the young man, paid him seventy-five dollars as a consolation.

La Farge had friends in New Orleans, and so he returned to the French Quarter and concentrated on completing *Laughing Boy*. With the encouragement of Houghton Mifflin, he finished the manuscript in May 1929, had it accepted, and then packed his bags and returned to the Northeast. The book was a success, gained adoption by the Literary Guild, and won the Pulitzer Prize in 1930. Because of an ungenerous trustee Tulane missed the opportunity of having La Farge on its staff when he became famous.

Blom continued to hold Oliver in high esteem. He considered the novel "one of the most beautiful things I have read in many a day." When La Farge married a rich New York girl the next year, however, Blom feared that the success of the book and the wealthy marriage "will go terribly to his head." But after Oliver and his wife visited New Orleans, Blom was reassured. "He is shining like a new, polished sun," he remarked, "and is very happy. I think he has passed the 'Sturm und Drang' period." Frans contributed some advice on details when the little theater of the French Quarter staged a dramatic version of *Laughing Boy* in 1932. Decades later, as we shall see, Frans turned against his former friend, though the reason is not clear.

In marked contrast to La Farge was another worker at the department, Hermann Beyer, who specialized in the study of Maya glyphs. Born in Cologne, Germany, in 1880, he trained in journalism and attended lectures in ethnology, sociology, and history at the universities of Berlin, Halle, and Paris. He went to Mexico in 1904 and began publishing articles on Mexican archaeology in 1908; as the years passed, he moved into the study of Maya hieroglyphs. From 1915 to 1926 he worked in Mexico, first as Inspector of Ancient Monuments and then as a professor at the national university.

Blom brought him to Tulane in 1927 to continue his researches. At the time Frans described him as a serious worker, "somewhat inclined to German pedantry, but with a profound knowledge of his field." All told, he estimated Beyer as "steady and square." With rare linguistic books available at the department, he believed, Beyer could make significant contributions to professional knowledge by working at Tulane. After Frans hired him for a year as a "try out," the German remained with the department almost until the time of his death.

Blom had judged the man correctly. Beyer labored conscientiously, made some discoveries in the field of glyphs, which were appreciated by specialists, turned out numerous papers, and edited the periodical *El México antiguo*. He was not the kind of man to attract public attention. He spoke rarely to groups in New Orleans and almost as rarely was he quoted in newspapers in regard to his professional field.

Despite some eccentricities, he had a few good friends. If he was dogmatic in his views about glyphs, he was congenial with those who knew him socially. He lived alone in New Orleans. He had left a wife and child in Mexico and apparently contributed to their support. Once near Christmas time he asked Frans for money, explaining that "a little boy is waiting for his Christmas gifts, and I owe three months to the lady." He weighed over two hundred pounds and consumed quantities of food. At one time the problem of weight took him to Battle Creek Sanitarium for a few weeks. Each day he took physical exercise, once using roller skates on the pine floor of a friend's dining room.

Frans respected and supported Beyer in his scholarly endeavors. When the German sought a fellowship to make a firsthand study of the Dresden Codex, the sponsors of the grant suggested that the document had been examined many times. "I do not agree with Beyer's theory," Frans countered, "but feel that his work is of the highest value. If it brings positive results, all is well. If negative, he has eliminated one line of approach which the rest of us do not need to go over again."

On another occasion Blom went so far as to defend Beyer in a reprehensible act. When Hermann studied hieroglyphs at Chichén Itzá, Morley generously loaned him sheets of rubbings at that site. Morley planned to photograph and publish those records. At Tulane, without telling anyone of his action, Beyer cut the sheets into small pieces so as to isolate each glyph. When he returned the package of snippets, Morley flew into a rage, then calmed himself and wrote a complaint—a reasonably mild letter in view of the circumstances—to Frans about the act of vandalism. Blom did himself no credit in his reply: "You are free to use abusive language to your mules, but that you should use such language to a colleague on an official matter does not flatter the institution with which you are connected." He blamed Morley for not instructing Beyer how to use the rubbings! "Until I receive a written correction of your abusive letter," Blom concluded, "I shall refrain from having further correspondence from you personally." Although Morley gave no "written correction," he wrote Blom a cool letter, expressing his sorrow and sadness over the actions of the two men at Tulane.

As the 1930s wore on, Beyer, who retained his German citizenship, began to champion Hitler and his policies.

After a visit to Germany in 1938, he became more vocal. Local newspapers reported him as declaring that Germany enjoyed pure democracy, because the people ruled. When friends had him to dinner in a restaurant in New Orleans, his pro-Nazi remarks were overheard and almost caused a scene. In the middle of 1940 Beyer offered to resign because of anti-German feeling; Blom attempted to arrange a part-time position of "roving associate" for the man, but the administration would not agree to the proposal. After the United States entered the Second World War, the government placed Beyer in an internment camp in Oklahoma, where he died in 1942. Through the good offices of a friend, his voluminous papers, including the manuscript of his magnum opus on glyphs, were saved, and are available at Tulane for the use of scholars.

Blom succeeded in building an organization to carry on research and to educate the public. He enlarged the library and the museum, and added staff members for specialized tasks as the need arose. In the creative administrative program he had in mind, expeditions played an important role. In 1928 he led the most adventurous and most dangerous exploration during his years at Tulane.

5

The Expedition of 1928

In retrospect the Gray Memorial Expedition was a daring and foolhardy venture. Blom led his party, including two college boys, over impossible mountains, through unmapped wastes, and into a cliff-enclosed cul-de-sac from which he refused to retreat. He stretched his self-confidence and optimism almost too far. Only later did he admit sheepishly that he had learned a lesson in responsibility for the lives of others, especially two promising young men from New Orleans. Fortunately, the expedition succeeded in attaining its goal, though it was a month behind schedule.

The story of the journey is little known, because the official record was never published. The manuscript diaries of three of the participants survive, however, and provide a narrative of heroic adventure. The party passed through exotic lands, faced danger on the trail, suffered from insufficient food, made archaeological discoveries, saw nature in its wild aspects, and visited the Lacandón Indians.

Shortly after La Farge and Byers returned from their expedition to Guatemala, Blom began to tell friends about a new venture he would undertake at the beginning of 1928. He acquired the money in an unusual way. John Geddings Gray, of Vinton, Louisiana, had been a civil engineer with an interest in exploring and studying the fauna of his state. After his death his children, Matilda, William, and Henry, agreed to give $5,000 to Tulane to finance an expedition as a memorial to him. Frans, a friend of Matilda, certainly had a hand in concocting the plan. It was a unique way to combine a memorial with a trip through his favorite Maya area. He planned the journey to include a little-known portion of the Chiapas region.

In selecting the members of the team, Blom either showed remarkable judgment or, as is more likely, enjoyed some strokes of good luck. He chose several persons he had met in Central America in 1925 to provide a knowledge of local languages. Ciriaco Aguilar, a twenty-eight-year-old Tzeltal Indian, joined the team at Encanto and became cook for the group. Gustavo Kantor, twenty-four years old, the son of a German father and a native mother in Guatemala, had also come to Blom's attention in 1925. In preparation for the expedition of 1928, Kantor came to New Orleans so that he would be with the team at the beginning in order to choose mules in Tapachula; he was put in charge of transportation.

Frans also selected two students from Tulane University to accompany him. He insisted on using fraternity men on the assumption that they had learned how to get along with people. One day Louis Bristow, Jr., who had completed only a year in medical school, received a call to see Wilbur Smith, professor of anatomy and also director of athletics. Assuming that he would be asked to collect tickets at a weekend game, Louis refused to heed the call. Some days later he received another request to see Professor Smith, who asked him if he wished to accompany Blom. The young man, twenty-one years old, was flattered with the prospect of foreign adventure, but felt some misgivings at becoming the doctor for the expedition. He handled the assignment with remarkable astuteness.

Frans also determined to have F. Webster McBryde, a sophomore in the college, as a member of the team. The student had already developed a deep interest in geology and had once queried Frans about the advisability of a career in paleobotany. Later Blom called him to his office and asked him to join the expedition as geologist. "Not even through my first year in the subject," McBryde later recalled, "I told him that I did not feel qualified—not one college credit and no experience. Without a moment's hesitation he asked, 'What *can* you do?' I said I had been taking pictures since the age of nine, and he snapped back, 'Good! You're the official photographer, then.'" Frans had him experiment with the four cameras which were part of the equipment. On the trip McBryde took many pictures and did excellent work.

After the team reached Mexico, three other men joined the party. Epifanio González and José Domingo Zamorra, Indians of Chiapas, became muleteers, and also proved to be adept assistants. Finally, the government of Mexico sent Don Carlos B. as official representative with the team.

Blom discovered that he could not avoid the shadow of William Gates. After the men left New Orleans in a Cuyamel Fruit Company boat and landed at Tampico, they went to Mexico City, where Frans had to secure clearance for his project from the Mexican government. His request to carry three firearms in order to secure food in the wilds of Chiapas met a flat refusal from the war department. "After a lot of trouble and a sheer stroke of luck," he explained to Dinwiddie, "I found that the Department of War had Gates up as an exceeding undesirable, that he had been caught in smuggling of ammunition to the rebels as far back as 1915, and that he was suspected of contact with the rebels in 1925." In that year, when Blom was in Mexico with La Farge, he was listed as working for Gates and was apparently under suspicion. By exerting influence with the War Department and some individuals, Frans managed to talk his way out of the situation. "I finally appeased the God of War, and we got a permit even to import arms." Ever thoughtful of the young men in his team, he urged them to see the highlights of the metropolis and to visit the pyramids of Teotihuacán.[1] The team then went on to Veracruz and took train to southwestern Mexico.

At Tapachula, the starting point of the expedition, Frans collected supplies and acquired mules. He bought a group of fourteen animals which had already worked together; a white mule with a bell at her neck headed the team. He brought cameras, 15,000 feet of film donated by George Eastman, medical supplies, drawing equipment, notebooks, tents which could also be used to cover cargo, cooking utensils, canvas bags, a folding table, and collapsible cots. At Tapachula he acquired a supply of food staples, such as sugar, coffee, salt, rice, and beans.

He selected an unusual route. He determined to cut through the old Maya territory of southern Chiapas and then move into the Petén and Quintana Roo. Starting at Tapachula, he crossed mountains, stopped off at Comitán and Ocosingo, and then trekked eastward to Yaxchilán. This was the most novel and exciting part of the journey, because much of the area was little known. Pushing eastward through the Petén, he stopped off at Flores, visited Maya sites, then struck north through Bacalar and the *sublevado* country of unconquered Indians, and completed the journey at Chichén Itzá. He was in the field 197 days and traversed 1,475 miles.

On the trail he established a routine that varied little from day to day. In the morning Ciriaco rose first, built a fire, and heated coffee. Then he awoke Frans with a steaming cup. After Blom dressed "and drowned my morning grudge in the beverage," the other members of the team were aroused and greeted with coffee. A large breakfast provided strength for the entire day, for there was no midday meal. In the late afternoon the men came in from their work and ate supper before dusk in order to save candles and kerosine. After dark they sat about the fire, chatted, and then turned in for the night.

The men were free to express their personalities and enjoy themselves as they pleased. Ciriaco showed ingenuity in the way he used simple items from the forest to build shelves for his pots and to set up gun racks and clothes trees. Everyone also praised him for his versatility in turning the simplest foods into attractive dishes. Another member of the team suffered from nightmares, which was considered only one more personal idiosyncracy. McBryde painted pictures of birds by lamplight. And Epifanio and José insisted on music during and after the evening meal, though the phonograph had suffered from rough handling and sounded "more and more like mourners at a wake."

The phonograph crept into the equipment only with the reluctant consent of Frans, who "grumbled that he didn't like the idea too much." It appears, however, that he received some solace from the sentimental records that the young men played. "Blom would get a far-away look in his eyes to the wistful strains of the 'Indian Love Call' and 'The Little Gypsy Sweetheart' on the other side," McBryde recalls. There he stood, "hands clasped behind his back, looking thoughtfully and silently into the gloom of the forest, as the flames of the campfire cast deep shadows beyond the walls of our camp, walls of great trunks and leaves and vines."

The two college students adapted well to the demanding conditions of the work. Unaccustomed to a full day's exertion in cutting trail, they soon conditioned themselves to the requirements. Bristow displayed good sense in administering medicine to sick natives, and McBryde took photographs with care and patience. Blom, however, worried over McBryde's insistence on tasting every root and seed that he found.

Although Frans followed an itinerary, the party never knew what experiences each day would bring. On leaving Tapachula, they climbed around Tacaná Volcano, advancing in altitude from twenty-five hundred to eighty-three hundred feet within a few hours; on the way they passed from tropical forest land through a band of oak trees and then up into the pine belt. After descending the mountain, they traversed treeless hills, a barren valley, and a sun-baked plain. On overnight stays in villages they were quartered in anything from the local school to a customshouse or an old monastery. Three weeks after starting the journey, they arrived in Comitán, a town of ten thousand people, where they rested and prepared for the jungle ahead.

A week in Comitán provided relaxation and novelty for the men. While mules were being shod, Bristow visited every restaurant (the men always seemed to be hungry) and took in a movie, where a ten-part serial was shown at one sitting, with the audience shouting advice to the hero. On the day they left, the town gave a celebration for its patron saint with a grand parade, abundance of flowers, tolling bells, skyrockets, brilliantly costumed Indians, and the offering of a sheep to the saint. Three members of the team remained to photograph the festivities, while other members of the party took to the trail.

The first trying experience on the journey occurred between Zapaluta and Zapotal, when they crossed Pateras Canyon. The approaches to the tiny bridge over the gorge were "almost straight down and muddy as could be." Only roots, trees, and bushes prevented men and mules from sliding down the steep incline. A narrow bridge of logs spanned the twenty-foot crossing above the rushing waters sixty feet below. Natives tied leafy branches to the sides of the bridge to prevent the mules from panicking at the waters below them.

Because the small population of Zapotal was suspicious of the strangers and Frans needed their aid in preparing the difficult trails ahead, he used every device to make the people friendly. He dispatched Bristow to dispense medicine to sick villagers. He carried on friendly conversations and gave small gifts. On one occasion he mended two broken-down accordions for their owners. When the local "prayermaker" requested music to make the saint happy, two team members obligingly took the phonograph to the crude sanctuary and played raucous records again and again. Once Bristow was startled when he found Blom "kneeling before the saint. At first I thought he was working some kind of hokum to get something, but he was only doing a little request painting on the saint where the paint had peeled off." When the atmosphere became more congenial, Frans made the most of his opportunity to learn about the local culture. He asked Bristow to have a patient return for treatment, because Blom "wants to get all the information he can out of these people." On another occasion he had the medicine man of the place come to his quarters and "started pumping him" for facts about the surrounding country. "And he got plenty," reported Bristow. Frans later explained that "the medicine man knows something about the Maya calendar that was in use at the time of the Conquest." After several days of "good works" Blom learned about the route ahead and induced a group of natives to advance and break trail for the expedition.

The team found the most difficult passage out from Zapotal. Several days of rain made the route a muddy slick, even where the trail had been cleared. The path lay over a mountain, and "it took us four hours to advance one mile," Frans complained. Six men and fourteen animals struggled to reach the top in traversing the steep, muddy incline. "The mules turned somersaults, and boxes got bumped and knocked around, ropes got tangled up. . . . Fifteen times our pack animals rolled down over the side of the trail. Fifteen times we got them on their feet and reloaded them," Blom explained. Sixty feet from the top of the mountain, roots and soil formed a deceptive cover over a split in the rocks, and Bristow had a difficult and dangerous time getting the mules over that spot. The foot of one kicking animal "just missed my head by inches several times, as I rolled sideways down the mountain," explained Bristow. Frans also had a narrow escape, and saved himself by holding on to a tree. Less interested in his own danger than in the outcome of the climb, he exclaimed: "It was a wonder that neither men nor animals got more than a few minor bruises."

At the end of that day, camp offered little rest for the men. Probably because no better site was available, someone chose "a terrible place, right on a slope, so steep that it was hard to make our boxes stand, and still harder to find a level spot for the cots; we slept with our beds at all kinds of crazy angles."

The next day it was the same story over again, with mud and stalled mules. It had rained all night—"tents are soaked, blankets clammy, notepaper soft"—and it rained again in the morning, when they took to the trail. Animals slipped and floundered in the mud, and mired creatures had to be unloaded so they could be extricated. In desperation the men finally built a bridge of trees and logs over a ditch to ease the passage of the mules.

A new and ominous problem, hunger, began to appear from the beginning of March, and it increased during the next three weeks. Blom had arranged to buy staple supplies in the large towns on the route, but he did not realize that slow traveling would delay his schedule and deplete the food supply between towns. On March 1 an early sign of hunger appeared. When three of the men had to repack a stuck mule, a cake of sugar fell into the mud. "We washed it off and scraped the dirt off, and . . . ate it," Bristow remarked. Every member of the team spent more and more time hunting and fishing to provide food for meals. By March 13 conditions began to look serious. Ciriaco brought in hearts of palm and roasted them. "We'll have to use them for bread in the future, because our tortillas have run out," said Bristow. "Our kerosene is out too, so we get to bed early these nights." At that time the remaining staples on hand would last only five or six days. "We ate our last bit of rice for supper tonight. It will be necessary for us to do some heavy shooting. . . ."

More crises developed as the food supply ran low. The Indians from Zapotal who had cut trail completed their assigned time and returned home. In addition, Blom discovered that the party had reached a mountain and could find no way to cross it or go around it. "We searched the forest for a pass," he explained, "and climbed to the top. There we stood dumbfounded, spellbound." Across the river below them was a cliff four hundred to five hundred feet high, "a sheer wall of white limestone." For days the men went out in small parties to search for a route around the barrier, with no success. They spent more time hunting and fishing in order to save the staples, which were dwindling at every meal.

To complicate matters, two men could not be counted on for full physical labor. McBryde injured his foot with an unfortunate swing of the machete and for some days he could do no more than lounge around camp and fish until the foot healed. Then one night Blom awoke with a pain in his neck and arms. He examined himself with a mirror and discovered that he hosted a beef worm. The insect lays an egg under the skin; the egg hatches, grows, and moves around, causing pain. The next morning Ciriaco, expert in such matters, performed the minor surgery of cutting out the worm. On recovering from that affliction, Frans bruised his knee on a rock and had to take a day off to recuperate in camp.

Although Blom was always optimistic, he finally had to admit that the team faced a crisis. On March 18 there was no meat in camp, and one man went fishing. Everyone searched for a way around the barrier. On the nineteenth they searched again. They found a steep pass, and several men began to clear the way in that direction, but Blom decided that it was too steep for the mules to use and ordered an end to the operation. In regard to food, he remarked that the dwindling staples "have become something of a necessity, it seems." With confidence, he noted that his men would not starve, for there were fish in the river and game and palm hearts in the forest. But he failed to mention what Bristow revealed: they had no more fish hooks and only sixty shells for the guns. Frans kept his own counsel for the time being, though he admitted privately that "it looks serious to me."

After the evening meal on the nineteenth, he called all hands together and presented the uncomfortable facts. Everyone agreed that Kantor and José should take two mules back to Zapotal for a supply of food. Frans gave them most of his money, and in the morning they set out. They were expected to return in a week, because the trail back to Zapotal had already been cleared. It is interesting to realize that Blom never considered taking the whole team back to Zapotal; he had laid out a route over the mountains and he determined to follow it.

After the two men set off on the morning of March 20, Blom, unworried and hopeful that everything would come out all right, rested in camp because of his bruised knee. It was a rare occasion when he could enjoy the forest. "Last night it rained slightly," he wrote. "The night was filled with a most complicated sound. The rain dripped on the tent top like the working of an engine of a steamer. Millions of frogs were holding a concert, which sounded like the whistling of a strong wind in telegraph wires, and insects were producing a shrill whining." For a moment he thought of the predicament of the expedition, and then he longed to examine ruins again. As he sat in camp, he found the place full of peace. "There is something deeply attractive in being absolutely alone in the forest, a quiet which is being deeply intensified by the rush of the water in the river." A few days before he remarked that the jungle was so peaceful "that I wonder why people want to live in towns and noise."

The search for a way around the barrier continued, and the staples ran low. "For days we hunted the mountains. For days we went out early in the morning to find a pass and returned in the evening, tired and unsuccessful." On the twenty-first Frans observed that "there was a sad spirit over the outfit, two men gone for good, and the rest of us sitting in the rain without being able to move."

Everyone felt more dismal than ever on Saturday, March 24. In the afternoon the men returned with no news of a pass. For supper Ciriaco mixed canned milk with a block of bitter chocolate, "but we do not have

much of it left," Blom noted; and they ate some of the
small fish caught the day before, "not very savory." Only
a pot of beans remained in the larder. They discussed
the usual subject, ways of getting around the barrier.

Suddenly their gloom changed to joy. They heard
hoofbeats on the trail. "Kantor's head appeared above the
bushes, with José's right behind," McBryde remembered. "They were driving the two mules loaded
with sacks of food" and some curassows (game birds)
they had shot on the way. The two men had made the
trip of eight to ten leagues each way in four and a half
days, not seven.

In addition to supplies, Kantor and José brought news
of a pass around the barrier. The trail cutters from
Zapotal had known the route the whole time, but they
feared that if they revealed it, Blom would force them to
accompany him. Back in Zapotal one of the Indians gave
Kantor instructions on how to go around the barrier.

Everyone celebrated that night. They overindulged in
cheese, posole, sugar, tortillas, coffee, and sugarcane. "It
developed into a great eat," said Frans, "and now I
realize that we were somewhat hungry." Everyone was
in high spirits, and Blom praised Kantor and José. "It
shows what type of men we are so fortunate to have, and
speaks well for the future success of the expedition." As
part of the celebration McBryde and Bristow indulged
for the first time in cigars made of the strong native leaf.
"They smoke a little, complain, and smoke again," Frans
observed with amusement.

Celebration was in order after many days of hunger
and despair. Nor could they know that at the end of the
next day they would be in a different mood, solemn and
thankful. They rose late on the morning of the
twenty-fifth. McBryde, accompanied by Blom and
Bristow, mounted a cliff to secure panoramic views of
the country before they left it. McBryde moved out on a
ledge, set up his tripod and camera, and took pictures. As
he turned for a moment, he heard Blom shout, and
instinctively he grasped the tripod, which had begun to

fall forward. The near loss of a valuable camera did not appear in Blom's story for that day. He *was* concerned, however, over the accident that befell Epifanio.

The incident occurred in the most natural way. Some of the men attempted to cross the river filled with rapids in order to get to the elusive pass on the other side. They undressed, and as they ventured into the water to find a way for the mules, Epifanio's foot slipped and he was swept into the dangerous rapids. Fortunately, he managed to grasp a rock in midstream and crawl to safety, but he was marooned. On learning the news, Blom was "thunderstruck," fearing that he "had lost a man in the rapids." He rushed to the scene faster than Bristow had ever seen him move. By that time Epifanio had been on the rock, exposed to the hot sun, for some hours.

Instinctively, the team members went into action. Although no orders were given, some hands "got all available rope ready, coffee was set to boil, blankets prepared, and then we undressed and went out into the rapids," Blom explained. The men managed to get the rope to Epifanio, and he tied it securely around his body. Then he plunged into the rushing river. Could he keep his head above water and his body free from the jagged rocks? "For what seemed a long time the water played hand-ball with him, but soon he ducked up on a boulder, safe among us," with only a few bruises. Everyone gasped at his courage and marveled at his escape. They poured coffee into him, contributed clothes to replace those he had lost, treated his bruises, and wrapped him in blankets. Frans expressed his relief in an understatement: "I was certainly glad to see him in camp again."

In the days that followed the men solved troublesome problems as if they were no more than incidents of daily routine. The ingenious Ciriaco—what would they have done without him?—found corkwood trees in the forest. They cut them into lengths of fifteen feet, peeled off the bark, grooved them at the proper places, and used bejucos (rubbery vines) to lash them together to form a raft. Blom accompanied two of the men on the first trip across the river. Ten times they brought the raft back and forth until they had carried all the baggage to the other side. On the far bank, where they landed the boxes and bags, they picked up the trail they had been seeking for so many days.

Getting the mules across caused more trouble than the baggage. The men struggled for two days to induce the bell mule to go into the water. "She had a mind of her own," as Bristow remarked. They tried to pull her over with the raft, "but she would just turn around and go back to shore, carrying the raft with her." Finally the men found another crossing, which they thought would suit the mule; the banks sloped gently and there were no rocks or rapids in the river. Eight times they drove her into the water, and each time she stubbornly returned to land. "Finally, Kantor undressed and led her in and started swimming, pulling her rope, and she followed. . . ." The other mules advanced behind her.

The men moved on along the trail, never knowing where the next problem would occur. "We made about two and a half leagues today," Bristow noted on March 30, "more than we've made for a month." Soon they came to the junction of the Santo Domingo and Jataté rivers, and they had to find a way to cross the Jataté.

With considerable trouble they rigged up a corkwood raft, but this time it did not function satisfactorily, because the logs were too heavy. The trial trip turned out badly. When the men on the raft met the cross current of the Santo Domingo, whirling water "drew the raft down till we stood in water to over our knees. . . . I thought we were going overboard," Blom remarked. With the aid of Ciriaco's paddle and the stock of Frans's rifle, they maneuvered into a backwater and caught a rope thrown to them from shore. Blom concluded that "we would not dare risk to send the cargo across on that raft. . . ." So he dispatched three men to the forest to find new logs for another raft, a task which would require a day's work.

With time on his hands, he relaxed in camp, as Bristow sat nearby cleaning a gun. "It looked black again," Frans admitted. A day to make a new raft, and another day to cross the bad current, if a crossing were actually possible, "and who knows how many days to San Quintín? . . ." Putting aside the unhappy prospects, he took up a book, as he sat facing the Santo Domingo River ahead of him.

Help came out of the blue. As he looked up from the book, he could not believe his eyes. There in front of him were three canoes, manned by Lacandones with hair down to their shoulders and dressed in long, loose tunics. They stood in the canoes, paddling slowly. Bristow took one glance and exclaimed, "Lacandones!" Blom agreed, and added that they were very lucky to meet those Indians. "They were our means of getting information about trails; they were our means of crossing the river—if they did not flee." Frans rushed from the tent, shouting and waving his arms. The lone man in the first canoe came to the bank while the other canoes crossed to the opposite side and waited. Frans had determined that if he could get hold of one man, he would hold him as hostage until the remaining four men and an old woman crossed to the camp. The Indian came closer, landed, and without the least fear spoke in Maya and began to examine everything in camp. Blom carefully placed himself between the man and his canoe so that he could not escape. There was no need for the precaution, however, for the other Lacandones eventually came to the camp.

Near pandemonium ensued. Some of Frans's men turned on the phonograph and started trading with the visitors, hoping to detain them. Others brought out cameras to record the sight. Ciriaco and Kantor were called in from the forest to aid in translation. With signs, gesticulation, grunts, and some Spanish, Frans agreed to trade several machetes, which the Indians wanted more than any other article, for carrying his cargo across the river in their canoes. Members of the team hastily began to dismantle their tents and pack the baggage; "our men took our cargoes across in their canoes; the Indians smilingly helped in this work." In addition, despite the difficulty of communication, the Lacandones indicated the trail Blom sought on the other side of the river.

Before the equipment had been packed and moved, Frans's men had their troubles with the Indians. Peaceful though they were, the Lacandones were also acquisitive and desired as gifts any items that took their fancy. "They strolled about, fingering everything, including ourselves," Frans noted. "What they wanted they would just take and, as we were immensely grateful for their turning up, we let them have most" of what they wanted. When McBryde emerged from the woods, two Lacandones seized his shirt, which was checked with bright colors, and nearly tore it off. "They were here, there, and everywhere . . . and it was all we could do to keep track of everything."

Bristow, accustomed to the idea of private property, soon drew the line. When the old Lacandón woman came to the camp, "she was all 'gimme,' too, and wanted everything in sight." The American flag took her fancy, and she insisted on having that "pañuelo" (handkerchief). Bristow noted that "she was really peeved when we wouldn't give it to her." He "soon got disgusted with this curiosity and inquisitiveness." When one Indian "tried to pull a towel out of my box, I was highly tempted to throw him in the water, and did hit one with my arm, and knocked him back about three feet, when he tried to pull my hair."

As the last of the baggage was moved to the other bank of the Santo Domingo at dusk, only McBryde took in the scene and had the patience to describe it:

> It was an unusual picture, weird and beautiful, which presented itself as we crossed the river in the twilight; the long canoes shooting gracefully through the rapids, with one of the men in either end and working his paddle rhythmically, long hair and loose robes flowing together as he bobbed in sudden vigorous jerks. We were about mid-stream when a

flock of macaws, eleven pairs, passed overhead, their long plumage redder than ever in the light of the setting sun. The whole scene bore a hue of rose reflected from a bank of clouds in the west. It was certainly a perfect ending to a perfect day.

Once more the food staples began to run low. Before meeting the Indians, the men were eating chocolate and boiled maize. They secured a few wild potatoes from the Lacandones, but not as many as they wanted. A few days later they had curassow meat, "the first meat we've had for some time." By April 9 any food satisfied them. Ciriaco baked green bananas, "but they were not so good." Then Blom and Bristow tried baked bananas with wild honey, which went down better. Coming upon an abandoned lumber camp, they found some cans of beans, left by the former owners at least a year before. The beans were "worm eaten and tasted like sand." The famished men put mustard on the beans to kill the taste and then mixed them with baked bananas. McBryde found a squash, which provided a morning meal. On the eleventh the men foraged the forest and found potatoes, pumpkins, and some corn, which provided food for four meals.[2]

They arrived at Finca La Martinica, the first inhabited place since Zapotal, on April 14, after two weeks of near-starvation diet. Everyone ate and overate—tortillas, eggs, beans, rice, and chicken. Bristow rose from the table "tighter than a balloon." Hungry for sugar, the men devoured quantities of it. Then they walked to a sugar mill, and indulged in sugar candy and cane juice. "I have done few more foolish things in my life," complained Bristow. When they returned to the finca, they devoured a meal of pork, tortillas, and coffee.

They rode on into Ocosingo, a place of a thousand inhabitants, on April 17, never dreaming that they would remain there for two weeks. At once Blom wired to Matilda Gray for $1,000 to complete the expedition. Delays had caused unexpected expenses, and he would be out of funds by the time he reached Flores. At the same time he sent a message to President Dinwiddie to support his request to Miss Gray. The telegram arrived in New Orleans about the time that Oliver La Farge warned the president that news from Blom was a month overdue. It happened that all messages from Ocosingo had to be telephoned to San Cristóbal, the nearest town with telegraphic facilities.

Blom waited and waited for a reply. The little town of one-story white plastered houses with red tile roofs had little to offer the visitors except rest. All of the men but McBryde had haircuts and removed their beards. Bristow made some effort to measure Indians, a task which he had been performing whenever he had an opportunity, but the natives of Ocosingo were so drunk that they would not hold still long enough for him to secure the data. After struggling with five inebriates, he "gave it up as a bad day." For a brief period Frans fell ill. Soon he recovered and passed some time visiting the Indians of Sivaca.

Every day he inquired at the telephone office for the money, but it failed to come. Ten days after sending the message, he learned that someone had stolen a thousand feet of telephone wire outside the town and that no one had bothered to repair the damage, so the money had to be sent by mail from San Cristóbal, which took a full week. Bristow found the long wait getting on his nerves. "I had much rather be in the mountains cutting trail than hanging around here doing nothing."

As soon as the money arrived, the group set off on the remainder of the journey. Although there were interesting experiences ahead, they had already passed over the worst terrain in the little-known region. The days of hunger were over. Traveling along the trail still required physical strength, but the troublesome mountains were behind them. Also from now on the team was able to follow the schedule Blom had laid out for the journey.

There were two more experiences with Lacandones before the party left the Chiapas region. Back at the crossing of the Santo Domingo River, Frans had managed to have some conversation with the Indians who helped to ferry the cargo over the river. Noting only one old woman in the group, he mentioned casually that there were Lacandones to the north who had wives. He never imagined the result of that remark.

Some weeks later, when the party was back on its route, Vicente and José, two young men from the Santo Domingo River group, appeared and asked Frans to direct them to the Lacandones with women. The young fellows "wanted wives, either by purchase or theft, and they wanted them promptly." Convinced that Blom was traveling toward the Lacandones with women, the youths attached themselves to his party. Frans was willing to buy wives for them, but none were available. The several groups of Lacandones were hostile to each other, so when Blom was about to visit the Lacandón settlement at Jethá, he had to dismiss the young fellows and send them back to the Santo Domingo River area.

A local intermediary provided Frans with the opportunity to take his men on a visit to Jethá. It was a remarkable experience. A guide announced the coming of the strangers. Blom bore gifts, and McBryde brought the motion picture camera. During the visit the natives went about their accustomed tasks, while McBryde photographed everything in sight and Bristow took measurements of the few members of the settlement. When gifts were exchanged, the Lacandones always presented bundles of tobacco leaves, their staple crop. The strangers ate the food offered to them and enjoyed a demonstration of the use of the bow and arrow. "They let us walk around freely to inspect everything," Blom noted, adding that only the "idol house" was off limits to the strangers. Frans came away from Jethá not only gratified by the rare opportunity to record the life of the fast-disappearing people but also amazed by their kindness and personal freedom.

After weeks on the trail, the team enjoyed a respite of eight days in the picturesque town of Flores on an island in Lake Petén.[3] "The town treated us grandly," remarked

Frans. A "football game was played this afternoon, and dedicated to us. I had to make the kickoff." He inspected a new library and the schools and gave an address to a local club. After resting and relaxing, everyone felt better. One evening "after supper, while we were sitting around," Bristow explained, "Mr. Blom went into a store across the street and borrowed a five-gallon hat, in which he gave us an original jig in the street, much to the native children's delight."

Frans admired the energetic Colonel Fuentes, new *jefe político* of Flores. "He brought among other things strange to the Peteneros some footballs, ordered the local youths together, divided them into two groups, and started them on football. The game spread at once, and now even the small children play around with footballs." But would the natives, "who have been living in a semi-sleep for a couple of centuries," be able to understand the good intentions of the new official? The *jefe político* "sends all the kids swimming three times a week," Frans explained. "The Flores kids splash around the island all day long, but that they should be ordered to bathe, and even scrub with soap, seems cruel, according to the parents of the kids. They are protesting."

After the team left Flores, illness forced McBryde to drop out of the venture. When the men crossed Lake Petén in a mahogany dugout, "it was a magnificent day, but what heat!" exclaimed Frans. McBryde fell asleep, with his head and neck exposed to the blazing sun. At Ixtinta he suffered the first attack of fever and registered a temperature of 104 degrees. Although Frans had planned to take the entire team to Tikal, he could not do so because McBryde was immobilized. So Blom and an assistant made a hasty visit to the famous ruins. When he returned, he found McBryde suffering periodic attacks of fever; he had good days and bad days. Frans allowed the young man to accompany him to the ruins of Yaxhá, but that night McBryde was exhausted. Frans wanted to let McBryde realize that he was too weak to continue with the expedition. The sick man made his own decision to leave. Blom, who felt a deep responsibility for his men, admitted that he would be relieved "when I know him safe in the United States."

There was a relatively easy route out of the country for McBryde. The team went to El Cayo, British Honduras, to arrange for his departure. On June 25, two weeks after the fateful trip across Lake Petén, McBryde was placed on a boat that took him down the river to Belize. Twenty miles before the boat reached the city, however, a logjam impeded the passage; so McBryde hired an automobile to carry him to Belize, a journey of four hours. There he took a boat to New Orleans, where he regained his health.

As the team moved north into the *sublevado* country of the unconquered Indians of Quintana Roo, Frans was uncertain how the natives would receive him. At Bacalar he met General Francisco May, head of the *sublevados*, secured safe conduct, and also arranged to sell his mules to May after the expedition ended at Chichén Itzá. That was a fortunate turn of events, for May could just as easily have seized the animals. Trouble occurred, however, when the team reached territory not under May's jurisdiction. Some of the mules ate a few banana plants, which incensed the natives. Blom and a local leader engaged in a shouting match, neither one understanding what the other said. Then the Indians appeared with firearms. That night Frans saw to it that his mules were secured and that his men formed an armed guard around the camp. The next morning the team left without incident.

At the village of Chimila, Blom revealed two of his personal traits—the love of nature and the dislike of persons he believed to be religious hypocrites. In the evening he treated the members of his party to a movie, "Billie Dove in some kind of nightgown play with a Russian prince." "I could only stand a small part of it, and went home. It gave me infinitely more pleasure to watch the moon rise behind the old church and a row of royal palms." Less to his taste was a "longhaired Christ-Anton Lang-Oberammergau apostle loose" in

town, who sold pictures of himself on the cross. Blom
spied him at the movies, "and he didn't miss a hug or a
kiss on the screen. How I loathe an unhealthy-minded
cuss like that."

Two days later the party arrived at the Indian village
of Kaua. "In the evening there was an animated baseball
game in front of the church, and Louis [Bristow] joined
in to the great joy of the Indian players, several of which
were unsteady from drink." There was more to this
incident than Blom related in his diary. At first the
villagers had been cool toward the visitors. It happened
that Kaua was a center for the production of illegal liquor
on a large scale, and the travelers were suspected of
being Mexican revenue agents. Unaware of the situation,
Bristow joined in the baseball game. "All the English
they knew," he explained later, "was 'strike one' and
'knock a fly' and that sort of thing, but we had a fine
time." The villagers concluded that no revenue officer
could play baseball as well as Bristow, and they became
friendly. Later Blom's men learned that the natives had
been planning "to take us off to see some ruins and then
pump us full of lead." After returning home, Blom
gratefully acknowledged the value of Bristow's prowess
at baseball.

The investigation of archaeological sites on the trip
produced several discoveries, revealed new ruins, and
provided an opportunity to reconnoiter several well-
known sites. The first major ruins Blom examined were
extensive, though not productive of any discoveries except the avarice of the owner of the land. When Frans
learned of ancient remains at El Rosario Ranch, he applied to the owner for permission to examine the site. On
top of a hill he found large mounds, pyramids, and
ruined temples. The seven monuments and five circular
altars bore no inscriptions. During the inspection the
owner dogged the strangers at every step, expecting
them to uncover treasure in which he could share.

More important were the pieces of textile which Blom

discovered in an unusual way. He heard in Comitán that some local bee hunters had found old cloth in a cave. He could not let the opportunity pass, so he hired a guide to take him to the place. They reached the base of a cliff.

"Here is the cave." I looked up at the sheer wall and saw no opening to a cave. "There behind the tuft of grass." True enough, there was a small hole, but I would not call it a cave. Climbing up to the hole, I had the grass removed and put my hand into a small cavity the size and shape of an arc light. Inside was a lot of fine dust, a few potsherds and the remains of a squirrel's nest. Clinging to the cliff wall, with my head and one shoulder inside the cavity, I started to sift the dust. Acorns, sticks, dry grass, a potsherd, dust and more dust, and at last a piece of textile, not very large, to be sure. . . .

Bristow, who accompanied him, gave details. On finding the cloth, Frans "straightened up with 'Ah!', but there was more in the 'Ah!' than in most books. . . . He said 'textile.' A little more rumbling around, and he came down very excited. He smoked one cigarette after another. Kantor, who had been holding him, then poked his head in the hole and about five minutes later pulled his head out with a handful of rags, and said *más*. . . . I thought Chief would throw a small-sized fit, anyhow, but he disappointed me." On the way back to the ranch, Frans turned to Bristow and exclaimed, "Imagine a man going crazy over a few scraps of cloth like this." "But," said Bristow, "I was surprised that he was as calm as he was." Blom estimated the age of the cloth at fifteen hundred years; later scholars scaled the figure down to the preconquest period of some five hundred years ago.

In the same neighborhood he also found some chaltunes, those underground cavities which the Maya used for storage, and also some ball courts, another standard feature of Maya sites. He considered both items significant, for he believed that they had never been reported before in Chiapas.

On the shore of Lake Tepancuapán he went over the ruins of Chinkultic, which he had examined in 1925. His men used an automobile jack to raise a fallen stela and revealed a finely carved figure of an ancient worthy with a fantastic headdress. "An ugly fellow he was, with a hooked nose and tatooing on his cheeks, but a beauty in my archaeological eyes." In the meantime he sent Bristow to search for a cave on the farther shore of the lake. The young medico ran into a weird "cemetery" in a narrow fissure in the wall of a cliff. He "returned proud of his discovery, and carrying a collection of skulls, bones, and pots," Blom noted. Bristow measured the human remains in order to determine the size of the ancient Maya, and photographed the ceramic vessels.

Still another discovery was a unique type of tomb. At Tzajalob Frans examined a cruciform burial crypt, which had been uncovered a number of years before. This kind of tomb, common enough in Oaxaca, was unusual for that part of Chiapas.

Several other sites also attracted his attention. At Pestac, don Aureo Cruz showed him a monument with the date of A.D. 305. At the ruins of Toniná, Frans located some new monuments. At Yaxchilán, where his party camped in one of the old structures, he wandered over the site, copying inscriptions and photographing buildings and monuments.[4]

The brief visit to Tikal excited his admiration for the vast assemblage of structures at that impressive site. On reaching the acropolis, he rushed 150 feet up to the top of Temple I, carrying cameras with him. At the top he took a panoramic motion picture view of the other great pyramids of Tikal. On returning to the acropolis, he copied inscriptions from the stelae. For overnight quarters he used Temple 14, which had sheltered famous archaeologists in the past. There by the light of a candle he found some wall sketches (sometimes called graffiti or "doodles"), which Teobert Maler had not reported. "The night was clear with multitudes of stars in the sky. . . . Far away to the southeast lightning flashed." He wrapped himself in a blanket and before falling asleep contemplated "the outline of the great Temple V against the night sky. . . ." In the morning he took photographs of the carved lintels over the doorway of Temple III, because they were deteriorating under the assault of termites and malicious chicleros. Lack of water ruled out a trip to nearby Uaxactún, where he had worked in 1924.

The remainder of the journey, through the Petén and Quintana Roo, produced no surprises in archaeology. At San Clemente he photographed the red hands on the walls of Maya buildings. Among the ruins on the shore of Lake Yaxhá he found two stelae which he believed were unreported, and as he moved northward he mapped the site of Kaxil Uinic and found a ball court there. A great disappointment occurred after he paid a large fee to a guide to lead him to a new site; it turned out be to La Honradez, which the Peabody Museum had explored many years before. While examining a site at Tzotzkitam he turned a stela and found a finely carved figure, with evidence of red paint that had once covered the entire surface. The only remains of interest in the Yucatán Peninsula appeared at Kaua, where the walls of a cave bore paintings of serpents, human hands, and scrolls.

In later years he liked to boast that he sold his mules at the end of the journey for more than he had paid for them at Tapachula. That transaction, however, was only a small part of the financial picture of the expedition. Actually, he ran over his original budget by at least 20 percent. In 1925 he had paid a dollar for a hundred pounds of corn to feed his animals in Chiapas; by 1928 the price had risen to eight to ten dollars per hundred pounds. Moreover, unexpected difficulties on the journey delayed his progress by almost a month, and he had to ask for more money to complete the itinerary he had projected. Even with that supplementary aid he incurred a deficit.

In considering the adventures of the expedition and the ruins Frans visited, it is easy to overlook the most significant ingredient of the entire trip. Blom's expert leadership was the one element on which everything depended. He was alert to every aspect of the expedition, from the selection of the equipment and publicity for Tulane to the morale and safety of his men. Some weeks before setting off, he put the equipment on display in the department to arouse public curiosity. During the journey he prepared five field letters and sent them to Tulane as factual reports for the release of stories to the newspapers. He flew the Tulane flag and the pennant of the Explorers Club at every camp he established. On returning to New Orleans he gave sufficient information about the archaeological finds to satisfy the public, reserving the details for a paper presented to the International Congress of Americanists.

In the forests of Chiapas he exerted his gift for making friends and getting along well with th Indians, who could give him valuable help if they were so inclined. In a native village like Zapotal, he used his "whole catalogue of tricks," as Bristow somewhat cynically characterized his actions; and one could see Indians gradually warm up to him and eventually do everything he asked. Despite elaborate planning for the journey he went through almost unknown territory and always needed advance information about the condition of the trails ahead. Only the locals could provide those facts.

The unparalleled cooperation of his men must also be attributed to Blom. Those individuals lived and worked together for seven months, without evidence of "bush fever" or "cabin fever," terms commonly used to describe the irritations that can spring up among men in close quarters and explode into arguments and even fights. Blom set the example by controlling himself. In the early stages of the journey he realized that he was "riding" one of the students too much so he stopped the practice. Eventually he began to appreciate the young man's ability. Only twice did the leader reprimand assistants. Near the end of the journey one of the men complained that he was unfairly treated in regard to a box of crackers, and Frans "called him down." Even more justifiable was his anger when an assistant sent a weak mule to bring water to him at Tikal. Blom "cussed" him out "in a blue streak."

He was nonchalant, frank, and usually on near-equal terms with his men. When the need arose, he cut trail, herded mules and helped them over hard parts of the trail, and shot game for food. There is no evidence that he demanded special treatment. He spoke his thoughts freely with his men, though at several critical junctures he did not voice the deep concern he felt. Always optimistic, he determined to carry out the itinerary regardless of the difficulties. At the mountain barrier, which stopped his progress for days, he never considered turning back. With almost reckless self-confidence, he insisted that the team must go forward—and it did. He appreciated the diverse qualities of the different members of the team. The book he planned to write about the expedition was to be a cooperative affair, with each man making his own contribution. Unfortunately, the official report never appeared.

The months in Chiapas, Guatemala, and Yucatán provided the joy that Blom relished. Adventure made life interesting, trials tested his resourcefulness, and the natural glory of the forests gave him peace and contentment. When the party arrived at Chichén Itzá on August 5, the expedition ended. As the boxes were unloaded and lined up, Frans remarked wistfully, "It is with some sadness I looked at this—no more camps, no more trails for a while, the 'vacation' is over, and now it is time to go to work."

6

From Success to Failure

From all outward appearances Blom directed the work of the Department of Middle American Research successfully during the 1930s. He carried out an expedition to Uxmal, which resulted in the reproduction of part of the Nunnery at the World's Fair in Chicago in 1933. His staff grew until he employed as many as nine persons. He inaugurated a series of publications, published a book and numerous articles, and arranged an increasing number of exhibitions. At the end of the decade he was the key figure in a campaign to raise money for a building for the department.

Beneath the surface, however, something was undermining his spirit. He suffered more disappointments and defeats than he could bear. He went to pieces and took refuge in alcoholism. At first suspended from his work, a year later he lost his job. For some time he suffered personal humiliation and disgrace. Professional associates wrote him off as a man who had ruined his career. Everything indicated that Blom was finished.

The World's Fair at Chicago gave Frans the opportunity to investigate the ruins of Uxmal in Yucatán.

114

Through the National Research Council the department received a commission to reproduce the Nunnery as a preconquest structure at the fair, scheduled to open in 1933. Authorities of the fair provided $100,000 for the entire project.

Blom planned the expedition so as to make the most of an interdisciplinary attack on the problem. In addition to Frans as director, the party included R. H. Merrill, engineer from Chicago, and later Gonzalo Trujillo, engineer from Mexico; J. H. Thompson, head of the School of Architecture, Tulane University; Gerhardt Kramer and Herndon Fair, students of architecture from the same school; Enrique Alférez, sculptor, and William Hayden, assistant sculptor; Daniel Leyrer, photographer from New Orleans; and Ciriaco Aguilar and Pablo Pantoja as assistants. Frans preceded the arrival of the team in Yucatán, and with the aid of the Fairfield Aerial Survey had Uxmal and vicinity thoroughly photographed from the air.[1]

The expedition included more touches of "luxury" than Blom had enjoyed in any of his other forays into Mexico. As members of the party awaited the arrival of the equipment in Yucatán, the Peón family entertained them at Hacienda Uxmal, where they were "treated like royalty." The "royal" treatment had drawbacks. The eight men and other guests overtaxed accommodations. Some team members had to sleep in hammocks, to which they were not accustomed, and other men stretched out on the veranda. Kramer bedded down on a table until an army of spiders drove him to the floor.

The equipment, packed in 194 bundles and boxes, was carried on nine carts. In addition to the usual supplies of canned food and tools, Blom brought folding cots, mattresses and bed linens, four rubber bathtubs, seven cameras, two and a half tons of plaster for molding, a radio, and a portable power plant to supply electricity for thirty-five bulbs. Although the members dressed in overalls, flannel shirts, and sombreros for work, they brought evening clothes in case they might be invited to

formal festivities on the way to or from Yucatán. The
Mexican railways, moreover, furnished all transportation,
including a special Pullman car for a visit to Chichén
Itzá. According to Blom's standards, this was exploration
in grand style.

After the team members arrived at Uxmal, drove bats and
swallows from the rooms, and set up quarters in the Nunnery, daily life quietly fell into routine. The first night in
the Nunnery, however, belied the luxury which the men
expected to enjoy. The bats returned to their former home
and attacked some of the men. Then everyone moved cots
outdoors and slept under the sky. The men put in days of
hard work, with the temperature hovering around 120 to
125 degrees. They rose at dawn, breakfasted, and worked
until noon; after lunch they wisely adopted the local custom of a siesta until three, and resumed work until five
or five-thirty. After the evening meal, they received news
from the outside world by radio, often put in more work,
and retired by ten. Sometimes the party gathered on the
roof of the Nunnery in the evening to survey the country; from that vantage point they could count forty buildings and mounds.

There was some trouble with the local supply of labor
and with finding the right kind of food. "We have at least
been able to drive up two natives," Blom explained,
"and one of them is occupied all day long carrying water
for the household, washing, and not least for Enrique's
casting" of the molds. Blom considered the local natives
lazy. Laundry had to be sent to a town twelve miles
away, and vegetables and poultry had to be brought from
the same place, because the natives around Uxmal grew
only tomatoes and oranges. When good food was
available, Ciriaco Aguilar, cook on the expedition of
1928, performed gustatory miracles at Uxmal. Everyone
remembered the turkey wrapped in banana leaves which
he baked in a hole in the ground, lined with hot stones
and covered with earth.

Gerhardt Kramer and Herndon Fair, the two college
students, made the most of their stay at Uxmal by

visiting other places in Yucatán. They enjoyed a fiesta in Muna, and when the expedition was about to close down they made a backpack trip to Campeche. After four days of curious experiences, they took a train to Becal, and then decided to walk the remaining thirty miles to Uxmal. When they arrived at 11 P.M., Blom rose from his cot, thrust a flashlight into their faces, and inquired sleepily if they had been to Becal. Assured that they had just come from that place, he remarked dryly, "That's funny. We heard that they were expecting a couple of crazy Americans at Becal, and they saw you and threw you in jail. We thought you were there still."

At Uxmal the team concentrated on collecting every bit of information for the reproduction of the Nunnery. Artists copied the decorations, photographers took pictures, engineers surveyed the site and even adjoining areas, and Alférez and his assistants cast molds. All told, the men produced seventy drawings, over two hundred plaster casts, numerous maps, hundreds of photographs, and six reels of moving pictures.

As the specialists worked at their tasks, Blom interpreted his commission broadly and examined the entire site. With the help of Inez May, the caretaker, he found twenty-three unexplored groups of buildings and nineteen monuments with figures and glyphs, which he said carried the occupation of Uxmal back to A.D. 500. In exploring areas beyond the immediate site, he found remains from two to five miles away from the major settlement. He took the opportunity to visit some other ruins in Yucatán, discovered eight new stelae and a ball court at Sayil, and a doorway with glyphs at Mulux.

He took pride in several discoveries made by members of the team. Within the quadrangle of the Nunnery, careful measurements disclosed that the Maya had used false perspective. Although the inner courtyard appears to form a perfect rectangle, his men found that at the north end the side walls were moved slightly inward and the floor raised three and a half feet, probably for the purpose of enhancing the size of the enclosure.

Careful measurement also disclosed the use of negative batter: although the walls stood at a perfect right angle to the ground, the decorations on the walls projected farther out the higher they rose. Enrique Alférez, one of the sculptors, gave the explanation: "The edges of the undercut places throw a heavy and solid shadow, thus making the contrast between the outer and the deeper planes." Later investigation revealed the use of negative batter on structures at Kabáh, Labná, Labpak, and Sayil.

The team also contrived an improved method of photographing low-relief carving to bring out greater detail. With the use of powerful lights at night, they took pictures that produced a sharper record of the carved surfaces. This was hailed as a new discovery; the team did not know of Teobert Maler's night photography at the end of the nineteenth century.

The Nunnery, as it appeared at the fair in Chicago in 1933, disappointed archaeologists, including Blom. Officials considered it too costly to reproduce the entire Nunnery, and so they built only a portion of the north wall. The construction consisted of a wooden shell, covered with stucco and plaster casts, and treated to resemble stone. The two-story building had a broad stairway in the middle and smaller stairways at each side. The slick, clean finish of the exterior and the handrails for use of visitors appeared incongruous. The interior was no more than a drab, nondescript hall with displays of Maya artifacts and a reproduction of the murals from the recently discovered Temple of the Warriors at Chichén Itzá. Sylvanus Morley, who had reasonably good taste in such things, pronounced the building terrible and the color pestilential.

Although Frans was unhappy with the result, he was careful not to criticize it in public. When the building was in the planning stage, officers of the fair continually cut down the size of the original plan, and he made his irritation evident to them. Only occasionally did he express dissatisfaction to friends. In one letter he noted his sorrow over what had happened. With sarcasm he informed another acquaintance that "the Maya bastard on the Fair grounds seems to please the public."

Everyone at Tulane, it appears, was happy with the exhibit, or at least with the public notice the structure gained. Reports claimed that ten thousand persons a day passed through the building. Somehow Blom had managed to send a number of the staff members at one time or other to Chicago to see the exhibit. One wonders whether the "bastard" building was worth the money it cost.

One of the visitors to Uxmal during Blom's work there in 1930 was Robert B. Stacy-Judd, an English-born architect who crusaded for Maya-style buildings in modern American architecture. Two years later he planned an expedition to Yucatán and proposed to put Blom in charge of a reconstruction project, probably at the Adivino at Uxmal. As much as Frans wanted to get into the field again, he knew that he could not work under Stacy-Judd, because the project would feature "noisy advertising and ballyhoo," large expenditures of money (Frans had always tried to keep down the cost of expeditions), and personal publicity, which Blom opposed. He was wise in avoiding entanglements with Stacy-Judd.

About the same time T. A. Willard, the wealthy battery manufacturer who also followed Maya studies as a hobby, offered the department $1,000 on a matching basis for the exploration of the site of Mayapán. Although Blom did not consider the place a spectacular site, he believed that archaeological work there would be "certainly of great importance." He was unable to raise the additional money, however, and never worked at Mayapán.

In 1935 Frans went on his last Tulane archaeological expedition. The Danish National Museum secured money for an expedition, sent Jens Yde from its staff, and chose Blom to lead the project. The aim of the joint venture was an examination of western Honduras for evidences of ancient Maya civilization. Prentiss Andrews, a Chicago lawyer and amateur archaeologist, went along at his own expense. Before leaving New Orleans, Blom gained notice by declaring that the journey would be "a great, big picnic." He also explained that the members would not take guns, "because they scare the natives, and they're dangerous." The three men started at Tegucigalpa and went north to San Pedro Sula. Then they flew south to Copán, where they visited Gustav Stromsvik, who was restoring that site under the auspices of the Carnegie Institution of Washington, and Alfred V. Kidder, head of the historical division of the same institution. From there Blom and his men made a mule trip north to San Pedro Sula. On that leg of the journey Frans announced the discovery of a mound and some carved stones on an island in Lake Yojoa east of the Ulúa River. That find, he claimed, extended the eastern limits of the Maya area. Although the investigators aimed only to reconnoiter the area for evidences of Maya culture, the results were disappointing. The only published reports of the expedition were written by Yde.

Several personal impressions of the expedition appear in Frans's diary. The airline service in Honduras attracted his attention. TACA (Transportes Aeros Centro-Americanos) began in 1931 with practically no capital; four years later it owned thirteen planes and was worth $250,000. Blom wrote an appreciative article on the subject, which appeared in English, Spanish, and Portuguese.

He was distressed at the singular lack of care for historical records in Tegucigalpa. Looking about the library of the National Archives, he exclaimed, "What a mess! It breaks my heart to see documents and books all thrown around in bundles without rhyme or reason. I wanted to get a librarian in there right away." A few days later he had a greater shock when he visited the National Museum. There in the corner of the patio he saw stacks of papers, newspapers, and pamphlets "unloaded by the National Library and being used . . . to make papier-mâché. It is pitiful to see the interesting materials go to waste." The final blow came "when I went to the toilet and found two bunches of copies of government telegrams, mostly referring to revolutions, hanging on a nail—for useful purposes. I pocketed them."

If civilized people acted carelessly about their past and Indians lacked artistic taste in weaving and pottery, Blom found beauty and consolation in nature. Even in the capital city "the evening was pleasant and cool, the sky a velvet blanket scattered with stars." After he left Copán, he mused: "I like to be in the big jungle again, with its rich growth, variety of plants, and strange-looking vines." A rare experience occurred as he moved through the Callejones Valley. "The trail wound along a small stream. We were in the shade of the tropical forest, of luxuriant beauty. At one place a whole limestone cliff rose up and the top of the cliff—what glory!—was covered with a solid mist of purple orchids. What a pity that such abundant beauty can only be enjoyed by a few people who venture in to these far-away places."

The expedition was no more than an interlude. At the department he continued to be busy with all kinds of tasks. Now and then he undertook projects of a local nature. Once he favored Newcomb College girls with the adaptation of a Maya legend, so that they could celebrate May Day in elaborate Maya costumes. On another occasion, as he flew out of New Orleans, his sharp eye detected a zigzag pattern on the ground of Chalmette Park. When he later examined the place, he discovered breastworks from Civil War days, which gained an article in the local newspaper. He gave some attention to local and state archaeology, though without great enthusiasm. He and La Farge gathered arrowheads on the shore of Lake Pontchartrain, and Frans planned to share them with some museums in the north. Later he collected some artifacts in the northern part of the state, on which he wrote a short paper which was never published.

Another paper called for anthropological and ethnological research in the state. The last reference to local work appears in 1929, when he told a friend that he "went out to look at a Louisiana shell heap yesterday, and found it thoroughly uninteresting." In archaeology his heart was with the Maya of Central America.

He conceived the duties of his position as broad in scope, directed toward the advancement of scientific knowledge, the information of the lay public, the cultivation of donors, and keeping the department running smoothly. He spoke to small groups in New Orleans, usually about his latest expedition, gave more serious papers before professional groups like library organizations, and delivered scholarly reports to fellow professionals in the International Congress of Americanists and the American Association for the Advancement of Science. For several years he held annual seminars on archaeology at Tulane for visiting scholars. Much time was spent in drawing up reports in search of grants from foundations, buying rare books and manuscripts when they became available, and answering inquiries that ranged from requests for bibliographies from high school students to laymen's queries about esoteric subjects in Maya archaeology. Too easily forgotten is the amount of time expended on the operation of the department. It appears also that the university administration expected to gain as much notice as possible in the local newspapers, and so there was the task of seeing that any item worthy of notice was made available to the press.

He took extensive trips, which usually combined professional work with pleasure. In 1930 he spent ten weeks in Europe, where he visited his parents for a month, attended the Americanists' congress, visited the Trocadero Museum in Paris, devoted ten days to helping T. A. Joyce classify pottery from British Honduras, and was the guest of Charles Dawes, U.S. ambassador to Great Britain. At the professional meetings Frans sometimes gave papers or served in an official capacity.

He was elected honorary secretary of the Americanists in 1930. At the first meeting of the International Congress of Archaeological and Ethnological Sciences he served on a committee on film documentation relating to anthropology, and at the second meeting he headed the section on American anthropology. He was chosen a fellow of the American Association for the Advancement of Science, and presented a paper when that organization met in New Orleans in 1931. In Europe in 1933, when he and Mary spent several months on vacation, he again performed some professional duties. He examined the exhibits in the Central American Hall of the Trocadero, and addressed the Société des Américanistes de Paris in a special session.

In perspective, it appears that his activities in the department varied from important tasks to trivial routine items which had to be reported to the administration. The cultivation of potential donors was certainly a significant part of his work, and he carried it on in various ways, from visits to northern cities to a large friendly correspondence with many people who showed interest in the department. The acquisition of rare books, manuscripts, and artifacts he managed with interest and alacrity, although the lack of money restricted his success in some instances. Much time went into the writing of reports to obtain grants, an activity in which he enjoyed considerable success. The correspondence of the department, however, indicates the many routine matters with which he had to deal. There were requests for fans, a notice that he would dismiss the staff when the temperature rose to 92 degrees, a plea for fire extinguishers, a request for insurance on $298,000 worth of material in the department, haggling over pay for the janitor, complaints of a leaking roof, and a careful report on each worker's vacation time.

By the mid 1930s he was jumping from one project to another. In 1935 he prepared pamphlets for a tourist agency in Guatemala, and two years later carried out a similar assignment in Honduras and Costa Rica. Sudden-

ly he announced a five-year project in which members of
the department would explore the "geography, geology,
history, and archaeology" of Honduras. It sounded like
an echo of Gates's program a decade earlier. It is not
clear what prompted the plan, but it seems that
Honduras never forwarded the contract authorizing the
project. At the department he set up a weekly staff
meeting open to the public. He participated in a local
radio program about Cortés, with the script by Maurice
Ries, editor of the department. Unwilling to overlook
small things, Frans held a contest for the best poster to
encourage people to visit the department; he received
eighteen entries, and planned to place the posters in
local hotels.

Beginning in 1937, he spent much time arranging
exhibitions of Maya artifacts. In that year he supervised
an exhibit in New Orleans, one at the Baltimore Museum
of Art, and a large display at the Greater Texas and Pan
American Exposition in Dallas. The last exhibit utilized
six thousand square feet of floor space and received the
grand prize for the best display. A little later he managed
exhibitions at the Detroit Fine Arts Museum and at the
Golden Gate International Exposition in San Francisco.

In 1938, Blom had to fight two movements that
threatened the effective work of the department. In line
with his recommendation of a decade earlier, the
administration changed the department to an institute.
Along with that change, however, went the provision that
the institute could offer courses for graduate degrees. In
public Frans put a good face on the situation. But he was
certainly unhappy with the development, because he
believed that teaching interfered with research. Staff
members were likewise alarmed, for they feared that
they would be replaced by a teaching faculty. Although
Blom was slated to give a course in Middle American
archaeology in 1939, neither he nor his workers taught a
course as long as he was director. Soon another threat to
the unity of his organization appeared in the attempt to
merge the specialized library of the institute with the

university library. As late as July 1940 Frans staved off the action with the support of President Rufus Harris. But the following year, when Frans was on leave, Harris changed his mind, and the books and manuscripts were moved to the main library, where they were still technically under the administration of the institute.

In spite of his energy and many activities, Blom voiced relatively few opinions or ideas. Remarks about fellow workers in archaeology sometimes occur in personal letters, and they have a negative cast. George O. Totten's volume, *Maya Architecture*, appeared to him to be "a fearful mess. . . . It is really a scandal, and the book on Maya architecture is still to be written." He condemned Spinden's *The Reduction of Mayan Dates* but approved that scholar's correlation of the Christian and Maya calendars. Spinden floored his associates with his vast knowledge. When the two men met in Mexico, Spinden lectured Frans on his correlation system. Frans had to admit that "as I have not got his magnificent memory for dates, I was not able to check him. I, therefore, laid low while he was talking."

Blom differed with Morley on the reading of some glyphs, and he did not quite know what to do about it. On the expedition of 1928 he wrote to Tozzer, "Shall I let this loose . . . or shall I keep my mouth shut, and let the coming students labour under the burden of having incorrect material to study from? I am now leaning toward bringing out the whole bag of tricks and getting the mess cleared up. It is Maya research and not Morley's name I am working for." Tozzer gave him good advice: publish your results for the sake of scientific knowledge, but do it quietly and without fanfare.[2] Then Blom made a curious admission. "I have found several slips of my own on this trip, found monuments in places where I had been before, etc., which all irritated me, and I am glad that I can correct this myself." He did not realize the implicit injustice of the position he had taken: expose another man's mistakes with indignation, but thank God that you have discovered your own errors. In fairness it should be added that a few years later Frans made a generous public acknowledgment of the valuable work Morley accomplished in the project at Chichén Itzá.

When Charles Lindbergh made flights over the Maya area in 1929, scholars generally hailed the event as a new way to find ruins hidden in the forest. Although Blom joined in public approval of the flights, he had private reservations. "Frankly, I cannot see the scientific value of the Lindbergh exploit," he confessed to his friend Tozzer, "but it is great for publicity for the Mayas and will undoubtedly help us." He was close to correct, for aerial reconnaissance did not produce the immediate results claimed for it, despite the enthusiastic statements by some scholars at the time.

All through the 1930s Blom carried on a one-man crusade to break up the "expedition racket." He maintained that explorers with questionable aims operated under the auspices of respectable institutions. As a result, "racketeers" secured low transportation rates and contracts to lecture and to write books. Moreover, publishing houses failed to examine the credentials of the authors and hence sometimes foisted volumes of dubious information on the public. He also claimed that in some instances the racketeers took advantage of unsuspecting people in foreign lands. Once he pointed to Frederick Mitchell-Hedges, Captain Stuart Murray, and, "to a certain extent," Gregory Mason as men of questionable practices, though he dubbed Richard Byrd "the king of them all." He cited Peter Keenagh's book on the Mosquito Coast as a prime example of irresponsible journalism.[3] Frans hoped to see a clearing house set up to screen the qualifications of explorers, but nothing came of his proposal.

Although Blom generally avoided controversial subjects, he did not hesitate to disclaim transoceanic influences on early American cultures. When a New Orleans newspaper baited him to answer the contention of J. Leslie Mitchell that Egypt was the source of all early civilizations,[4] Frans replied with mock seriousness that he could not claim the broad knowledge that Mitchell possessed when he generalized on early cultures. A little later in his book *The Conquest of Yucatan* Blom dismissed all theories of transoceanic contacts. Once he gingerly suggested that the noncalendrical glyphs probably represented phonetic signs, but he was tentative about it. He was more positive about the aesthetic aspects of Maya art, for he considered artifacts as artistic creations rather than the product of a savage people, a point he made in comments on the exhibition in San Francisco.

He advocated a comprehensive approach to the study of archaeology. Glyphs, buildings, and monuments were worthy of study, he remarked, but the attempt to reconstruct the daily life of the ancient Maya required a knowledge of "their food supply, their roads and rivers, their tools and household goods." At least in theory he considered archaeology a multidisciplinary study, drawing upon contributions from geology, geography, zoology, botany, and climatology. In this respect he voiced an approach which was already becoming widespread in some circles of archaeology and is the dominant methodology today. Although he never carried out the multidisciplinary approach on an elaborate scale, he made a promising move in that direction in assembling specialists in various fields at Uxmal in 1930.

He firmly believed that prehistory, which spanned a long period of time in the history of mankind, taught valuable lessons. He never explained the lessons he had in mind, except on one occasion, as we shall see. Actually, he wanted to see archaeology taught in the schools. Conventional history, he asserted, contained "too many hatchets and cherry trees." He advised that the modern historian should follow the businessman in graphing events so as to determine cycles of occurrences over a period of centuries.

For the same reason he was convinced that the general

public should visit museums as a way to acquire knowledge of prehistoric peoples. Once when he went to the American Museum of Natural History in New York, George Vaillant showed him some duplicate artifacts in storage. At once Blom called on Clark Wissler, the curator, and proposed "that the museum should rent show windows in the principal subway stations and exhibit a few peace pipes and war bonnets." His reason for that curious suggestion ran this way: "Papa would wait for the subway, and decide to take son to the museum next Sunday." The idea was too much for Wissler; and "my suggestion was pooh-poohed."

Blom sometimes liked to put forth ideas in ways that would catch public attention. He achieved the greatest success when he declared that Columbus missed his opportunity by not visiting Yucatán, where he would have found an amazing civilization. If few persons knew about the Maya and Yucatán, everyone was familiar with Columbus. Many newspapers quoted his remark, some published editorials about it, and there were a few rebuttals.

Frans reiterated the idea that archaeologists could learn the traits of an early culture by examining deposits of refuse. When he addressed an audience on the subject in 1935, he entitled his paper "History below the Surface." For that occasion he requested a photograph of a dump heap at the World's Fair to illustrate the theme. The next time he spoke on the subject, he changed the title to "History in the Garbage Can." When part of Claiborne Avenue in New Orleans was improved by filling in a canal to form a beauty spot, he made the headlines with "Blom Sees Orleans Dump Heap as Archaeological Trove." The article repeated the theme that the archaeologist finds his materials by examining refuse deposits. He could hardly have wished for greater publicity for his pet idea.

He had one last fling at his favorite theme when a new building was proposed to house the department. He announced that the structure would contain two dump heaps, one of 2,000 years ago from a Maya ruin, and the other of the past half-century, containing carriage wheels, electric bulbs, old automobiles, and other discarded objects of contemporary civilization. When plans for the building were issued, they provided for a dump heap on the main floor. The structure, however, was never erected.

Several times he gave his views on contemporary civilization, generally in negative terms. He characterized his own time as the age of the unfit, "for letting the healthy and fit starve and treating the diseased and broken to luxurious sanitariums and penitentiaries." He had grave doubts about government aid to the poor, asserting that many "loafers" flourished without working. A local newspaper editorialized on his remarks under the title "Too Much Coddling."

When he visited Europe in 1935, he found the outlook black. He had seen armies in France and Germany, and he felt the hatred of one nation for the other. Only internationalism, he claimed, could reduce the malevolent force of nationalism and lead to peace. He blamed the schools of Europe for using biased textbooks, which taught that hatred. As an aside, he criticized education in the United States as too dogmatic and theoretical. He repeated some of these ideas in an address in 1938. History, by which he meant prehistory, could teach contemporary man how to avoid physical degeneracy and save himself from destruction. Men, he sighed, learn "nothing from the past." This time a newspaper took some exception to his view that the present is the age of the unfit.

These ideas were but superficial indications of his major concern that the public school curriculum failed to include archaeology. A knowledge of prehistory, he insisted, cooled the passions and taught valuable lessons. Certainly his own knowledge of prehistory did not entirely cool his passions. Four days after Hitler invaded Denmark, Frans exclaimed to a friend: "It was a terrible shock to hear the news from Denmark, and I won't get

over it until the last damn Nazi is out of the country."
Later he worried whether German bombs were falling in
Aalsborg, where one of his sisters lived.

Blom's publications in the first period of his career
varied from brief popular articles to longer, scholarly
studies. He produced several books, a large number of
articles and monographs, and a few leaflets. In addition,
there are manuscripts which never appeared in print,
and also occasional plans for other projects. We shall
look first at the books, and then consider some of the
other items.

The first volume, *I de Skore Stove,* which appeared in
Copenhagen in 1923, is a narrative of travel and adventure in Mexico, intended to appeal to young people
in Denmark. Blom transcribed and summarized the diary
he kept from the time he left New York early in 1919
until July 4, 1922. In a matter-of-fact style he conveyed
the novelty and exotic flavor of Mexico by relating his
daily experiences. As the story proceeds and he moves
into the hinterland of southern Veracruz, Tabasco, and
Chiapas, he shows increasing interest in traveling
through the forests and a growing passion for the
occasional Maya ruins he encounters. The narrative is
full of descriptions of landscapes, towns, people,
conditions on the trail, and overnight accommodations.
Some photographs, reduced too much on the pages of the
book, supplement the text. Blom's remarks on Maya
sites, especially Palenque, indicate that he was well read
on the subject before he visited those ruins. In some
undefined way, however, the writing fails to convey the
high excitement that he certainly experienced from day
to day. He could have profited from editorial help in
revising the material from the original diary.[5]

Before submitting the manuscript to a publisher, Frans
took a prudent step. The text contained some unflattering
remarks about Mexicans, especially in regard to rebels,
bandits, occasional plundering, internal disorder, and the
irresponsible use of the military. To be honest, he had to

include the unfavorable items; on the other hand, he wished to return to Mexico in the future. So he turned the manuscript over to Manuel Gamio, head of the national department of anthropology, who had parts translated into Spanish. Gamio returned the manuscript without objections. The Danish publisher issued an edition of 2,000 copies. Shortly after the work appeared, Blom proposed an English translation to the Century Company, but nothing came of it.

If Frans aimed to entertain the reader in his first book, he combined serious archaeological reporting with interesting accounts of travel in the second work, *Tribes and Temples,* written in conjunction with Oliver La Farge as the official report of the expedition of 1925. After securing permission from Alfred P. Maudslay, Blom dedicated the work to him, "the first to explore the Maya ruins in a modern scientific way...," and noted Maudslay's "monumental collection of material for future research" published in the *Biologia Centrali-Americana.* Departing from the stereotyped approach of a scientific report, Frans included personal experiences as well as archaeological. He hoped that the volumes might "help to awaken the interest of the public in the history of the ancient American people...." When he sent the manuscript to Tozzer for a critical reading, he explained another aim. "Gates destroyed many good leads," he wrote, referring to potential donors to the department, "and I hope to reestablish certain promising connections by giving them a book that they can get a little fun out of."

He wrote the two volumes in about ten months. That was a good record in view of the temporary misplacement of La Farge's notes, the struggle between Frans and Gates in the winter of 1925-26, and his consequent assumption of the duties as director of the department. The two volumes appeared in 1926-27.

Tribes and Temples is an imposing work. Samuel Zemurray, who paid the cost of publication, must have been willing to provide unlimited funds. The two

volumes contain 551 pages, 5 maps, 7 plates, and 374
figures. Linguistic material fills many of the 10
appendices. Often unnoted are the small drawings by La
Farge, which are used as chapter tailpieces. Four
thousand copies were printed, with fifty numbered
copies on special paper. Unfortunately, the work never
gained interest beyond archaeological circles, and copies
remained on hand for several decades. They are now out
of print and hard to find.

A peculiarity appears in the absence of the authors'
names from the title page. If the reader turns a page or
two, he finds a list of the members of the expedition:
Blom as chief, La Farge as assistant, and Lázaro as guide.
Frans later told a friend that he deliberately omitted the
authors' names from the title page on the grounds that
the accomplishments of the expedition were more
significant than the names of the participants. It seems
that La Farge wanted his name on the title page. Was
this omission a way of depriving the younger man of a
natural satisfaction? Blom never followed the practice
with his own later publications.

Frans lost the opportunity to publish a book about his
adventures of the expedition of 1928. During the journey
three publishing companies offered him contracts for the
story. He sounded out President Dinwiddie on the
propriety of accepting one of the offers, indicating that
the scientific results of the trip would be published by
Tulane. Dinwiddie generously told him that it was a
personal matter with Blom. In the end, Frans did not
accept any of the contracts, and the university was
unable to raise the money to issue the scientific report.
The only extended account of the Gray Expedition was
an article by Blom in *Holland's* magazine, which had
limited circulation. Frans lost an excellent opportunity to
tell the world the personal story of his most adventurous
travels.

In 1930 he set out to write a popular book on the
Maya. The time was ripe, for he had just been advanced
from associate to director of the department, and his

expeditions of 1928 and 1930 had been well publicized. In June he signed a contract with the New York publishing house Convici Friede and received a $250 advance on royalties. He announced that the book would appear that fall. There was a delay, however, and in 1931 he explained that the volume would appear at the end of that year. It seems that Blom had misjudged the task before him. Writing a book from extensive field notes was one thing; composing a manuscript on a broad subject like the Maya was another. He discovered how little specific, factual information he had at his command, and admitted that he spent much time reading on the subject. He sent to the publisher some text, illustrations, and a design for a jacket. The publisher, however, was so displeased with the text that he asked to call the whole thing off, and in addition he mislaid or lost the manuscript and illustrations. Blom insisted on another $250 if the contract were broken; the outcome of that claim is not known. Two and a half years later Convici Friede recovered the manuscript and returned it to him.

Frans persisted, and eventually saw his book, *The Conquest of Yucatan*, appear in 1936. He approached the Houghton Mifflin Company and explained the history of the manuscript. The first publisher had refused it, and a second publisher lost interest because of the cost of reproducing the illustrations. It is doubtful that the manuscript he submitted was the same one he had prepared in 1931. Houghton Mifflin issued the book. No figures on the sale of the volume are available, but at the end of 1938 the publisher said that it was selling about a hundred copies a year.

The Conquest of Yucatan is an acceptable work for the general public for which it was intended. The style is simple, clear, and interesting. If Frans used a ghost-writer, as is sometimes rumored, it was a wise choice. Close inspection reveals some curious things about the book. The thirty-two chapters average less than eight pages each, a fact of little significance except that it betrays Blom's difficulty in presenting a large mass of material. There is, moreover, a discrepancy between the title and the contents of the book. He treats the conquest in the first half of the volume, and then follows with a description of Maya culture, which is extraneous to the title. The discrepancy is pointed up by the fact that he later translated chapters 21-30 and chapter 32 into Spanish and published them as the life of the ancient Maya.

Reviewers generally found imperfections as well as merits in the volume. Herbert Spinden provided the most perceptive criticism; he regretted the lack of an overall grasp of the details and the failure to reveal "a larger and more significant pattern of events." It happened that Spinden had a remarkable ability to grasp generalizations from a mass of facts, though few of his associates in archaeology possessed that unusual gift. Perhaps Spinden was setting too high a goal for the average book. Among the reviewers, only Philip A. Means gave the volume unqualified approval.

Blom copyrighted *The Conquest of Yucatan* in his own name, a wise move since in later years he was able to arrange for translation of parts of the volume into several languages, apparently with some financial benefit to himself. The dedication of the volume is also worth noting, although it appears commonplace at first sight. Frans acknowledged the help of teachers, friends, and his wife. This was one of the few occasions during the early period of his career when he admitted a debt to those who had aided him. He was not ungrateful for the help of others, but generally he was so self-confident that he tended to overlook acknowledgments.

His shorter writings varied in subject matter and treatment. His monographs on the Maya ball game, on Gaspar Antonio Chi, and on commerce and units of money among the Maya are serious studies, still valuable. The early papers given before the International Congress of Americanists also provide good summaries of his discoveries. Although the exposure of fake codices is a negative form of scholarship, it is a necessary task, especially when a fraudulent work is published with the appearance of authenticity and finds its way into serious collections, as happened with Gates's edition of the Gomesta manuscript. In several papers Frans exposed such frauds.

It is easy to overlook the labor he expended on the scholarly journal *Maya Research* (1934-36). When the Hyatt Foundation proposed the quarterly and provided the money to subsidize it, Frans was happy to become editor. After the support was withdrawn, he continued to publish the periodical for an additional year. He even accepted articles for a fourth year, but that volume never appeared. Again in 1940 he hoped to revive the journal by charging $200 a page for advertisements for four issues, but he did not carry out the project.

He was always ready to spread the news of Maya art to the informed public. His essay on that subject in the *Gazette des Beaux Arts* was illustrated with a fine display of photographs. Although he offered to forego his compensation as author to subsidize the reproduction of the pictures, he received 1,200 francs from the magazine. About the same time he began to collect pictures for a book on Maya architecture, which a publisher wanted him to produce. We hear no more of the project. From a commercial point of view, it would appear to have been a fairly risky endeavor considering the poor economic conditions of 1933.

There are some curiosities among his shorter writings. The leaflet *Are There Laws?* begins with the provocative question "Are there laws governing human progress and retrogression?" Frans simply used the arresting sentence to direct the reader's attention to archaeology. The Maya area, he explained, is "richer in antiquities than ever Egypt was"; there are two thousand known archaeological sites in Mexico, only forty of them mapped, and no more than a dozen excavated. He referred to the specialists working in the department, and concluded that archaeology "is the art of making dead men tell tales. . . ."

Sometimes a negative tone crept into his writings. *Art and Archaeology* asked him to prepare a note on two books. Emma Lindsay Squier's *The Bride of the Sacred Well*, a volume of short stories, elicited a brief, favorable comment from him. In the case of Miles Poindexter's *The Ayer-Inca*, however, Blom reveled in denunciation, and the editor printed the merciless criticism in order to support the reviewer's freedom of speech. His review of the Morris-Charlot-Anne Morris work on the Temple of the Warriors criticized the artist Jean Charlot for his use of symbolism and archaeology. When Frans wrote an extended notice of William Gates's edition of the Gomesta manuscript, he was particularly sarcastic. Although Tozzer modified the sharp tone of two of his reviews, much of Frans's biting language still remained. When Brentano's asked him to prepare a foreword for Phillips Russell's *Red Tiger*, he submitted a half page, noting earlier travelers in Central America and remarking that Russell's book lacked the length and detail of those of his predecessors. Little wonder that Brentano's refused to use the foreword!

A publishing project launched late in 1935 had the distinction of beginning and ending its career with a single item. Frans announced that Midameres Press would issue rare documents. Although members of his staff cooperated in the venture, it was not an official part of the department. Plans called for the reproduction of Lieutenant James Cook's travels around the Yucatán Peninsula in 1769, to be followed by the Ordenanza of 1524. The brief Cook item was issued in facsimile, but no succeeding volume appeared.

In addition to the abortive projects already noted, Blom could point to a number of other items that never got into print. The World's Fair failed to make good its promise to issue the official report of the expedition to Uxmal in 1930. Frans' diary of the journey to northwestern Honduras in 1935 remains in manuscript. The two attempts to write literature to attract tourists to Central America likewise failed to appear, and an essay on ancient Maya women was rejected for an important volume on archaeology.

He spent some time in the mid 1930s drawing up material for tourist purposes. In 1935 the Long travel agency in Guatemala commissioned a number of pamphlets, each one on a place of interest in that country. Blom and his assistants prepared the manuscript of some half-dozen pamphlets. The travel agency never used them. Likewise two years later he and two members of the department were sent to Central America to collect data for a book to interest tourists, which Frans entitled *In the Shadow of Volcanoes*. The manuscript was written, but at first the United Fruit Company, one of the sponsors of the project, delayed publication on the plea of difficult financial conditions in 1937. Blom was optimistic, especially after Houghton Mifflin prepared the manuscript for the press. Two years later, however, the fruit company lost interest in subsidizing the volume, and it never appeared.

Frans was annoyed over the rejection of a scholarly paper he prepared for the Tozzer festschrift, *The Maya and Their Neighbors*. The list of contributors to that book reads like a Who's Who of Middle American archaeologists. Frans submitted a paper entitled "Cherchez la femme Maya, or Women's Place among the Ancient Maya." To his amazement, it was returned as unsuitable for the volume, and he assumed that the editors considered it too frivolous and perhaps too frank in a brief reference to prostitution near the end of the essay. He sent a copy of the manuscript to Professor Tozzer, who praised it.

In later years he revived interest in the paper. After settling in Mexico, he asked a worker in the department to send him the manuscript. As late as 1961 he added twelve pages of notes to it and translated it into Spanish. A reading of the paper today suggests that it was rejected not because of the subject matter but because of the poor presentation; it is little more than a compilation of passages from the early Spanish writers in Mexico. He had an interesting subject, but he lacked the ability or patience to mold the factual material into a smoothly flowing narrative.

As Blom wrote books and articles and carried on other professional activities in the 1930s, he struggled persistently to secure adequate quarters for the department. Beginning in 1932, he proposed that the Nunnery should be reproduced on the Tulane campus to house the Department of Middle American Research. The following year he suggested that the structure stand at the corner of Claiborne Avenue and Audubon Boulevard Tract, where tourists driving through the city would see it. The air-conditioned two-story building would cost $400,000, with an additional $100,000 endowment for maintenance. The president and two trustees, he remarked, were "intensely interested in my plan and they encouraged me to go forward with it." The proposal, however, encountered opposition from other trustees. When Frans received permission to solicit funds for the structure in 1934, some board members objected on the grounds that other departments of the university had needs of more educational value. By this time the cost of the project was estimated as high as $750,000. If Blom solicited contributions, he had no success.

In 1935 he changed the plans and proposed a reproduction of the Castillo, the temple pyramid at Chichén Itzá. The structure was designed to extend 200 feet on each side, rise to 104 feet, and contain five stories on the interior. Three years later the idea began to gain administrative favor, and preliminary preparations for a funding campaign got under way. By that time Frans enlarged the plans so that the Castillo would contain eight floors in an air-conditioned, windowless building. The cost had risen to more than $2 million.[6] Frans and an assistant took off for Chichén to gather architectural and pictorial material about the original Castillo.

The campaign to solicit money for the building began

in 1939, with plans to extend the drive into 1940. Tulane employed a fund-raising firm to manage the affair. Attractive brochures explained the need for the building, and a separate folder indicated the cost of each room to attract individual donors. Samuel Zemurray gave money to launch the campaign and acted as general chairman of the campaign committee. Several of Blom's workers and a professional motion picture man went to Central America to make a four-reel film, *Middle America,* to be shown to audiences over the country.

The campaign centered upon Blom as the dynamic director of the institute. The brochures emphasized his past accomplishments. He went out on speaking tours to large cities, and presented the film with accompanying remarks to create interest among potential donors. Although he made a foray into Texas, he spent most of his time in the North and Midwest. To outward appearances, all was going well.

Sometime during this period, however, Blom succumbed to alcoholism. It is not certain when it occurred; perhaps it came on gradually. The effects were so obvious that the university administration felt compelled to take action. Friends recall different episodes in the story. One former associate reports that when he went to hear Frans speak in Chicago during the building campaign, Blom appeared so unstable on the platform that the houselights went on, the performance was canceled because of the speaker's "illness," and the modest admission fee was refunded. Another associate says that the representative of the fund-raising firm who traveled with Blom wired to Tulane to withdraw him from the speaking tour. A third associate reports still another story. When the president of Tulane took some important visitors to the institute, intent on making a favorable impression on them, Blom was absent. Hastily summoned, "he arrived in a disheveled condition, with rumpled clothes and a two-day growth of beard," and other indications that he had been disturbed while under the influence of liquor.

Whatever the precise reasons, the administration felt

that it must take action. In November 1940 Blom was placed on "indefinite leave of absence." It was not announced that he had also been demoted from Director to Associate in Archaeology. Obviously, this was a drastic warning to the man to reform his ways lest he lose his job.

At this juncture a good friend made a noble attempt to save Frans. F. Webster McBryde, at work on a project in Mexico, easily induced the ailing man to join him. "He needed to get away, and he knew it better than anyone else," remarked McBryde. The two men spent some time in Oaxaca, and then they went on to San Cristóbal, "one of his favorite places."

The effect on Blom was remarkable. "When he arrived in San Cristóbal, he seemed to come to life," McBryde reported; "his old youthful enthusiasm revived." Although the men stayed in the same hotel, Frans secured a room as far as possible from his companion's quarters. When McBryde learned that Frans was drinking on the side, he entered Blom's room and removed the bottle.

"Every day we would go out to an Indian village, such as Tenejapa, usually an hour or two away by mule. He took those trips well, as they were easy rides by open trails, and the mountain air was invigorating. It all brought back his most pleasant memories, and, as I had hoped, the therapy worked wonders. He improved noticeably day by day. After a few weeks I could not detect that he was drinking at all. He really seemed to be cured by the time we left."

In San Cristóbal Frans took his friend to the Penagos house on the edge of the town, which he decided to buy as soon as he had the money. "He ran his hands over the beautifully carved door, and was really enraptured. I think that house, as much as anything else, helped to revive him." A decade later the house became his home.

After Frans returned to New Orleans, he reverted to his old habit. In November 1941 he was asked to submit his resignation for reasons of ill health. It was accepted at once, and he received his salary for the remainder of the academic year.

Why did Blom go to pieces in his late forties, an age when most professional men are rising to the peak of their performance? The reasons must be inferred from his actions. In the late 1930s, he suffered a series of defeats. Undoubtedly he could have withstood any one of the problems, but they piled up, and it is a reasonable assumption that the cumulative effect defeated him. He remarked in late 1934, "I am having hard sledding here" because of increased work, cramped quarters, and more people using the department. About the same time, when he complained of the failure of the trustees to approve some action, he admitted that "some days I feel thoroughly discouraged and impatient," a significant statement in view of his perennial optimism. His publications fell off in quantity and quality. *Maya Research* lost its foundation support; his later attempt to revive it required a subsidy of $1,000 a year, which he could not raise. The five-year project for Honduras never got under way. Instead of exploring, he spent time writing pamphlets and a book to attract tourists to Central America. His divorce was a hard blow to his pride. Then he faced the possibility of having to teach, which he did not like. The attempt to revive the exploration fund was vetoed by the administration; the building campaign forced him into the uncomfortable role of public speaker.

Perhaps the most significant reason for his failure was his prolonged absence from the forests of Chiapas. His last trip to that region had occurred in 1928. The brief return in 1941 had a tonic effect on the man; unfortunately, he could not remain there long. The depression of the 1930s and the lack of money for expeditions to Chiapas sapped his inner strength; his spirit was breaking, and he had no way to restore it.

The picture of his collapse is not complete without considering another aspect. Somehow Frans lost his nerve. In the earlier years he had developed extreme self-confidence, perhaps too much self-confidence for his own good. Everything he did reinforced his personal esteem. Then, beginning in 1936, he was trapped in meaningless activities, with no prospect of returning to the Chiapas highlands. His innate optimism finally gave way. For the first time in his life he could not help himself. He fell into despair.

His actions from November 1940 until September 1943, the darkest period of his life, are not clear. The few things that are known of those years indicate his hopelessness. No longer did he have money to buy books. Months before he was placed on leave, all the utilities were disconnected in his apartment because he failed to pay the bills.

Letters written by a close and well-intentioned friend in the early part of 1941 reveal Blom's troubles. He suffered from the old sinus affliction; later he believed that he needed an operation for appendicitis. He had no regard for the proper use of money, and could not adjust himself to his modest salary. When he received almost a year's salary in advance, it appears that he used it unwisely. Once he took visitors from the North to Antoine's for dinner and let them pay the bill because he had already spent his money foolishly.

He had lost the will to struggle. Instead of facing reality, he imagined that some high-paying job was about to come his way and conjured up other bright prospects for the future, all without the least basis in fact. He assured inquirers that everything would come out all right. If someone remonstrated with him, he laughed and gave no answer. He indicated that no one ever had to help him and that by his own will he could accomplish the impossible. The friend advised him to clean his apartment and open the windows for air and sunlight, eat normally, find diversions by driving in the country and attending movies, and write on subjects of his interest.

After his resignation he was denied access to the institute. He insisted that he had left some personal possessions there. On one occasion he was allowed to reclaim certain photographic equipment. He insisted that the university was holding personal property of his worth $1,215, so the administration had him sign an agreement to accept $750 to settle all future claims.

He attempted to find a job. The United States was at war and could use men with the languages he spoke fluently and without accent. There was no doubt about his pro-Ally feelings. "I am rather rabid on the subject of being anti-German," he remarked. He applied to the army, navy, and civilian service agencies. In fact, one of his friends in government service arranged a job for him in the Office of Naval Intelligence in Mexico. It is possible that lack of United States citizenship thwarted his employment. Although he applied for naturalization right after Pearl Harbor, he had to wait many months to secure final papers. The delay discouraged him, because he felt the immediate urge to join in the war effort.

At times he recovered sufficiently to do some writing. He is reported to have spent seven months in the middle of 1942 working on a book on the ancient Maya; this was probably one of those optimistic bits of information he passed on to his friends. By the end of the year, however, he had produced a brief note on Lacandón arrows he collected back in 1928 and an English translation of the *Popul Vuh.*

Apparently he spent some time at the Latin American Library of the University of Texas. Once he reported that he had an opportunity to carry on research there, "but I feel I have no right to spend my time on things of the distant past, when my familiarity with Latin America should be of present usefulness" (a reference to the war). He became familiar enough with the manuscripts of the University of Texas to annotate a printed catalog of those holdings, mentioning errors in the listings.

In the spring of 1943 he informed a friend of his activities. He had just recovered from an operation on his sinuses and had spent some days in a hospital to recover from the bites of ants. "I am now staying with friends in the country," he observed, "but will be back in town next week." He had transcribed a document for publication. As a by-product of that work he had begun to compile a dictionary of unusual words found in documents of the period of the Spanish conquest. In mentioning the *Popul Vuh,* he regretted his failure to learn the Quiché language. In passing, he remarked that his personal library was in storage. It is likely that he had to resort to that expedient when he moved from his large apartment to the more cramped quarters of the first floor at 511 St. Ann Street.

Eventually he lost all his personal possessions. Although the details of the story have not come to light, enough is known to reconstruct the general outline of that debacle. He failed to pay his rent and his income taxes. To a friend he confided the story of his library. "The business of my books being sold is a very bitter thought to me, which still breaks my heart. When I left Tulane, I was paid a year's extra salary, they were so eager to get rid of me. I was paid on December first [1941], which means that I, according to the tax authorities, had made double salary in a war year. . . . As I never have had to do with lawyers before, I did not know anything about all this. I blissfully went to Mexico, and then heard that because of not having declared correct and gone to Mexico without advising duly, I was fined and heaven knows what more. As I was out of reach of mail, my books were seized and sold. Nice, isn't it! It made me very bitter, and I don't think that you will blame me if I do not intend to set my feet in the U.S. any more in my life. . . . This is the story and I hate to be reminded of it. And please do not mention it." Two years after arriving in Mexico, he wrote to a bookstore in New Orleans, asking if they were willing to send him family albums and personal files left over from the sale of his books.

The fate of his personal belongings was another story. When the unpaid rent ran up to $110, the owner seized his remaining personal effects—clothing, silverware, maps, and a few books. Some years later a faithful friend, formerly an employee of the department, paid the delinquent rent, salvaged the clothing not damaged by mice and moths, sold the silverware, and sent him the maps and books plus $40 left over after balancing accounts.

Blom had fallen as low as a man can go. Self-confidence, which had carried him so far in the past, deserted him, and he shunned the aid of the few friends who cared for him. Could he ever recover?

7

The Uphill Climb

Frans Blom spent the last twenty years of his life in Mexico. He recovered his self-control, found a faithful woman to help him, adopted a revised set of values, and strove to create a new career to satisfy his desires. This was the surprising part of his life. At Tulane he displayed conventional professional success, but in Mexico his achievements revealed unsuspected personal resources and disclosed his true interests. Because his rise was slow and his accomplishments unspectacular in that second career, many of his former friends, especially those in archaeology, never fully appreciated the significance of his later years of self-fulfillment.

Blom had to start at the bottom, and the uphill climb was difficult. He was in a foreign country with relatively few friends, and many of his former associates in the United States quietly lost interest in him. In addition, he lacked affiliation with a professional institution. Entirely on his own, without financial resources, he had to work at menial jobs and seek grants for expeditions.

He began the second career with some assets, which in the end did help him. He retained his professional knowledge of archaeology, and he made use of it. He found a few friends in important positions in Mexico who were willing to help him. Drawing upon his knowledge and interest in Chiapas, he determined to explore those highlands as often as possible. Although it seems insignificant, he saved himself time and money by avoiding the pointless frivolities of teas, receptions, and formal affairs. There is no doubt that at the beginning of his new life his greatest asset was Gertrude Duby, a woman who provided the support and encouragement he needed and who believed in him and helped him to achieve his aims.

Born in the canton of Berne, Switzerland, in 1901, Gertrude Duby, generally known as Trudi, had studied horticulture, gaining practical experience by working in the gardens of a Swiss castle for a year, and had attended a school for social work in Zurich and taken courses in sociology at the university of that city. She traveled in France, England, and Germany to learn the languages of those countries, and wrote articles for periodicals in Switzerland.

During World War II she came to the New World. Strongly anti-Nazi, she devoted some time to aiding victims of Hitler's Germany. By the end of 1940 she was in Mexico, a country which had fascinated her since childhood. At first she aimed to raise the cultural level of workers in the textile and tobacco industries of western Mexico. She gave some attention to the Otomí Indians, and for a time Zapata's agrarian movement also interested her. Finally she devoted herself to the Lacandón Indians of Chiapas, who became her major passion.

Trudi was an unusual person. An attractive woman, she knew how to dress with flair, and took great interest in clothes of unique material and design. Spirited, independent, and determined, she was also practical and down-to-earth. She could shoulder her share of the burdens on an expedition, operate a household efficiently, and, when the occasion called for it, she could command others effectively.

Fortunately, Trudi joined Frans at the beginning of the expedition that inaugurated his new career. He received a grant (from unrevealed sources) to search Chiapas for supplies of wild rubber for the United States government, because the supply of that vital item had been cut off from the East Indies. When he left Mexico City on September 24, 1943, he was the lone passenger in the plane, and the pilot obliged him by flying twice over the ruins of Monte Albán. After a stop at Oaxaca, he flew to Tuxtla Gutiérrez. There he met Governor Rafael Gamboa, who impressed him favorably as a man of ability and foresight. From him Frans received a document requesting all municipal authorities in the highlands to aid his work. Planes flew to Ocosingo at irregular intervals, depending upon the need to transport cargo. On Wednesday, September 29, Blom boarded one of those planes for Ocosingo, where he would begin the expedition into the forests.

Trudi was waiting for him. Governor Gamboa had given her permission to accompany Blom on the expedition. She and Frans had never met before, though they had heard much about each other through some intermediary, who has never been identified. As the plane swooped down on the landing field at Ocosingo, "a reformed cow pasture," as Frans dubbed the runway, all the inhabitants of the town were on hand to meet it; the arrival of any aircraft was always an important local event. Trudi was in the crowd.

Trudi saw Frans descend from the plane—a tall man, with jaunty, self-confident bearing, blond hair mixed with white, and casual attire of drill trousers, Chamula-style shirt, and an Indian knapsack hanging from one shoulder. With a quick glance over the crowd, Frans had no trouble spotting her, for he saw an "attractive looking woman, who certainly did not fit into the picture, the city-way she was dressed in tailor-made gray flannel and turban."

"You are Gertrude Duby," he said in a matter-of-fact way, and remarked that he had heard much about her.

"And you are Frans Blom," she replied confidently.

They spent several days together. Frans was fifty and Trudi was forty-two. It was not a case of young love, which must constantly be reaffirmed in words; mutual understanding provided the requisite assurance. Some days after her arrival they climbed a steep mountain behind the town. That night Blom recorded his happiness—in an indirect way, it is true—in his diary. "After a while we scrambled down the steep slope. There were many wild flowers, red and blue, strong in color and pale shades. A small mountain stream chuckled along near the trail. It sounded happy." There was an unusual atmosphere about the scene, and he had to think twice to determine what it was. "One thing that impressed me this afternoon, as I came down the mountain toward the town, was the quiet. There were no noises, no motors exhausting, no automobiles honking, no mechanical noises. The broad valley lay stretched at our feet—a complete calm that was restful." Finally, he got to the major point of that day's entry: "La Duby is the kind of person with whom you can feel in close relation without having to do conversation. I like that gal."

Under the unusual circumstances one might expect that Ocosingo took on a new meaning for Frans, but not so. It had lost the liveliness he had enjoyed there during the visit of 1925. "Then there were gay marimbas," he remembered, "now there are none. Silence lies heavy over the town, a few anemic light bulbs flicker—and a million stars shine through the black velvet of the night sky. It is the silence that is so beautiful."

When he set out on the expedition the following day, Trudi was with him, although he had long declared that he would never allow a woman on his expeditions. After accompanying him for several days, she left to attend to business in Mexico City, with the understanding that in about two months she would rejoin him at Yaxchilán. She did return, as we shall see, and remained with him thereafter.

Frans and Trudi settled in Mexico City in 1944 after
the end of the expedition. They rented a small apartment
at Los Alumnos 48, Tacubaya—"not much more than a
terrace," Frans explained. But from the terrace they had
a view of the great volcanoes, Ajusco Mountain, and
nearby Chapultepec Park. The apartment had two rooms,
with kitchen and bath, and the terrace full of flowers.

They held open house on Saturday and Sunday
afternoons at four, one day for scientists and the other
day for laymen. Various languages could be heard at
those gatherings; and Trudi, an accomplished linguist
herself, was a charming hostess. For Frans this was a
change from his habits in New Orleans, where he had
restricted himself to a small coterie in the French
Quarter and a few wealthy women. If he was searching
for individuals who might support his expeditions, there
was also the genuine pleasure of associating with
informed persons. In later years he enjoyed the same
variety of visitors in San Cristóbal.

How he supported himself, at least until 1947, is not
quite clear. The grants he secured for expeditions could
hardly have netted him more than the expenses of each
trip. In 1945 he complained to a friend that he had "lost"
many months just in order to make a living. He
conducted classes in English, guided tourists, and in
some unexplained way helped with summer school
classes. In his free time he wrote numerous articles for
newspapers.

Conditions improved somewhat by 1947. His friend
Gamboa, now head of the national Department of
Health, gave him an office job. When Frans complained
that he had too little to do, Gamboa told him to perform
his work and not to worry about himself. The job must
have been undemanding, for Blom carried on numerous
outside activities. He conducted a class of 220 students
in a summer school. On weekends he hired a
thirty-passenger Greyhound bus and took sightseers to
Texcoco, Puebla, and Oaxaca. That experience taught
him that there was money in the tourist business, and in

later years he was always alert to the importance of attracting tourists to Chiapas. In the late 1940s he explained that he was giving talks at a summer school, though he offered no details about the work.

More important than the jobs he held was the new outlook on life he developed. Learning from past experience and guided by inner desires, he sought simplicity in ambition and in life-style. He scaled down his wants to essentials, adopted casual clothes, took an interest in a broad variety of people, and arranged for excursions to the jungles as often as possible. He told a friend that after leaving Tulane he had become a free man. Not only had he escaped from the frustrations of his former job, but in Mexico he achieved a new maturity of outlook.

An increasing appreciation of other people emerged as one aspect of that outlook. In the 1920s and 1930s he assumed that he was a self-made man who could carry out tasks without reliance upon friends. After 1943 he became more reflective and began to appreciate the ideas and thoughts gained from association with others. Looking back on the days at Harvard, he now remembered ·the "people who helped me . . . Pilgrim Father Tozzer, the incredible Roland Dixon, the Hooten magnificent," as well as Samuel Lothrop and Carleton Coon.

He admitted that occasionally he was lonesome and would enjoy hearing from former friends. Just who those friends were is not clear, for he realized too well that many acquaintances of the Tulane years avoided him. One day on the streets of Mexico City he saw Matilda Gray, the wealthy woman he had known so well during the years in New Orleans; "she tried to pass me up, but I stopped her." He did not reveal the nature of the conversation. He also felt out of touch with developments in his professional field; he asked one archaeologist to send on copies of his published articles. "My long stay in the backwoods has separated me from recent atomic brain bombs," he explained.

He esteemed simplicity in everything he did. Once he
had a chance to secure a position, apparently in a
museum in New York State. The employer "wanted to
offer me a job as No. 2, but as it involved too much 'fish
and soup' and white ties, I just let it go." He boasted
that now his work meant "blue jeans, a khaki shirt, an
old Stetson and the smell of mule sweat, frijoles and
tortillas, and what's beyond the next mountain range."
"No fooling with tea parties," he remarked, "no
clowning for audiences, and most of all no begging for
money. I get a job and I do it."

The desk work in Mexico City lacked the thrill of
traveling through the forest. He disliked "paper, carbon,
a slow stenographer," and "the nuisance about living in
a city." "What cheers," he added, "is the end of a mule
which is headed for the bush." He revealed also that
"somehow the older I get, I become more and more
restless about going and seeing, and recording what I
see." Compared with urban life, travel on the trail had
advantages. "When you ride along on a mule, you have
much time to think. It is like one of those Alka Seltzers
of the harried people."

He sought invitations to guide expeditions. He queried
a well-known North American archaeologist as to
whether he had any work for him to do in Mexico.
"Nobody knows better how to cuss a mule in Spanish,
Aztec, Maya, Tzeltal, Quiché, etc. I ain't boasting." To
another friend he wrote in a similar vein: "If you have
some field men who want to take an old mule skinner of
Central America, just let me know. Show me a mule and
an expense account, and I am on my way. And with no
desire of getting rich—just the rent, the home, etc., and
the chow."

Blom had the good fortune to arrange a number of
expeditions. We have already mentioned the journey
through Chiapas in 1943-44. Then he studied the disease
onchocerciasis two years later, followed by travels in
Tehuantepec and Oaxaca. Sometime during this period
he searched for amber for William Spratling, an old
friend of New Orleans days who was becoming a famous

silversmith in Mexico, but no record of that venture has come to light.

Frans also remarked that he "climbed the Paricutín with Dr. Nils Nilsen, Secretary General of the Royal Geographical Society of Copenhagen...." Some years earlier the volcano had erupted and buried a town. "Got about 100 feet from looking down into the crater, and it got wild, and what a slide we made down the ash cone. Injured my spine and burnt the bottom out of a very good pair of pants...."

There were other expeditions in the latter part of the 1940s. In 1946 he was scheduled to make a five-month jaunt through Chiapas and Tabasco to study the irrigation system of the ancient Maya, though it is not clear that he made the journey. About the same time four tourists hired him and a plane to visit Bonampak and Yaxchilán. He and Trudi traveled through the Lacandón territory in 1946, with a return visit to the region in the fall of the year. The Bloms were able to contribute 1,000 pesos toward the 12,000 which the expedition cost. Late in 1949 Frans explained that Alfonso Caso, director of the National Institute for Indian Affairs, and the state of Chiapas were about to send him on a three-year survey of the Lacandón forests.

Blom was at his happiest during the major expeditions of this period. Unpublished diaries of 1943 and 1948 provide abundant records of his feelings and experiences. In an indefinable way those journals have a more intimate, personal quality than the accounts of the earlier travels when he was at Tulane. In the 1940s he was more sensitive and appreciative of everything about him.[1] We shall consider his experiences on the trail in 1943 and 1948 and then give briefer notice to the unusual mission of 1945.

Blom never indulged in self-pity. When he encountered hardships, he described them, but he did not dwell upon them or refer to them in the future. Whether experiences were good, bad, or indifferent, he took all in stride as part of the day's work. When he made entries in the diary, he emphasized what he had done, not what he had failed to accomplish. In fact, he was not above turning a misfortune into a virtue. When funds for the expedition of 1948 were less than anticipated, he explained how he solved the problem. "There wasn't enough to buy more than five pack animals, so we went on foot for six months. But this has its advantages. One sees more of the ground indications and doesn't have to get down from the mule every time suspicions turn up."

He took pride in making careful preparations for an expedition. If he was ever caught short in the jungle without some item he should have brought, he never admitted it.[2] Aside from staples like sugar, salt, and coffee, which he carried with him, the other food came from hunting in the forest. For recreation on the 1943 trip he brought two books, *Don Quixote* and the chronicle of Bernal Díaz del Castillo, which provided diversion before he retired at night. Apparently he had no books on the journey of 1948, for he complained, "I wish I had something other than Blom's writings to read. He gets boring in large doses."

On the trail the time of rising and retiring varied with the circumstances. He liked to make the most of the early morning hours by getting up at dawn. But the more members he had in the party the later the group started off on the day's journey. When he had three assistants in 1948 he complained that "breakfast never gets ready early when we are in camp." Because his helpers were still sleeping by 6 A.M., he resolved "to turn them out at dawn from now on." That day the party took off at 8:30, "an ungodly late hour." His routine after the evening meal changed from one expedition to another. In 1943 he liked to sit up reading and writing until he fell asleep. Five years later he revised the routine. When night fell at 7 P.M., he went to sleep, woke up two hours later and attended to his records, and then turned in for the remainder of the night.

There was no typical day on the trail, for every part of the journey offered new experiences. On leaving Toniná in 1943, the trail took him into oak forests, then into the pine belt, where the trees stood apart and soft grass covered the ground "like a well-kept park. It was cool, and the wind sang in the pine tops. I did not hear a soul on the trail. A pair of cardinals went by. . . ." When Trudi and two native assistants accompanied him in 1948, Blom described an ordinary day. They crossed the Jethá River in the morning. After a shower the sun appeared. They started off on a muddy trail, "beaten up by oxen and mules, but we soon came in on the untraveled forest trail. We were all on foot. . . . Saw fresh tracks of tapir."

Sights and sounds of the tropical night intrigued him. "Not a drop of rain all night," he noted in July 1948, "but bright, white moonlight falling through the tree tops creating the most amazing effects." Twenty-four hours later "the rain passed on, and when night came the forest was silent. Not a whisper in the leaves, only the chattering of a few belated parrots as the darkness closed in on the jungle." On another occasion he observed that "the night is filled with noises. There are different kinds of owls; some hoot lugubriously and others sound like human beings. Sometimes two owls keep up a hooting conversation. One rarely hears animals. Only when it has made the kill, the jaguar or cougar warns the forest that it is ruler. Insects chirp along most of the night. Always there is the murmuring of the *arroyo* or the rushing of a river near camp."

During brief pauses on the trail Frans was aware of everything. ". . . I sat down for a smoke. A light breeze made the branches rub against each other, giving out a mournful note. Then the breeze stopped. Not a leaf stirred. It was completely silent. Only a woodpecker tapping on a hollow tree, an occasional bird call, the distant murmur of the river. The loudest sound was the beating of my heart. Some time went by. Then suddenly I had visitors. A family of spider monkeys had discovered me and were discussing excitedly what kind of an animal I might be. I left them still arguing."

Overnight accommodations varied from a crude camp of his own making to quarters he might find along the trail. In 1943 he described his camp as "a lean-to of sticks, covered with grass, palm fronds or large leaves. The floor is the earth, the kitchen is a wood fire burning on the floor, and the roof is not always free from leaks. Comfort is minimum, but why go to a lot of trouble when one moves to a similar camp the next day?" He preferred sleeping in his hammock, which he rigged up with a net to protect him against mosquitoes. Over the net he threw a rubber poncho in the event of rain or heavy dew. Once he tried a bed of sticks on the ground, but found that it was hard on his bones, and "at last one sleeps out of sheer fatigue." In a chicle camp he found that four layers of sacks made a comfortable bed. He used the hammock, however, most of the time.

An incident during an overnight stay in San Antonio in 1943 illustrates Blom's confidence in handling potential trouble. He stopped at a house for wayfarers. "Six beds in a room for travelers," he explained. "A boy with fever in one, and a very drunk muleteer in another. Muleteer vomited all over place. He cleaned up floor with his hands. Told him to wash down floor. He did this, cursed and made gestures, pulling his machete out of scabbard; didn't directly threaten, but made it clear that he would like to let me have it. Placed several chairs in his way, so that he would fall over them in the dark if he woke up to go for me. Nothing happened."

After he left San Antonio persistent rain slowed his progress. Waiting for better weather, he killed time in one settlement repairing the radio of a local family. And he renewed acquaintance with don Pedro Vega, a wealthy ranch owner he had met on former expeditions. In a search for ruins, Frans accompanied Vega's son to a mountain top where the view was "so splendid that only silence was the answer; words would have been small and poor." Then he expressed his inner feelings: "There is good reason why those of us who have once visited Chiapas must always return. It is the beauty of the country."

He pushed on the trail despite the constant rain. Experience, however, had taught him how to proceed.

"Don't argue with a mule when on a muddy trail. It knows a darned sight more about trails and especially about muddy trails than I do. A mule picks the best spots and won't go ahead, because it knows it's going to get stuck. Leave the trail to the mule, and the mule to itself, and enjoy the landscape." Frans followed his own advice. Soon the rain stopped, and he looked about him. "I saw a pair of red-crested woodpeckers hammering on a hollow tree trunk; a couple of humming birds hovered over the trail and then flashed away sideways. Spiders had spun fine cobwebs across the trail, and I would ride into them. They tickle your face. Lots of flowers of all colors. I didn't know the names of them, unfortunately. A small coral-colored mushroom. Some wild papaya."

In the afternoon he arrived at Las Tasas, a chicle headquarters of five grass huts without walls. He sat down to rest. In the trees above he saw "a party of those amusing little devils, the spider monkeys. They can be very entertaining and they are very curious, but they can also be most annoying. They will come out on a branch right over your head and deluge you with a shower of urine; so be wary when you look up at them."

After rain and mud he arrived at Agua Escondida. Although it was no more than a sinkhole with dense trees, he relaxed to contemplate life in the jungle. "There is nothing like sitting one quiet late afternoon in the great forest watching the animal life. It slowly gets darker. Birds are busy. The parrots, always in pairs, screech overhead as they go home to roost. . . . As I returned to the small clearing by our camp, a flock of twenty-four macaws, flying in pairs, passed by, looking like a fleet of airplanes against the evening sky, and their red and yellow plumage shining in the light of the setting sun."

By this time he had hired two Tzeltal boys to accompany him, because one of them claimed to know of ruins. The boys, however, proved to be a nuisance the night he camped in a "half-rotten shelter" near the Cristolino River. Hardly had Frans gone to sleep when

the boys aroused him with frightening noise. They
reported that they saw the tracks and heard the roar of a
jaguar. He told them to go to their hammocks, for a
jaguar does not attack a sleeping man. And then he
mused, "Man smells too rankly to a jaguar and anyway
the king of the local jungle knows that man is not his
best friend." All night long the boys sat stiff with fear,
and the next morning they would not leave the camp for
fodder or firewood unless they traveled together.

Sometimes unfortunate luck dogged the members of
the expedition. A bad day and a bad night plagued them
in 1948. During the day an unripe aguacate (avocado) fell
from a tree and almost hit Frans. Then Rogelio, the
helper, cut a deep gash in the ball of his right hand, and
blood streamed out. Blom applied sulfa and bandages,
the best he could do at the time, because the supply
train with medicines was six hours behind on the trail.
To complicate matters, Enrique, the other helper, had
been blinded by a glob of mud kicked up along the trail;
by the end of the day, however, he had recovered his
sight. After the hammocks were put into place, it was
discovered that "they hung right under the aguacate
trees." Misfortune continued during the night. Blom "did
not sleep until 2 A.M., woke up at 4, and got up at
daybreak. . . . After dark some animals roamed the
aguacate trees above us and pushed the unripe fruits
down on top of us. One actually hit the nylon strings of
my hammock and they sang like the strings of a breaking
harp."

The most unnerving nocturnal experience occurred at
the settlement of Jordán in 1943, when the Tzeltal boys
traveled with him. Frans found

> one house with a family and a large grass-roofed
> house for travelers. It looked good to us. We would
> have gone through to Tecojá, but my ankle was now
> double the thickness of the good one. Later I
> wished we had gone on. The woman of Jordán made
> supper for us, and as the place swarmed with
> mosquitoes, I took cover in my hammock under my

mosquito net. Sometime during the night it started to rain. I woke up when a small river came running down the hammock ropes into the hammock. There was not a dry place in the house, so we fanned the fire and made coffee.

The rain stopped, and wrapped in my rubber poncho, I went back to sleep. Again I was wakened, this time by the boys yelling "Ronda," and, lighting my small petroleum torch, [I saw that] millions of small white ants were crawling on the outside of my mosquito net, and I lay there hoping fervently that they would stay outside. The Ronda is not the big Army ant, but it's a darned good imitation. Suddenly those ants decide to go on a raid. Millions of them charge forward, killing every insect they find on their way. When the Rondas come, even the large animals take flight. Their bite gives a stinging pain. If you put your bare feet on the ground, they will be covered with these vicious little animals, and your feet will feel as if they are being burned. Fortunately, they did not come inside my mosquito net. Outside, the two boys stamped and cursed and. finally jumped out into the pouring rain. In about a half hour the attack slowed down. Soon they had all gone to other fields to plunder. That somehow took all desire to sleep out of our systems for a while and called for another cup of coffee. At last we slept out of exhaustion, heavy with restless dreams.

He relished the food that the forest provided. The cojalite was a favorite bird, to be found everywhere. More to his taste was the pheasant, "nearly as big as a turkey—and what swell beefsteaks!" After tasting the breast of the pheasant, he boasted, "Don't think we can't live high in the jungle!" Although the Indians liked to eat spider monkeys, he drew the line at those animals. "It's too much like cannibalism," he remarked. He followed the policy of killing wildlife only for food. When Rogelio López, the native assistant, was with him in 1948, Frans made the point clear. "I told Rogelio to go slow with the shooting, as we had meat for several days, and I am much against murdering animals for sport. Not ten minutes later I saw him lift the gun and bang away. This time he shot a female deer, after which I took the shotgun away from him. All day long we met more game, and Rogelio would look back at me with sad and inquiring eyes." When Frans returned from that expedition, he told a friend that "we traveled with two shotguns and a handful of fish hooks, and with the help of fruit and vegetables from our Lacandón friends, we lived like kings."

In planning expeditions extending over months, he could not always prepare for unexpected illness. In the summer of 1948 he contracted rheumatism in his left arm and shoulder. A week later he found a physician who gave him an injection. Five days later the trouble reappeared, but after that he said nothing about it, and presumably he recovered. On the expedition of 1943 he suffered twice from severe illness, not counting a sprained ankle, which mended in a few days. By the time he reached Tenosique, sores covered his right leg and foot. It was no consolation to learn later that he suffered from bedbugs, which had probably feasted on him in one of the chicle camps. He applied iodine and gave himself a case of poisoning. Only in the hammock did he feel comfortable. He called in a doctor, who used salve and bandages. The bites swelled, and for eleven days he suffered from pain, so much so that he had to take drugs to sleep at night. When he began to improve, he took a plane out of Tenosique. "The dreary place looked quite charming from the air," he remarked, "and a casual passerby would never dream of the deadly boredom of the town."

When he arrived at El Cedro he felt better, and the town appeared colorful and lively:

> After dinner we watched a baseball game. Here with forest-clad mountains around us, with the smell of the tropics rising from the ground, was a gay crowd of players and spectators as enthusiastic as

any big league show. Yells, cries, boos and howls, and the technical language was in English. "Out," "streek" (strike), etc. Gradually, we talked to the men. Some were out of work and there was little chicle in their section; others were passing through from one camp to another. Some quite little kids were playing with crude, homemade airplanes. A faded chiclero woman strutted along in slacks and in high heeled shoes. Silk stocking, by gad! Chickens, dogs and mules interfered with the baseball game. . . .

Then came nightfall. A chicle plane came and left. "The noise of the propeller faded away, someone started to play a guitar, and a group began to sing. It darkened. Lights blinked in the huts, and the chicleros started their monotonous noise so typical to the tropical night. Across the runway is another camp; singing voices and laughter come across to us. It is Saturday, but no drinks, no noise, no hilarity. Just long Mexican love songs and tinkling of a guitar. . . ."

Frans recovered sufficiently in five days to set out again on the trail. Once more he was happy. "I enjoyed it out in the open. A clear and silent night. The tree tops made a lacework above, and the stars looked as if they were tied to the points of the branches. Now and then a lightning bug blinked. To the song of the cicadas I went to sleep." He continued on the trail, and some nights later he noted that "there was a new moon early in the evening, and it scattered polished silver on the floor of the forest." Wandering through the jungle, he confessed that this "life suits me better than any town." By the time he camped out the following night, the pleasure had ended. It rained, everything was damp, and he had to sleep in wet blankets. He stopped short to rebuke himself: "What the heck am I squawking about? There are no Japs in this jungle." Rarely did he refer to the war raging in other parts of the world.

He settled in the chicle camp of San Pedro and relaxed. At that place he described the complications of taking a bath, which he correctly termed "quite a performance." "Armed with a machete to cut a trail to a deep pool, one sets out with soap, towel and a sheet to cover one's nudity. Not that there are any people who would be shocked by your nudity, but there are gnats and mosquitoes who quickly attack every exposed spot." On finding a suitable place, you "proceed to undress and at the same time to take cover. It's a job. Once under water to your chin, you find that the gnats attack your ears and also that the soap will not lather. Then emerging after a while, the fight is on again, and you return to camp thoroughly uncomfortable and scratching."

By this time, early December 1943, Trudi had completed her work in Mexico City and determined to rejoin Frans on the expedition, though she did not know where he was traveling in the forest. She took a plane to Tenosique and then to El Cedro. No one in Cedro could tell her a thing about him.

The lack of information only increased her determination to join him. She decided to take the trail south to San Pedro. She hired a guide named Hilario, although she had been warned that he was peculiar and subject to epileptic seizures. At that moment two Yucatecans were also setting out for San Pedro to collect chicle; so she and Hilario joined them. On the way Hilario nervously whispered his fears to her: the two men were bandits and they planned to murder him and Trudi. That news made little impression on her; she worried over what to do if she failed to find Frans at San Pedro. Travel was at its worst—rain and mud, dangerous tree branches, hanging bejucos, and spines projecting from the side of the path.

On the outskirts of San Pedro, she met Carlos Frey,[3] then attached to Blom's expedition, and she realized that she had chosen the correct destination; her man was in San Pedro. She worried about her appearance. Her blouse was torn in several places, and she was splattered

with mud from head to foot. At four in the afternoon the
party entered San Pedro, and she announced her presence through the chicle camp. Blom emerged from a hut
and saw her "dressed in a red flannel shirt, a straw sombrero, and cakes of mud." To her great pleasure, he advanced and like a gentleman kissed her muddy hand.
She had found him, and she remained with him until the
end of the expedition.

Unaware that the most difficult days lay ahead, Frans
and Trudi enjoyed more than a week of pleasant travel,
accompanied by Carlos Frey and Pepe Centurión as assistants and one mule to carry the baggage. When the
mule became exhausted, Carlos and Pepe were assigned
to take it to a chicle center and to bring back a good
animal. For unknown reasons days passed before the two
men reappeared. Although Frans and Trudi were alone
in the forest, they were competent to care for themselves
under normal circumstances. "I fixed camp," Blom noted
on December 17, "and Duby took care of the food question. She is a brick on the trail, always ready to help."

An unforeseen event, however, occurred at the most
inauspicious moment. On the morning of December 18
Frans woke up shaking with malaria. He insisted on
taking to the trail. They covered the excess baggage to
protect it from rain and left it in camp, loading
necessities on their backs. The journey became a
nightmare. "Duby carried her pack, the small frying pan,
and her hammock, which is somewhat heavy. I carried
my hammock and blankets, my heavy rubber poncho, my
notebooks, medicine, a set of dry clothes, beans, rice,
coffee, salt, two plates, and the two smallest cooking
pots. . . . What a walk! I had forgotten that malaria made
you so weak. Sliding and stumbling, getting stuck in the
mud, my cargo slipping from side to side throwing me
off balance. Step by step, and at every step using up
strength against the suction of the mud. . . ."

In the crisis Trudi showed heroic qualities. Realizing
that it was impossible to reach San Juan that day, she

adopted the only sensible plan. She put her load down, shouldered that of Frans, and accompanied him to an advance point on the trail. He hung his hammock and crawled into it. Then Trudi returned to bring the second load of baggage, a trip requiring three hours. Rain continued to fall, and night came on. She lighted a small lantern and, loaded with baggage, set out to return to Frans. Rain, mud, and fallen trees confused her. When she thought she had returned to the place where she had left him, she called his name and received no answer. At each bend of the trail she expected to see his hammock. She lost the sense of passage of time and of her place on the dark trail. Must she wander in the jungle all night? At last she came upon his hammock, where he burned with fever. The only drinking water available came from the rain dripping from the leaves. The night could not end early enough to please her.

Eventually, they reached San Juan, where Frans was laid up for days with the enervating sickness. He attempted to overcome his weakness by sheer willpower. Once he arose to provide firewood, but soon gave up the task. "Most of the day I sat still." In the late afternoon he and Trudi "walked out into the forest and sat on a log at the edge of a clearing. . . . Across from us a dozen tree tops flamed red in the setting sun, as each was covered with a wonderful parasite that ranges in colors from red to pink, and which blooms at this season." That night was bitterly cold. In the morning "I managed to contribute nine pieces of firewood, and that sent me back to the hammock out of breath. . . . I went up to the trail and went into the forest. . . . I managed twenty minutes' walk in the forest, but stumbled a lot."

At last Carlos Frey arrived with a horse for Frans and a mule to carry the baggage, and they proceeded to El Cedro. After a local medico gave Frans injections of atabrine, he began to improve. As soon as possible he insisted on visiting some nearby ruins. But it began to rain when he arrived at the site, and he decided to return; "it was bone-freezing to ride back to Cedro in our wet clothes, and a pleasure to get on dry clothes, and drink a cup of steaming black coffee, spiked with 'White Mule.'" This is one of the rare references to the use of liquor during the expedition. On New Year's Eve there was a celebration in El Cedro, with turkey for the midnight party. "There was much laughter and singing, all in the most sober way, as there was not a single drop of liquor in camp."

For months he had no news of the outside world, and he showed little interest in the daily events of the war. At the end of October, after repairing the radio for a family in El Cedro, he tuned in and listened. "It was strange to hear the war news after weeks of isolation." Some months later, near the end of the expedition, suddenly his curiosity was mildly aroused. "After a trip like ours," he remarked, as he waited for a plane out of Santa Clara, "one builds up a thirst for something printed; even a year-old magazine is welcome."

Early in January 1944 he and Trudi took the trail from Santa Clara to Anaïte in preparation for a visit to Yaxchilán. Mud hindered them so much that they spent eight hours covering fifteen kilometers. Trudi "sloshed along with her inexhaustible energy, but even she at one point felt pretty tired." Frans had not fully recovered from the malaria. "I thought I knew mud. Now I know it," he exclaimed. "I was surprised how much strength the malaria had sapped out of me. The long and boring rest at Cedro should have built me up; on the other hand the food was not exactly strength-building."

Frans ended the expedition by taking Trudi on her first visit to Yaxchilán. He, too, enjoyed the experience, for he considered that site the finest Maya ruin. Then they went on to Tenosique and left by plane. As the aircraft bore them away, he took a parting shot at the town he despised. "Tenosique is deadly, depressing, sterile. If the whole world exploded, Tenosique would not know or care."

Statistics of travel intrigued Blom. On one of his later expeditions he meticulously noted the number of minutes from place to place on each day's trail. More informative was the general rate of travel on the expedition of 1948, which he provided for a friend. "A man with fresh animals," he explained, "and good ones at that, can make 6 to 7 kilometers per hour on the first few days, that is, if he can feed them corn every day. On long trips and with scarcity of fodder, as the case is when you travel in the forest, it is good to do 1.5 kilometers per hour." The rate, of course, was slower on mountainous trails, during rain, and in crossing streams. He found that on the Usumacinta River a large canoe went downstream at 8 kilometers per hour and upstream, with the men pulling the boat, at 2.5 kilometers per hour.

Although Frans enjoyed following trails through the jungles of Chiapas, he was not prepared for the frightening experience of the expedition of 1945. The journey involved the predictable trials of traveling through heavy growth, traversing muddy trails, and crossing mountains, but those difficulties faded into the background after he arrived at his destination. What he saw moved him more deeply than any other experience he had had so far in Mexico.

One day late in 1944 or early in 1945 Manuel Gamio, director of the Inter-American Indian Institute in Mexico, called Frans and Trudi to his office and proposed an expedition. It had nothing to do with archaeology, map making, welfare of the Lacandones, or the life of the chicleros or mahogany loggers. Gamio talked about a particular fly, *Simulium ochraeum,* which bit human beings and infected the bloodstream with a disease. The organisms traveled through the body and some of them usually settled near the eyes of the victim and eventually caused blindness. Generally, a tumor appeared on the person as an outward sign that he had the disease. Gamio sent Frans and Trudi to examine a section of southeastern Chiapas, where the Indians suffered from the scourge. There was no remedy; and if the victim did not have the tumor removed, he was sure to lose his sight.

The expedition was exploratory in nature, that is, the members of the party were prepared to do no more than examine the situation and trace the habitat of the fly. José Parra, a specialist in disease-bearing insects, brought scientific knowledge to the investigation. The Bloms provided their skill in traversing the forests, and Hector Arévalo acted as aide and muleteer.

The journey led inland over mountains and occasionally through settled areas. Beginning at Huixtla near the Pacific Coast, the party traveled north to Motozintla, followed the Cuilco River, and passed through Nuevo Amatenango. Turning eastward, they climbed mountains of scrub oak, where orchids occasionally appeared in the trees. Then came mountains covered with pine, and the party continued upward to four thousand feet. Looking down on the Tapisalá River, they saw the town of Unión Fronteriza. The area was lush with tropical growth. Orchids flourished everywhere. There were plantations of oranges, lemons, coffee trees, and bananas; pineapples, sugarcane, and corn abounded. They saw houses with gardens, grazing cattle, chickens, and turkeys. It was a land of natural bounty and tropical beauty.

At first, Unión Fronteriza appeared like any other Mexican town. The visitors learned quickly, however, that it had a peculiar, tragic quality. When they presented their credentials to the municipal officer, he stumbled over the words and then stopped reading; he was going blind. Everyone in the town suffered to some degree from the same affliction. There was no trouble about quartering the visitors in the schoolhouse, which was empty because teachers would not remain in the stricken village. Sightless old men used canes to find their way along the streets; younger persons, suffering from the early progress of the disease, shaded their eyes against the tropical sun. Now and then a doctor had appeared in the village and removed tumors from some of the people, but the bite of the fly quickly reinfected them. Everyone in the town was doomed to blindness. Blom's party could offer no medical aid; they had been sent only to examine the situation.

Never had Frans felt human suffering so poignantly. Later he told a friend that he had been bitten by the dangerous fly on the trip, but had been operated on before the disease became dangerous. This provides some explanation for the personal references in the passionate letter he sent to Gamio after returning from the journey. "It is easy to say that there is no remedy for onchocerciasis," he began. "It is easy to believe that it is a remote danger. *I* have seen that the sickness is spreading. *I* have seen that we are not safe in our houses. *I* fear the advance of evil among ourselves, and no doctors have convinced me otherwise. I've seen them combat yellow fever, but no one can convince me that human intelligence cannot find a remedy" for this disease.

He called for persistence and dedication:

> But it won't be done in the medical center of Huixtla, a place created only so that the doctor in charge can show off his fine clothes. It will not be done by laws and ordinances. It must be attacked seriously. We must penetrate the suffering settlements. We must give better pay to the nurses and doctors who carry on this mission. We must make them enthusiastic. Finally, we must select fanatics, as fanatic as the Catholic *frailes* of the Conquest. . . .
>
> My cry is preparation and prevention—that the laboratories seek a remedy, but that meanwhile we prepare ourselves.
>
> Pardon me, *querido maestro*, but your commission made me see incredible suffering. I saw the old blind men who asked for schools for their sons. The

badly paid teachers flee in view of the blind
sickness. I have seen even young men who do not
see the beauty of their land. I've seen abundance of
orchids forming a covering in the trees, which they
cannot see.

This was unusual language for Blom. Writing to
another correspondent, he admitted the effect the
experience had on him. "Please forgive me, but that trip
made me somewhat of a fanatic, which means violent. I
have seen people who cannot see, and I want to help
them." When he and Trudi wrote a description of the
journey for *Natural History,* he contrasted the tropical
beauty of the land with the frightful scourge that blotted
out the enjoyment of that beauty. This was not a mere
literary device; it came from his own experience. "When
we were talking to the people with the smarting eyes
and knowing that soon they would be blind, there stood
a can on the table overflowing with flowers." He added
another detail not revealed in the article. "Unión
Fronteriza was our first sight of the horror. . . . Toward
the end of the trip we saw something even worse:
onchocerciasis combined with elephantiasis of the face.".

Without realizing it, Frans had broadened his experience and deepened his feelings. Rationalist that he
was, with a belief in the power of human intelligence
and faith in modern medicine, he found himself faced
with a problem of human tragedy. There is no evidence
that he grappled in his mind with the larger aspects of
the problem in a philosophical way, but it is certain that
the trip to Unión Fronteriza matured his outlook on life
and developed a latent humanitarianism.

After completing the assignment on onchocerciasis,
Frans and Trudi continued the expedition into Tehuantepec and Oaxaca. He found eight ruins, brought to light
a lienzo of the period of the Spanish Conquest, and examined some sixteenth-century churches. Unfortunately
he never drew up a report of that expedition. It seems
that he had secured $1,500 from the governors of Chi-
apas and Oaxaca to meet part of the expenses of the

journey. He placed the money in the hands of a governmental official in Mexico City, but when Frans returned from the expedition, he learned that the official had diverted the funds to other uses. Thus he had no money to draw up and publish a report.

As Blom traveled through the jungle with Trudi at his side, he found life worth living again. His spirits soared; self-confidence and optimism reappeared. In enjoying nature, he also revived his interest in Indians and Maya ruins, which seemed to be part of the natural landscape.

8

Interests and Activities

The expeditions of 1943 and 1948 provided the setting for the development of Blom's latent interests. He showed a greater concern for the Indians, especially the Lacandones, than in the past. He revived the search for Maya ruins in the jungles of Chiapas. And the expeditions into those regions inspired him to map the area, stimulated him with new ideas, and provided source material for his writings. At last he could devote much of his time to the forests, which inspired most of his activities in the last period of his life.

One of the most notable changes in emphasis in these years appeared in Blom's deep concern for the Indians. Formerly, he had esteemed their patience and hard work; now he broadened and deepened his interest in them. His earlier curiosity developed into humanitarian concern.

The formal religious practices of the Indians struck him in different ways. If the ceremonies involved only small offerings and invocations to their gods, as was the case with the Lacandones, he had no objection. He was in fact respectful of their sanctuaries, and he believed that their religion formed an integral part of their simple way of life.

Other practices, however, aroused his contempt. If celebrations of a religious holiday got out of hand or demoralized the people, he condemned the practice. When he visited Tecojá in 1943, he described the local natives' celebration of a holy day in unsympathetic and sarcastic terms:

> On Nov. 1st it is "Todos Santos," All Saints, one of the most important of all Indian religious days of the whole year. Very convenient. Instead of praying to each saint individually, one can placate all of them at one shot. Weeks beforehand Indians have the great day on their minds. They work for pay so that they can get money together to buy food and liquor for the celebration. November 1st is All Saints and November 2d is All Souls. On the first day they get drunk and on the second they carry food and liquor offerings to place on the graves of their relatives, and get some more drunk. Ofttimes they kill someone they don't like, and thus contribute to the graveyard celebration. On the third there is a universal hangover, and a couple of the most outstanding village sots are found asleep among the tombstones and crosses in the graveyard. By the 4th everybody is sick, and nobody has a cent. All that is left is the expectation of next year's All Saints.

Frans developed a lively interest in the Lacandón Indians. Back in the Tulane days, during the expeditions of 1925 and 1928, he had considered them as ethnological curiosities, descendants of the ancient Maya who had remained almost unchanged over the centuries. By the time of his expedition of 1943, however, he displayed a deeper and more humane interest in them. Perhaps he absorbed some of Trudi's strong commitment to aid them.

The Lacandones, numbering no more than several hundred individuals, lived in two separate groups in the vast stretch of the jungle between the Jataté and the Usumacinta rivers. The northern group clustered around Jetjá, and the southern group lived near the chicle settlement of Lacanjá and the region of the lower Jataté River Valley. Although the two groups had no relations with each other, the Bloms visited both settlements without trouble. The Lacandones were good farmers, expert hunters, displayed intelligence, and were peaceful and hospitable toward strangers who indicated that they wanted to help them.

It is interesting to read Frans's comments of respect and sympathy when he visited the Lacandones in 1943. "Their milpas are very clean, not a weed, not a blade of grass," he remarked, "and if one throws a fruit peel or the like on the floor of the milpa, they immediately pick it up and carry it outside the milpa. They clean their feet before stepping into the milpa, as they do not want to bring in seeds of weeds which may stick to their feet." In regard to their use of weapons, he noted that "though they now use shotguns, they are excellent with bow and arrow, which they make with great care. . . ."

At the same time he was upset over possible dangers to those natives. "The Lacandóns die like flies from scarlet fever, smallpox, grippe, as they have no resistance to those imported diseases. I roughly calculate that there are about 250 of them left, and with the death rate as it is at present, they will be gone soon." The other danger came from the chicleros, who easily cheated the Lacandones because the Indians had not learned the value of food and supplies in barter.

One of the major aims of the expedition of 1948 was to carry supplies to the Lacandones. Frans and Trudi displayed remarkable ingenuity in inducing agencies, individuals, and companies to make contributions to the cause. Medicines came from the Mexican Department of Health and Public Welfare and also from several Swiss medical firms. The director of the Trifolio Seed Company provided a generous supply of packaged seeds so that the Lacandones might cultivate new vegetables.

The head of the San Angel Paper Company donated paper bags for various uses. Money and color film came from the National Museum of Anthropology; the Bloms used the money to buy ethnological collections and the film to record various Indian types for the museum. Finally, the Pan American Institute of Geography loaned several instruments for Frans's work in map making. The Bloms bought necessary supplies and utensils for traveling over a period of six months.

They set out from Mexico City on May 8 with everything packed in a station wagon. After a stop at Tuxtla Gutiérrez, they continued until they left the highway for the forest. Then they packed the supplies on animals and proceeded on foot into the jungle.

Trudi was active in carrying on the humanitarian work. She knew how to deal with her native friends, and they respected her forthright manner. At El Real she handed out seeds, combs, and other items, and planted a vegetable garden for the natives. "The seeds which we have brought are very popular," Frans noted.

At another settlement some weeks later Trudi "gave a talk on fruits and vegetables for the children, who all have 'granos,' caused by the lack of vitamins. She also had something to say about letting the swine run loose, and urged them to build fences around their houses. They and their children live in mud and filth, and can't understand why they get sick. They pay exorbitant prices for patent medicines, sold by unscrupulous traveling merchants. It's a pity to see how these poor people get jipped all the time."

The next night the natives gathered in something like a town meeting. They had to decide what to do about a peculiar chiclero who was always threatening to kill people. After heated debate, the Lacandones agreed to let him continue to live in their neighborhood. Frans tells what happened next. "The more pleasant part of the evening started after Trudi told them all to shut up." The force of the statement can only be appreciated by one who has heard her give that order. She had stronger words in her multilingual vocabulary, but none carried the same whiplash of command. "Then she distributed the packages of seeds of radish, cucumber, watermelon, eggplant, etc. . . . ." On other occasions the gifts were sometimes used for barter. At one Lacandón village she "distributed red bandanas, beads, combs, mirrors, etc., to the women. The men got a file for their machetes and some small fish hooks, and admonition to bring maize."

The physical appearance of the Lacandones intrigued Frans. "Hair hanging down their shoulders, and dressed in their sack shirt of cotton of their own growth and woven by their women. These men were much healthier looking than those who live close to civilization. Their hands are delicate and of fine shape in spite of the fact that they are agriculturalists. Their bare feet are well formed, as they are unhampered by footwear. Their walk is balanced and like an even glide through the forest."

Chicleros and mahogany men, however, threatened their peaceful existence. Frans observed that the Lacandones "have good reason for hiding the entrance to their milpas and houses. The chicleros—may they be eternally damned—used to raid their fields, destroy or take away their crops and rape their women. They would bring in their mules and let them graze on their cornfields." With the Lacandones living in the Perlas River region it was another story, for they were losing their lands to whites who exploited the forests for mahogany. "Nobody should be allowed to settle or cut timber here," Frans remarked. At least outsiders "should be stopped from selling liquor to them."

Blom saw those natives as a part of nature. On passing some Lacandones on the trail, he noted that "they fitted perfectly here in the forest. Seemed to be part of the trees, the leaves and the gay singing of the small cascades of the little stream." Some days later, again passing two natives, he remarked that "they blended with the forest, and I have a vivid feeling that *they*, not we, belong here."

By this time he had developed a sensitivity even for

small things about the Lacandones. At the end of one of
the meetings which Trudi addressed, "the two women
with their babies got up, and as they walked away they
made a little song or signal to the gods to protect the
baby. It started with the most exquisite bird-like cry
repeated several times. It reverberated in the silence of
the forest, and will linger in our memories. . . ."

A striking defect which Frans could not explain was
"the amazingly little artistic expression among those
people. Granted that their bows and arrows are
masterpieces of artistic skill, one would think that they
would express themselves artistically in the decoration of
their household goods, but no. Occasionally, one will
find a gourd with some carving on its surface, usually
without meaning. I have seen a few spindles nicely
carved of wood, but that is about all."

On rare occasions the overly friendly natives exasper-
ated Frans. One evening in the fall of 1948 he had too
much of the Lacandones of Lacanjá, because they crowded
his camp quarters so closely. He wanted to copy fragments
of a mural he had found in the nearby ruins. When he
returned to his hut, the Indians swarmed over the place.
"All very nice," he exclaimed, "but they are decidedly
getting in my hair. It is impossible to do any work when
they are around, and I was working with the colored pen-
cils." At the natives' request, he found that "it was very
exciting to try the colors on their tunics. Result: I didn't get
a chance . . . to finish the job" of copying the mural. Then it
began to rain and there was no hope that they would leave.
"The big lazy brute Kin wanted to hang his hammock over
my desk, but I said no." "I believe," Blom concluded,
"that I am due a vacation from Lacanjá Lacandóns. . . ."
This was an unusual instance of frustration, and it occurred
because the Indians interefered with his work, which they
did not understand.

His general feeling appeared more accurately when he
noted a few days later that "we now have been accepted
by Lacandón society, which is a damned sight more than
a lot of other society which I have met in sundry places."

On returning from the expedition of 1948, the Bloms

made several reports. Trudi submitted an account of nutrition among the Lacandones to the national Ministry of Health and Public Welfare. Frans joined Trudi in drawing up recommendations to aid and preserve the Lacandones. They advised that the northern and southern groups should be concentrated in a single area. To preserve the dwindling population, they believed that the Lacandones should intermarry with the neighboring Tzeltal Indians. Finally, they strongly urged the Mexican government to take over all trade with the Lacandones to insure that the natives received the supplies they needed and to prevent exploitation by traveling merchants. Unfortunately, the recommendations were impractical, because the two groups of Lacandones disliked each other, and they despised the Tzeltal Indians; moreover, the Mexican government was not ready to institute a paternalistic economic policy for a few hundred Indians who had stubbornly resisted racial intermixture.

Blom's sympathy for Indians stirred his disgust with other groups in the Mexican population who took advantage of the oppressed natives. Although he carefully kept his opinions to himself, he railed out against the exploiters in his diary. During the early stage of the expedition of 1943, he enjoyed renewing his acquaintance with several prosperous ranch owners. Blom did not criticize those wealthy families for showing initiative in developing their lands nor did he oppose their elegant behavior as such. But their unknown and unpublicized actions stirred his anger. Their "charming hospitality" and "gracious manners," he declared, covered numerous cruelties. The powerful men often illegally claimed Indian land and then forced the natives to pay rent and personal services for the right to till their soil. It was "the story of the Conquistadores—mean, cheap, cruel exploitation." Near the end of the journey he lashed out against another group. "All mahogany and chicle operators, Spanish or of Spanish descent . . . are a bunch of ruthless thieves, who first plunder the neighborhood before they work their own property or concession."

He threw another light on the ranch owners when he visited El Real in June 1948. "These finqueros [ranch owners] are all related and friends," he explained, "but when it comes to business they cheat each other ruthlessly. There are constant jealousies, and some of them are perverted and crazy." "One man poured gasoline on a neighbor's cattle and set them on fire." Murders were common, and no punishment was meted out. "Their chief income comes from cheating the Indians, and though many of them have no education at all, even to not being able to read and write, they carry big pistols and call themselves civilized. Obviously there are exceptions, but these are few."

When Blom visited eastern Chiapas five years later, he expressed his disgust with the ladinos, Indians or part-Indians who adopted some aspects of modern culture and hence considered themselves superior to less Hispanicized Indians. "That lazy and arrogant set of ladinos," he exclaimed, "doesn't care a damn, and spends their time talking about how lazy the Indians are, how civilized they are themselves, and make their money by robbing the Indians at every turn." Only a few days later he let out another blast: "The Chiapas ladino is a thoroughly despicable person, [of] narrow mind, superstitious, dishonest, fanatic Catholic of the worst kind, and even though he can read and write with difficulty, he talks about himself as being civilized."

Another group that stirred his ire were Protestant missionaries, especially those of a zealous evangelical disposition. When he learned of the presence of a missionary among the Lacandones, he asked why such a man should impose "his conceit and ignorant self-satisfaction on people who never asked him to come anyway. . . . What a weak and rotten lot all of those conceited missionaries are!"

His antagonism was at its height when he witnessed the arrival of a Baptist missionary at El Real in July 1948. The plane

brought Don Felipe, American and missionary, who

16. Blom and an assistant, 1948. *Courtesy Gertrude Duby Blom*

17. Blom after a fall in the mud, near the Lacanjá River, 1948. *Courtesy Gertrude Duby Blom*

18. Temple 33, Yaxchilán. "Yaxchilán stirs me more than any other of the Maya cities," wrote Blom. *Photo by Teobert Maler from* Peabody Museum Memoirs 2, *pl. 42.*

19. Group at Na Bolom, early 1950s. Adults, from left: Bor, Roberta Joughin, Frans Blom, Gertrude Duby Blom. The children are Bor's sons Kayum and Kin. *Courtesy Arthur Gropp*

20. Blom in Lacandón jungle, 1951. *Courtesy Gertrude Duby Blom*

21. Lacandón Indians. *Courtesy Gertrude Duby Blom*

22. Zinacantán Indians near San Cristóbal. *Courtesy Gertrude Duby Blom*

23. Chamula Indians near San Cristóbal. *Courtesy Gertrude Duby Blom*

24. A Lacandón Indian. *Courtesy Gertrude Duby Blom*

25. Blom excavating near San Cristóbal, 1951. *Courtesy Gertrude Duby Blom*

26. Frans Blom, Chiapas, 1948. *Courtesy Gertrude Duby Blom*

27. A view of the valley in which San Cristóbal is located. *Courtesy Gertrude Duby Blom*

28. The colonnade on one side of the main patio, Na Bolom, showing Trudi's flowers. *Courtesy Gertrude Duby Blom*

29. Gertrude Duby Blom in the 1960s. *Courtesy Gertrude Duby Blom*

30. Part of the library at Na Bolom. *Courtesy Gertrude Duby Blom*

lives among the northern Lacandón with his wife and a new-born baby. He is a husky guy with very little education, of the unattractive American type who says "folks," etc. Obviously more fitted to be a truck driver or a mechanic than to spread his special version of the Bible among the "heathen" or "Romanists." But he was bright enough to find himself a soft job, good pay, plenty of food and special trips on airplanes when he needs it. Judging from his Spanish accent, he is not very fit to do linguistic work among the people and would even do well by himself if he learnt to speak his own language, Americanese, a little better.

His name was Philip Baer, and he came from the Instituto Linguistico de Verano. "We talked to him a little as he unloaded a cargo of canned goods."

Three weeks later, after Frans had the opportunity to see Baer in action, he modified his harsh judgment of the man. He and Trudi met Philip and his wife in a Lacandón settlement, and Blom admitted that the couple were doing some good "without forcing their mission work" down the throats of the Indians. He learned that Philip and Mary had been in the region for four years and "in a quiet way have helped the Indians, both the Tzeltals and the Lacandóns." Frans, however, was not completely convinced about Philip. "He is not over bright and much more suited for a labor job, but here he is using involved philosophical terms to describe the Lacandón language." The Baers generously invited the Bloms to a meal, which Frans described as "vegetarian and tasty."

Trudi praised the constructive work that the Baers carried on among the Indians. It is interesting that Frans made no more unfavorable remarks about them; undoubtedly, their social service melted his opposition. Anyone engaged in disinterested activity for the Indians had his approval.

The Baers made every effort to fit into their surroundings. They lived in a house constructed in

Lacandón style, though the modest furniture was modern. Philip mastered the native language, learned much of Indian customs and beliefs, and saved many children during an epidemic. He brought in soap, salt, and other supplies and sold them to the Indians at cost as a way to save them from the unconscionable prices charged by the itinerant traders. He was also modest enough to admit that he had not yet penetrated many of the beliefs of the Indians.

Although Trudi did not agree with the religious views of the Baers, she found the couple simple, honest, and forthright. They came from humble origins, were willing to learn, and lacked the arrogance frequently found in North Americans. Philip's translation of the Bible into Lacandón left her unimpressed, for she reasoned that if the Catholics had not been able to convert those Indians, the Protestants could not succeed.

Although Frans was willing to consider the Baers exceptional, he could not give up his opposition to missionaries in general. After he moved to San Cristóbal, he had reason to revive his animosity against Protestant evangelists who invaded the strong Catholic region in which he lived.

After Frans returned to Mexico in 1943, he resumed work in archaeology, though with changes in scope and emphasis. In the 1920s and 1930s his interest had ranged over the entire Maya area and he had traveled in several countries. In the last two decades of his life, however, several modifications occurred. No longer did archaeology absorb him completely; it competed with other passions he cultivated. He restricted the geographical scope of his investigations to the region of Chiapas; because of the lack of money he was no longer able to make regular visits to sites in Yucatán and the Petén.

From another point of view, he made the archaeology of Chiapas his specialty. It was a wise choice, because part of the state seemed to be rich in Maya ruins that needed exploration. The sites he found and located on the map would be useful to future archaeologists.

He encountered some evidences of depradation at the sites he visited in Chiapas. He seemed in fact to take spoliation for granted. At Banavil his Indian guide had found pottery the preceding year. Likewise some missionaries had extracted bowls from the ruins of El Zapote before he arrived. At Santo Ton the owner of a nearby finca floored the corridor of his home with stones brought from the neighboring ruins. In the case of treasure seekers, presumably chicleros, Blom considered their activity in a faintly humorous vein. On the way to Cristolino in 1943 he saw evidence of their work. "Near the trail is a small mound partly excavated by treasure hunters. The greed for 'dinero' (money) hidden in the old ruins is both sad and amusing, because we know that the Maya had no 'money,' *i.e.*, gold and silver coin, and those greedy fellows who dig for treasure expend a lot of energy and sweat for nothing. But they never learn."

The manner in which he carried on explorations in this period is reflected in his diaries of the expeditions of 1943 and 1948. Like any man in the field, he made use of every promising source of information that might lead to undiscovered remains. At Tecojá in 1943 he hired two Tzeltal boys to guide him to the ruins of Trinidad.

Suddenly my boy, who was supposed to know where the ruins of Trinidad were, developed a blank spot in his memory, but after having attended to my mule he suggested that we should go for a "paseo" in the forest, a little pleasure walk. The rascal hit right for a narrow, winding trail, if it can be called thus, a mere hole in the dense undergrowth. We crossed the Arroyo Trinidad and climbed a hill. Nothing there. We continued, and climbed a much larger and steeper hill. I have been through a lot of thick underbrush in my life, but this was the toughest as yet. It just cut through, and most of the time we were bent double, and at times we crawled, but at last we came to the top of the large hill. We approached from the east. On top of the hill was a large pyramid of cut stones, with a narrow terrace on

the flat top. Then facing west, a stairway flanked the
smaller mounds. Further down, a terrace with three
mounds across, another terrace with mounds, with a
terrace at its north and south ends. The hill was
about 50 meters high, and all the way down to the
plain its west side had been terraced, each terrace
held by a slanting wall of cut stones laid without
mortar. I did not find any sculpture. There may be
some, but if there is, it will only turn up by accident
or when the whole large complex is cleared. There
were hardly any potsherds.

On two occasions on the same expedition he encountered informants by chance, which was not unusual for
archaeologists in the field. At El Cedro, a chicle center,
he overheard a man explain how he had traveled over
the region since 1907. When the stranger described ruins
near his camp, Frans joyfully exclaimed: "He is our
meat!" After Blom moved on to El Real, he came upon
an intelligent-looking Indian. Asked if he knew of ruins,
the native gave an emphatic "No." He displayed a pack
of expensive cigarettes, which he generously offered to
members of the group. "After puffing deeply and blow-
ing large clouds of smoke, he spoke in a way that let me
know that he was no darned fool Indian." He revealed
that he had worked some years at Piedras Negras with
the team from the University of Pennsylvania. After
Frans asked him about that project, the Indian then
"produced an amazing lot of first-rate information on the
Río Naranjo Valley. . . ."
Sometimes there were disappointments on the
expedition of 1943. The ruins of Toniná, which Frans
had examined in 1925, were completely overgrown. Near
Cristolino, where he expected to find "something
spectacular" because it was a likely place for a Maya
site, his surmise was wrong. He and the two boys
searched everywhere. "For six hours we beat through
the bush, looking for this and that, without results."
Another site he had to pass by because his sprained

ankle pained him too much to examine it. And on reaching still another site, he was deterred by rain. "There was no chance to work," he explained, "as notepaper would get wet; but we walked around."

Likewise on the expedition of 1948 he seemed to run into a number of dead ends. Only his eternal optimism kept him going during the disappointing days from June 4 to June 21. At one place a schoolmaster loaned him four boys to excavate a small mound. Although Frans tried to make a game of it for the youngsters, he was uneasy. "There is not much to show for the work, and I feel uncomfortable about using the school boys. It feels as if I had slave labor." He drew a sketch of the mound in his diary, but noted that he "found nothing." A few days later he put the young fellows to work on a smaller mound. The activity netted no more than a clay pot, two bits of obsidian, and a sherd. On another occasion he explained that "we came upon an artificial mound in a cow pasture. Nothing special."

Too often ruins turned out to be run-of-the-mill finds, with no surprises and no dividends for perseverance. At the ruins of El Zapote he found the usual hill leveled on top, several terraces, some mounds, a plain circular altar, and no buildings. "There is nothing very spectacular about these ruins," he sighed. "Their presence only fills out our picture of the Maya in the Zendales region." Going over the site a second time, he turned up three large stone blocks, which might have been altars, and a mass of stones that represented the quarry. He tried to find consolation in what he learned about the topography of the region. "The side trip," he remarked, "did not produce much in the way of archaeology, but gave me a clear picture of the Perlas River and its valley. A new piece of geography added to the map." At Santo Ton he believed that stucco decorations like those at Palenque had been used. The ruins at Huaca elicited only a few lines in the diary: "Nothing more, so we turned around."

At least Banavil provided unusual possibilities. When Blom found indication of many tombs, he was "inclined to believe that the entire group of structures compose a cemetery for the burial of the great." A few weeks of excavation would produce a good collection of ceramics, he surmised. "The only trouble about it is to get water carried up that mighty hill to the camp. Even a man much younger than I would lose his enthusiasm if he had to climb that hill a couple of times a day."

More promising were the ruins of Ojo de Agua, which he found on a tip from a chiclero in 1943. "I walked up to the Cedro trail and followed it to the hilltop pass. No signs of ruins. Then I turned into the forest and soon was aware that there was something. Down at the stream Trudi had noted a flat place, which would be good for a camp site. I had looked at it, and at once noted that it was part of a man-made terrace. Now more and more of the same kind here on top of the hill. I followed a low wall and then came to some rather large stone-built walls." Night came on and he and Trudi returned to camp.

The next morning the two explorers resumed the search. They came upon "a large terraced mound with retention walls. We first saw the back wall. Walking around to the front, we saw that the mound was crowned by two temples quite in ruins. A stairway led steeply down to the lower terraces, hidden under the trees. We also noted through the forest that the view from the top must have been magnificent. . . . Sliding down the ruined stairway, we came to a terrace on which we could see the stone heaps of two large buildings. 'There must be one over in that direction.' I pointed out the place to Trudi. Soon I saw this structure among the foliage."

The discovery of stelae added new interest. "A vibrating, excited voice yelled, 'Frans, a stela.' To my left stood what looked like a tree trunk, but it certainly is a fine stela about 2.5 meters high with a row of incised hieroglyphs, giving the Initial Series date 9-7-15-0-0, 12 Ahau 8 Yax.[1] The inscription is in perfect condition and simple to read. I brushed it off and observed the best time to photograph it. Then we went on and located a large ball court old style, with low slanting walls. . . ." In the days that followed they found more stelae, but without inscriptions. Blom mapped the site, drew the figures on the carved stela, and took photographs. The method of construction, he believed, bore out the relatively early date of the stela. "No mortar used in terrace walls," he observed. "I have seen no signs whatsoever of stucco wall coating or relief figures. No buildings are standing, and the debris on the top of the mounds does not indicate large roof constructions of stone."

He also spent many days examining the ruins of Lacanjá in the fall of 1948. Experimenting with new procedures, he learned how to bring out lines on stelae and to restore the original colors to murals. He dusted talcum powder over a stela, "then rubbed it with a dry cloth to spread the powder, and finally with a moistened cloth to take away the powder from the flat surfaces. The result was astonishing. The powder filled the incised lines and made every piece of carving stand out sharply. Then I photographed the monument, and should get some very good pictures." The next day he examined the stela with satisfaction. "Last night's rain had washed the talcum powder away, so that the method of bringing out the glyphs is safe." A small bit of mural in the Temple of the Columns led him to experiment again. He rubbed the painted surface "with medicinal oil to bring out the colors. It worked well." He reasoned that "what won't hurt a man's stomach should not hurt a painting many centuries old." Several days later he discovered that washing the mural with soap "again brought out more details."

When he decided to remove a few samples of stucco work and a few small pieces of obsidian for the state museum, he was careful to secrete the items. The Lacandones, who wandered all over his quarters, considered everything about the ruins sacred, and they would have been angered had they seen him taking away the smallest item. So he packed the specimens during rare moments when the natives were not present.

The only complaint of physical fatigue in examining ruins occurred in the early days at Lacanjá in the fall of 1948, when Frans was fifty-five. "One gets tired climbing and crawling up and down pyramids," he remarked, "trying to keep straight lines, peering into holes and stumbling over roots and vines while one's clothes are torn by thorns and brambles, but one goes on." His unceasing activity in examining those ruins day after day testified to his physical endurance.

There was no doubt that Yaxchilán provided the greatest array of remains in that part of Chiapas. As the climax of the expedition of 1943-44, he and Trudi visited the famous site. He described the event like a travelogue rather than as one would describe an archaeological investigation. They began the journey to the site some way down the river, avoiding the rapids of Anaïte. They set out after breakfast on January 6.

We boarded a long, slender canoe. We had contracted for two men to pole us up the river at 3.50 pesos per day (70 cents U.S.) and got 1½ men, one of the sons of Ulises de la Cruz and his son. The father of Ulises de la Cruz was one of Teobert Maler's men. There seems to be archaeology in the family, for Ulises is now caretaker of Yaxchilán.

The little boy, a swell little fellow dressed in his Sunday clothes, took the steering aft and his father did the pushing forward. . . . It was three leagues, about 10 km. to the ruins, but we made slow progress against the heavy current. The sun broke through and the picture of the river and forest was lovely.

. . . After about 4½ hours we beached below the house of Ulises de la Cruz, who lives by the ruins, and though we knew that one of the largest cities of the Maya lay right close by us, we could not see a single building, as they are all covered by forest.

. . . Ulises has cut some trails to the principal monuments and buildings, and he guided us from one significant stone carving to the next, as Duby is so interested in the fact that the Lacandóns still come here to give offerings to the big stone figure, which lies broken before the Palace, and which they call Muyál-Ha. The evening was pleasantly cool, with wisps of mist coming down the river like a filmy curtain, through which the moon was shining.

The following day they continued to examine the remains at Yaxchilán. "What one does not realize from Maler's map is the height of the hills that have been reshaped by man. . . ." "In the past when the ground was clear of trees, it must have been an impressive sight to approach the city, with its temples painted red, blue and yellow, as vestiges of paint still show."

After taking pictures of the ruins and enjoying a meal at Ulises' house, they took a cayuco down the river.

Pepe, son of Miguel, now had the prow as we were going downstream through the rapids. The forest passed by; sun and shade changed as clouds blew overhead, and the current carried us. An egret rose snow-white with lazy wingbeats. A large blue heron diverted its attention from its fishing to look at us. . . . Two snow-white hawks, a beautiful bird, circled slowly overhead. Some place downstream we met a brother of Miguel with a larger canoe and transferred to it. . . .

Then around the last arm of the horseshoe bend and into the box-cañon and the rapids. We rushed along as the water made whirls on both sides of us. The little fellow was rowing and kept on telling his father what to do. Anaïte came in sight too soon. In a great curve we swung into the shore, and again took up quarters with our young friend Ramón Cámera, who at once broke out with coffee and bananas. It has been two perfect days.

Frans added a note that the mounds and ruined buildings extended almost two miles along the river.

As early as 1943 Blom considered Yaxchilán his favorite site. "Tikal is majestic, Palenque is beautiful, Copán has strength, Chichén Itzá leaves me completely cold, and Uaxactún holds a bit of my heart, but Yaxchilán stirs me more than any other of the Maya cities. Its situation and plan as well as the fineness of its art thrill me."

When he visited Yaxchilán five years later, he complained of stupidities committed by authorities in Mexico City. A visitor who wished to take photographs of the place had to secure a permit from the national capital. More important were the directives issued by persons who had no firsthand knowledge of the site. Some official ordered that no trees should be cut down around the buildings. Frans pointed out that two temples had been destroyed because strong winds crumpled the trees over the structures. Another order prohibited the cleaning of stelae and altars; seeds, however, fell into the cracks of those stone monuments and sprouted into plants and trees, which tore the stones apart. He also noted that the caretaker and his wife were unable to keep the site in good order; two full-time men were needed to care for the area and to remove fallen trees from the paths leading to the monuments. Finally, he pointed out that a painting in the Temple of the Queen should be copied before it was lost. Not surprisingly, he observed that a good map of the site did not exist.

Blom could not quite reconcile himself to the unpalatable fact that he had not discovered the famous paintings at nearby Bonampak. It was the worst case of bad luck he suffered during those years. He believed that he had just narrowly missed making the discovery. As he later told the story to a friend,

> In 1943 I crawled into the chicle center of El Cedro in Chiapas. It took me eleven hours to fall on my face in the mud and advance five miles. I was so full of malaria. While lying exhausted in my hammock, the Lacandón Indians, who were my friends and trusted me, told me of some ruins only three hours away, where there were many painted figures on the walls of the temples. But a plane took the near corpse to a hospital, and I never got to

Bonampak. This gripes me, because I consider it the greatest thing archaeologically since Tomb #7 of Monte Albán found by Alfonso Caso.

It is curious that several other individuals also just missed finding the pictures at Bonampak. If some Lacandón Indians had always known about the buildings at the site, they kept the knowledge secret until 1946. A chicle foreman and his men camped at the place in 1945 and 1946, but they took no interest in the buildings. In February 1946 two Americans photographed the structures. They were John Bourne, an amateur explorer, and his guide, Charles "Carlos" Frey, who induced Chanbor, a Lacandón, to lead them to the structures. Chanbor did not take them into the temple with the paintings, and since the two explorers lacked the curiosity to investigate on their own initiative they missed the opportunity to make the discovery. Then in May 1946 a Lacandón led Giles Healey, photographer on assignment for the United Fruit Company to film "The Maya through the Ages," and Raul Pavón Abreu, director of the Campeche state museum, into the structure with the three rooms of paintings. Healey appreciated the importance of what he saw, photographed the painted walls, and notified Mexican officials and the Carnegie Institution of Washington. Abreu made no claim to the discovery.

United Fruit decided to capitalize on its good fortune. It provided the money for two expeditions to Bonampak, and a year after the discovery the company conducted a news conference in New York City, where Healey told his story to the world. That publicity stirred up Carlos Frey.

Frey was one of those curious characters who sometimes gravitate to far-off places like Chiapas. He was born in Illinois in 1915, the son of a coal miner. At the age of twenty-six he appeared in Chiapas, either looking for adventure or hoping to avoid being drafted into the military. He operated an unsuccessful farm near Ocosingo, married an Indian girl, fathered two sons, became

interested in Maya ruins, among other things, and traveled long distances on foot through the jungle. Chroni-
cally out of money, he sometimes acted as an aide or
guide to exploring parties. In that capacity Blom hired
him in 1943, but soon considered him unsatisfactory.
Frey had a disheveled appearance, and Frans condemned his lack of personal cleanliness. Five years later
Frans had occasion to check Frey's information on certain Maya ruins against his own findings, and he
concluded that Carlos was either "super dumb or
deliberately giving false information." Even after Frey's
unfortunate death, Blom dismissed him as a "moron."

The publicity emanating from the Healey press
conference in May 1947 convinced Frey that Healey was
making money from his discovery. So Frey put forth the
claim that he had a stake in finding the pictures, because
he had been in Bonampak before Healey. Frey, however,
had not been inside the building that contained the
murals, so no one gave credence to his claim. In 1949,
nevertheless, he convinced an official of the Mexican
National Institute of Anthropology and History to put
him in charge of an expedition to Bonampak. On that trip
he and a companion failed to clear the rapids in the
Lacanjá River; they were thrown from the boat into the
river and died.

Blom got caught up in a minor way in the controversy
over Bonampak. He circulated the story of how sickness
had prevented him from investigating the buildings with
pictures, which the Lacandones had told him about in
1943. That incident (which is not recorded in the diary of
the 1943 expedition) gave him no claim to discovery,
though it added one more claim prior to Healey's.

In addition, Blom was involved in an unfortunate
report that appeared in a Mexico City newspaper in
December 1948. After he returned from the expedition of
that year, a reporter in Tuxtla Gutiérrez drew up an
account of his work in the jungle, including a statement
that Frans had found paintings as great or greater than
those at Bonampak. At once Blom and Trudi sent in a

correction to the editor of *Excelsior,* disavowing such a claim. In the years that followed, Healey condemned Frans for suggesting the discovery of a site greater than Bonampak and for renaming on his map three sites Healey had explored. Eventually, Blom found the subject of Bonampak so unpleasant that he refused to discuss it with visitors.

After the discovery Frans made several visits to Bonampak. When he arrived there in March 1948 he found Augustín Villagra and Antonio Tejeda tediously making faithful copies of the paintings, which had been covered with a coating of lime deposited by water trickling through the ceiling. The two men applied kerosine to make the coating transparent for their copying work; then after some hours the kerosine evaporated, leaving a thin covering of oil, which preserved the pictures. Blom strongly applauded the method. He visited the site again in September with Trudi. On that occasion he found a head fallen from edifice No. 1, which he sent on to the Museo Nacional in Mexico City.

Like any perceptive man in the field, Frans received flashes of inspiration as he carried on his archaeological work. By 1943 he had already concluded that the ancient Maya always built at sites that commanded magnificent views. So confident was he of this generalization that he sometimes examined such places certain of finding ruins, and was disappointed.

One day in 1948 he looked at a native baked-clay fireplace in El Cedro and had an idea. The horseshoe shape strongly suggested a Totanac yoke, and the use of those yokes had not been solved. "Could they have been used for sacred fires?" he asked himself. "Should one today see signs of fire and heat on the handstones of the 'yokes'?"

As he wandered over the ruins of Lacanjá in the fall of 1948, several ideas occurred to him. Why had no stucco stelae ever appeared? "Elaborate stone ornamentation in the facades of buildings is common. Why not stucco stelae? To my knowledge, none has yet been found." On another subject he had a flash of understanding. "It is no wonder that so many Maya monuments lie flat on the ground," he exclaimed. "They are decidedly topheavy," because only a small portion of the stone was anchored in the ground. "For example, Stela #7 is 3.22 meters long, and of this only 45 cm. were planted in the ground." A more complicated line of reasoning began after he attended a Lacandón dinner where shelled snails were the pièce de resistance. He remembered that the natives burned the shells to produce a fine lime used in preparing the dough for tortillas. "Very fine lime," he mused. "Was this fine lime used to make the stucco decorations on the temple walls at Palenque and similar places?" Then he thought of other decorations. "Furthermore, does the 'caracol-bacab' have anything to do with this very useful snail . . .?" "A little god comes out of a conch shell on the Foliated Cross, Palenque," and the use of conch shells in other Maya decorations came to mind. There is no indication that he pursued these ideas.

An incident at Camp Quinteros in mid December 1943 suggested still another idea. When his kerosine can leaked, he tried the experiment of smearing some chicle on the hole, and "it worked." Noting that chicle is inflammable and produces an odor between that of copal and rubber, he surmised that the Maya could have used chicle for incense.

In regard to the larger questions about the Maya, such as the reasons for the rise and the causes of the fall of that civilization, Blom did not put forth speculations of his own. By 1943 he attributed the collapse of the Maya to deforestation and soil exhaustion, as explained by Orator S. Cook.[2]

Frans's work in archaeology during the first phase of his residence in Mexico appeared to be more of a promise than a fulfillment. He began intensive examination of the Maya area in Chiapas and found unknown sites to add to the knowledge of the region. The failure to discover Bonampak, however, continued to be a bitter pill, because that site lay within the region he had staked out for examination. Optimistic in spirit, he still hoped to make some startling discovery in the jungle he roamed over almost annually.

After returning to Chiapas in 1943, Blom also revived his interest in maps. A passion for correct cartography of the Maya area had begun, as we have seen, in the mid 1920s, when he and Oliver Ricketson compiled a list of sites with an accompanying map. During the years at Tulane he worked spasmodically to keep the project up to date.

In the second period of his life, he narrowed and intensified his interest in map making. Restricting his work to Chiapas, he set about drawing up an accurate record of the unknown parts of the state, based on his own explorations and measurements; the location of Maya sites became only one of the numerous features of the map.

During the expedition of 1943 he returned to mapping. The airplane flights he made during the journey excited him, because he could see from above the variations in topography, and sometimes he could even grasp the plan of a river system and its tributaries.

The few maps of Chiapas that were available aroused his contempt. "The official maps look fine and would be useful as wall decorations or lamp shades, but as maps they are absolutely useless," he snapped in 1943. "Rivers are either marked 25 or more kilometers from where they actually are or in some cases run up the mountains! Fine roads are indicated where there were mule trails 30 years ago, towns where there are only abandoned palm shacks."

Traveling again through the jungles five years later, he devoted more time to cartography. An official Mexican map issued in 1943 he condemned as "lousy." But he admitted to himself that he was just beginning to make sense of the geography of the region. As we shall see, he did eventually produce an excellent map of the unknown regions of Chiapas.

The few ideas Blom voiced during the 1940s, while still adjusting to life in Mexico, were projections of his earlier views in regard to education. He continued to believe that the lay public should be informed about prehistory, and his experiences in the jungles prompted some thoughts on the training of graduate students in ethnology.

He continued to attempt to popularize archaeology. Many of the articles he wrote solely for money were slanted toward arousing public interest in the subject. Not long after moving to Mexico he had a flash of inspiration for spreading the knowledge of ancient cultures, which came from the realization that museums had many duplicate artifacts in storage. He declared that those duplicates "aren't worth a damn as long as they lie in mothballs." So he tried to induce the Mexican government to make up standard collections of such objects, prepare pamphlets in English to explain them, and donate the collections to high schools in the United States. The project, he pointed out, would be instructive and also of great propaganda value for Mexico.

His own experience suggested changes in ethnology. By 1948 he had not learned the Maya language sufficiently to use it with the Lacandones so he had to converse with them in Spanish, in which they were not proficient. He believed that many other scholars who studied the Lacandones had the same problem, and he concluded that "the way we are getting information by speaking in a limping Spanish is highly unsatisfactory, and it makes me doubt all ethnological work done by people who do not speak the language of their subjects." Applying the criticism first to himself, he resolved that on returning to Mexico City he must ask Alfredo Barrera Vásquez to find someone to teach him Maya.

He then moved on to a larger defect in formal education. "Another objection is that most teachers of anthropology teach their students a rigid system or pattern of questioning and what to look for, with the result that the student overlooks a heck of a lot of interesting and important information, while he is looking." He believed that all students of higher education should be required to take a course in "How to Think for Yourself." In addition, students from urban communities should be taught how to use their eyes intelligently. Referring to three natives in his exploring party of 1948, he declared that they "are quick observers and see a lot of things, but they do not know how to use their observations, considering them of little value to others."

During these early years in Mexico, Frans carried on an active journalistic career in order to supplement his income. He wrote many articles for newspapers, drawing upon his knowledge of Chiapas and sometimes upon Mexican history for the material. In descriptive reports on the Indians or the Lacandón forests, he generally chose subjects that he believed would appeal to readers curious about that little-known part of their nation. As early as the first exploration of 1943, he made plans to write a book about the mountain men of Chiapas, such as chicle gatherers and mahogany loggers. Unfortunately he never succeeded in interesting a publisher in the project, and only a short selection from the manuscript appeared in print after his death. Much of the material for that book, however, went into numerous newspaper articles.

At first he claimed that writing for the general public pleased him. He remarked in 1944 that "freelancing is fun, though at times precarious." Soon the fun disappeared as he ground out page after page on the typewriter and worked hard to develop new angles for presenting the material. As time passed, he came to consider this hackwork, consuming time he should devote to more serious things. There is no doubt that journalism was precarious, for he was at the mercy of the vagaries of newspaper editors, and he could never be certain that an article would be accepted.

Although we have no accurate record of those fugitive writings which he produced solely for income, it appears that he turned out sixty to seventy articles in the period from 1943 through 1949. He got off to a slow start in 1943; thereafter, he placed from seven to seventeen items a year. Increasingly he sold articles to newspapers and periodicals in Europe; Trudi's work in journalism before coming to Mexico doubtless helped to open that market to him.

Occasionally he showed ingenuity in tailoring a subject to a particular magazine. He prepared an account of the preparation of salt for commercial use in Concordia, Chiapas. That was not particularly newsworthy; he showed, however, how the Indians who carried on the procedure formed a Star of David covered with salt. The article appeared with appropriate illustrations in the *Tribuna Israelita* in Mexico City. In order to avoid incorrect assumptions, he disclaimed any connection between those Indians and the lost tribes of Israel.

It is curious that he generally failed to market articles in the United States. During the expedition of 1943 he sent off an item to his friend Lyle Saxon in New Orleans, hoping that a literary agent would sell it. Later during the same expedition he submitted three articles to the *Saturday Evening Post.* Nothing, however, came of those endeavors. His approach to Charles Scribner's Sons about the proposed book on mountain men in Chiapas also brought a negative response.

In fact, the only popular article of this period to appear in the United States was published in *Natural History.* It told of his visit to Unión Fronteriza in 1945 in the search for the effects of onchocerciasis. He made it clear to the editor that he must be paid for the article, because "I have to earn money to buy my frijoles." In presenting the story, he coupled his interest in the natural beauty of the region with the frightful effects of the disease; he gave the article the appropriate title "Orchids and Onchocerciasis." Even with this article, which was more effective than many others he wrote, he had trouble. The editor did not like the title, probably because of general ignorance of the name of the disease, and he changed it to "Darkness to All Who Dwell There." More important,

Frans supplied numerous photographs as illustrations and their use would have greatly increased the pay for the article, but the editor considered the pictures unsatisfactory and failed to use them.

Blom was always alert to new subjects that might be turned into articles. On returning from the expedition of 1945, he told a friend that he had accepted a commission to produce a series of articles on the contributions of American scientists to research in Mexico. How he expected to collect the information he did not explain; apparently he was willing to tackle any topic that could be turned into money. The articles on scientists never appeared.

Frans and Trudi also published several books during this period. Her account of the Lacandones, just under a hundred pages, appeared in Mexico as part of a series of popular books. Drawing upon the visit to the Indians in 1943, she gave a factual description of the Lacandones and included some of her personal experiences. The book is written with charm and simplicity and illustrated with numerous drawings. Frans held the rights to his book *The Conquest of Yucatan.* He arranged for a Danish edition, which was published in Copenhagen in 1946; he later reported that it sold out in two months. "That's nice, and father is very proud," he remarked. Frans said that the book was also published in Italian and Russian, but no record of those editions has been found. The latter part of the *Conquest,* describing the life of the ancient Maya, was published in a Spanish translation in Mexico, and some years later it also appeared in Guatemala. When he proposed an English translation of Salvador Toscano's *Arte precolombino de México y de la América Central*[3] to a publisher in the United States, he received no encouragement.

It is surprising that in addition to the large number of popular articles he wrote, Frans was also able to turn out some serious works. He prepared an edition of Tomás de la Torre's travels in Chiapas in the sixteenth century. He wrote a description of the lienzo of Analco, coming from the time of the Spanish conquest, and he produced an attractive account of the engineering achievements of the ancient Maya. In addition, two brief reports on the expedition of 1948 appeared in Mexican journals devoted to the Indians.

He also prepared an edition of Francisco de Aguilar's story of the Spanish conquest. Although he was paid for it, he doubted that it would be printed, because it told too much of the bitter truth about the Spanish invaders, whom he compared with the Nazis. No record of its publication has been found.

It is interesting to realize that Blom had no respect for Malinche, the native woman who joined the conquerors. When a North American friend planned to write about her, he warned the author not to be carried away by the subject, because Malinche "was a hard boiled gold digger, hungry for power."

Some of the items Blom wrote during those years remain in manuscript. Either he found no appropriate place to publish them or they were rejected. An account of the Zona Romano in Chiapas, running to thirty-seven typed pages, describes the geography and resources of the area; he prepared a similar description of the Tierra Zoque. A list of Maya ruins found in Chiapas became the basis for later additions and eventual publication in the future. His work on a map of the unknown regions of the state was but a preliminary attempt, which he later completed with more detail. He also brought together John Lloyd Stephens's observations on Chiapas and translated the selections into Spanish in 1945, but he failed to publish the work.

False documents had always intrigued Blom, and he enjoyed exposing them. When he learned that a Miss Haddow owned the lienzo of Tlascala—that is, a contemporary copy of the original—he borrowed it for close study. Suspecting its authenticity, he asked his friend Hans Lens, a paper manufacturer in Mexico, to examine it. Lens reported that it was made of modern cotton, and Blom found that all the figures had been traced. He considered it a "delightful fraud." "As far as deliberate fakes go," he said, "here is a fine example. So intriguing and so nearly good as I have ever run into." Relishing his exposure of the document, which had been published as an authentic work in 1892 in *Antigüedades Mexicanas,* he said that "the pleasure and the fun have all been mine." It is too bad that his exposure did not appear in print.

An interesting brief manuscript, prepared in 1945 and submitted to the director of the Chiapas museum, described a project for archaeological studies in Chiapas. Frans called for the preparation of a map and of plans and photographs of the ruins. He stated that a year of exploration should be devoted to each zone of the state. Great discoveries, he believed, would be made, which would challenge Yucatán's claim to being called "the Egypt of the New World."

Frans was building a new life according to his real desires—communion with nature, association with Indians, and seeking out undiscovered Maya sites. Only one thing remained to make that life complete. He wanted a permanent residence in the highlands of Chiapas.

9

San Cristóbal—Home

Blom's second career culminated in San Cristóbal, Chiapas, where he lived from 1950 until his death thirteen years later. He bought a house there and enjoyed the style of living he had always longed for. He made expeditions into the jungle, established a research center, relished the company of visiting scholars, aided the Lacandones, and continued to turn out publications. He called it "a dream of twenty-five years which came true." San Cristóbal, surrounded by mountains, rises almost seven thousand feet above sea level and is a natural entry to the highlands of Chiapas. The Pan American Highway connects the town with the outside world. Although Frans worked hard during this period, the labor brought a pleasure he had never experienced in Mexico City or New Orleans.

He acquired the home through a peculiar turn of events. When his mother died in Denmark in 1933, she left him a legacy of $2,200. For unknown reasons he failed to receive the money until late in 1949. Then Blom bought the Casa de Penagos in San Cristóbal for $1,600, and used the remainder of the legacy to make the building suitable for comfortable living.

The Casa de Penagos had an unusual story. Many years before, Sr. Penagos had constructed the building as a seminary to train local youths to carry religion to natives of the surrounding region. Before Penagos turned the structure over to the church, he died, and his heirs, uninterested in the project, decided to sell the property. There were drawbacks for a prospective owner, because the place had no modern conveniences and the rooms lacked windows.

Despite the deficiencies Frans realized that he could make the place into an attractive home. He installed running water, toilet facilities, and electricity, built a fireplace in each room, and pierced the outer wall with windows. Eight rooms, three halls, a chapel, and three patios provided ample accommodations. He boasted that Chamula Indian labor cost only two pesos a day. After the modern conveniences had been installed, Blom, who liked to work with his hands, often took care of the repairs himself. Behind the house were two acres of land filled with fruit trees; Trudi soon terraced the soil, which rose to a considerable height, and planted flowers and vegetables. At the rear of the lot Frans built a shelter for saddle horses and mules.

Proud of his home and determined to give it an individual character, he devised a distinctive name and symbol for it. He was amused that the Lacandón Indians, unable to pronounce his name correctly, called him Pancho Balum. Then he remembered that in the Tzotzil language, which is spoken by natives in the neighborhood of San Cristóbal, "Bolom" means jaguar. Remarking that "Bolom isn't far from Blom," he named his home "Na Bolom," meaning House of the Jaguar. "Then I remembered a gay little jaguar, which strides along on a frieze at the ruins of Tula, Hidalgo. This I copied and colored, and then had it made into tiles in Oaxaca." He placed several of the tiles on the front wall of the building as a unique symbol. It was not long before everyone in San Cristóbal knew the location of Na Bolom.

Even before he moved into the house, he had decided to make it a research center for scholars specializing in Chiapas and Guatemala. To carry out the plan, he began to assemble a library of volumes bearing on those regions, "not only in the fields on anthropology and archaeology," he explained, "but in every other field of research which in one way or another touched Chiapas." Appropriately, he named the library for Fray Bartolomé de las Casas, early Spanish friend of the Indian.

The project, admirable as it was, could not be executed on the meager and uncertain income he received. So he put aside his pride and appealed for the donation of books. In September 1950 he sent out a circular in Spanish and English, asking for publications from friends, governmental agencies, and scholarly institutions. It was a bold venture, and it succeeded. Five years later he declared "that a good working library is in existence." About the same time he joyfully announced receipt of a copy of the *Encyclopaedia Britannica* as a gift from the publisher. "More than 95% of the study material" in the library came as gifts. In 1958 he counted four thousand items in numerous languages, with Spanish and English predominant. He assured the public that he did not consider the books his personal property but as a trust, and that he had arranged for the collection to remain permanently in Chiapas.

On occasion, his unfortunate past made it difficult to collect the proper titles for the library. The Carnegie Institution sent its publications gratis to scholars as a means of disseminating the latest research. The recipient was not expected to make money by selling the volumes. After Frans moved to Mexico, he was cut off the mailing list, and he complained about it. Alfred V. Kidder, in charge of the historical section of the C.I.W., told him the unpleasant truth: when Carnegie officials saw some of their publications advertised for sale as "from the library of Frans Blom," that is, books he had received when he was at Tulane, they took the drastic action. After Frans explained that he had reestablished his work in archaeology, Kidder was willing to restore his name.[1]

Some other persons were not as understanding. When Blom appealed for institutional publications without charge, one well-known archaeologist in New York City was cool to the idea. He argued that Frans had already built up his personal library of scholarly works in New Orleans, had lost it through his own fault, and was now begging for a second gift from institutions.

In addition to printed books, Blom realized that numerous documents on Chiapas and adjacent regions existed in manuscript in European archives. He was willing to pay the cost of securing microfilm copies of those sources. For two years he corresponded with Charles Upson Clark, who had searched European archives for a long time, as to the location of pertinent documents on Chiapas.

Within a decade Blom assembled a significant collection of manuscript records. Nineteen hundred pages of film on Indian languages of Chiapas came from the Bibliothèque Nationale in Paris; later on, Jacques Soustelle arranged to send him a copy of the Brasseur de Bourbourg material from the same library. The Archives of the Indies in Seville yielded three thousand pages on film, which Blom pronounced "interesting stuff." All pertinent material at the University of Pennsylvania, including the Berendt manuscripts, also arrived on film, as well as Antonio del Río's report on Palenque from the British Museum. With the help of Professor Norman McQuown, the Department of Anthropology at the University of Chicago supplied a copy of recent research that the department had carried on in Chiapas, and also donated a microfilm reader to Na Bolom.

An amusing incident occurred when Frans received a film copy of Jean Frédéric Waldeck's diary from the Newberry Library in Chicago. He told Ruth Lapham, the librarian, that he rushed to read the diary, for he knew that Waldeck, at an advanced age when he stayed in Palenque, had a mistress; Frans expected to find some "dirty linen" in the record. To his dismay, there had been an error; the film contained only the pages of a staid book on English literature. If he eventually secured the Waldeck diary, he had another disappointment in store, for portions of the record are illegible and there is scant notice of the mistress. It also appears that Blom had not encountered a rather recent article by H. C. Cline throwing doubt on Waldeck's self-proclaimed longevity.

The growing collection of volumes in the library presented some problems, which Blom had not considered when he began the project. He asked Arthur Gropp, former librarian of the department at Tulane, how to protect the books against insects. More pressing was the need for a trained librarian to care for the collection. Frans lacked the money to pay a professional and vainly hoped that some qualified person might care to work at the job without pay. Sometime over the years the books were cataloged and arranged on the shelves in a logical system; the daily work of adding volumes had been carried on by nonprofessionals. On the advice of friends, Frans accomplished a significant saving of taxes. The library gave him the basis for claiming Na Bolom as a nonprofit educational institution; thus he avoided the property tax levied on a private residence.

He regarded the research center also as a depository of the living history taking place about him. He made a deliberate effort to secure a pictorial record of costumes and ceremonies of the natives of Chiapas. "My trip into the mountains," he remarked in 1955, "was for the purpose of making colored moving pictures of some Indian festivals. Some of these fiestas are magnificent and most colorful. . . ." He deplored the way the Indians were succumbing to the attractions of civilization. They "go to town and buy store clothes. It is very sad to see how fast the beautiful costumes are disappearing, and for that reason I do all I can to build up an archive of color film of these fiestas while it still can be done." The gradual abandonment of the native dress pained him. "There are times when I say to hell with progress, and I am glad that I will be dead when the tourists are dressing in Indian costumes, and the Indians" go about in machine-made clothes.

Drawing upon his ingenuity, he devised several ways to make his home produce an income. He arranged to admit visitors for a fee to view the place, and he also provided rooms for overnight paying guests. Mexican religious paintings that he had acquired decorated the chapel. Artifacts from archaeological expeditions and from the excavation of Moxquivil were scattered in various rooms; later they were brought together in display cases in a museum. The largest room, with a huge fireplace, served as the library and was also used to entertain guests. In the main patio, surrounded by columns, Trudi cultivated a profusion of flowering bushes, which climbed to the roof of the surrounding gallery.

In the earlier years each visitor paid a dollar to inspect the house between the hours of four and six in the afternoon. Frans or Trudi conducted the guests from room to room, explained the objects, and sometimes showed a film of an expedition or of Indian costumes. The visit ended in the library, where coffee was served and Frans sat by the fireplace and reminisced about his expeditions. By the mid 1950s he found the entertainment of visitors a chore. He complained that "they surely can tire you out and spoil the day's work."

Because the Bloms were multilingual, they enjoyed the international character of the visitors. As early as 1953 Frans boasted that persons from nine countries assembled one day in the library. Some years later he described another occasion: "Not long ago we had an afternoon visit of two Danish ladies (who insisted on talking Danish to me) with their Mexican husbands, a French couple, three Americans and one Englishman, one Swiss from Berne (my wife's dialect), and Count Magnus Möerner with wife, he being the director of the Swedish Latin American Institute in Stockholm. The Tower of Babel had nothing on that afternoon."

The admission of afternoon visitors still continues at Na Bolom, with some changes. The fee has been lowered, college students escort the callers about the place and explain the exhibits, and coffee in the library is omitted.

Frans also fitted up accommodations for paying guests at his home. In the beginning he prepared three rooms, and charged $2.50 per person for the overnight stay, three meals, and a hot shower. Refusing to use commercial advertising, he relied only on personal messages in a newsletter that circulated among archaeologists in the United States and on word-of-mouth reports by travelers who had visited Na Bolom. After the peso declined in value from 8.5 to 12.5 to the dollar, he increased the rate to $3 a night, and by 1960 the fee rose to $5. He complained that traffic on the Pan American Highway caused inflation throughout the area. Each guest quickly learned that he was not in a hotel and could not expect auxiliary services. It seems that in the early days Frans attracted only a few guests; by the end of 1955, however, he indicated that the rooms provided an important part of his income. Eventually he added another room and could accommodate eight guests at a time. The meals, served in a large hall which could care for several dozen persons, were remarkable for garden vegetables, unusual dishes, and quantities of food. Frans presided at the head of the table and Trudi at the other end. All told, the accommodations were good and inexpensive according to North American standards.

The guest book, occupying a prominent place on a table in the center of the library, provided a record of the numerous and varied individuals who came to Na Bolom. Frans eagerly watched the pages fill up with signatures and avidly counted the number of countries represented by visitors. He reported twenty-eight nationalities during the year of 1956.

He hoped that he could finance Na Bolom without relying upon tourist trade. At one time when his resources were low, he feared that he might be reduced to the tasteless role of catering to the uninformed and uninterested traveler. When one of his plans to make money collapsed, he admitted sadly that he might "have to herd dudes" through the house for a fee, "and sell trinkets." He observed wistfully that "people get rich on that, and it would give money to work out our program of being useful to scientists," but he shuddered at the thought.

He believed that San Cristóbal and the surrounding country appealed only to serious travelers. "This is the real Mexico," he asserted in 1953, "though most visitors don't care a damn. They go to Cuernavaca and Acapulco to meet other Americans in barrooms." In the early 1950s, when few people called at Na Bolom, he confessed that "sometimes it is tough, but we carry on." He insisted that the distance from Mexico City, "two long days' automobile ride," eliminated most of the undesirable tourists from Chiapas. "Those who come this way are interested in our provincial colonial town and our very colorful Indians dressed in their beautiful costumes."

Frans had only contempt for the crude, aggressive American tourist, whose manners matched his ignorance; he refused to take in that type. A guest in 1961 saw Blom turn away a traveler and his wife from Chicago—the man was "loud and pushy"—declaring that all rooms were taken, which the guest knew not to be true. Frans's desire to make Na Bolom a haven for serious visitors has come down to the present time. Some guidebooks continue to explain that only professional persons who expect to stay more than a night are welcome.

As another way to make money, he planned to set up an annual summer school for college students from the United States. The prospectus for 1951 declared that instruction would be in "Practical Field Experience and Field Work." He limited the enrollment to twelve persons, required them to have a knowledge of Spanish, and he set forth the activity of each day from July 1 to August 15. The student had to arrange for academic credit with his teacher in the United States. The total cost of $250 per person included tuition, bed, board, and transportation to various places after the student arrived at Tuxtla Gutiérrez.[2]

The project ran into trouble from the start. The printer in the United States lost the copy of the announcement, "and I sat incommunicado out in the forest," Frans moaned. After the announcement had been found and printed, it was not issued until June 1. It is not surprising that only three or four students showed up, and Frans and Trudi took them on field trips to Indian villages. "They seemed to like it," he concluded.

In 1952 the announcement was issued on time, but another obstacle appeared. This time Frans called the project a School of Anthropological Field Work, with conditions and plans similar to those of the preceding summer. The project, however, failed disastrously. "There won't be anything of the summer school," he complained early in May. "Not a single student has written. This may be because I don't give credits—the great god credit!" He had failed to recognize the rigid system in United States universities in granting credit for transfer courses. By 1954 he gave up the idea of a summer school, though he indicated his willingness to take groups of students on field trips. Perhaps he was a decade or so ahead of his time, for anthropology and archaeology gained increasing attention in collegiate circles in the 1960s, and the practice of sending students into the field for practical training during the summer became more common.

Although he believed wholeheartedly in the rich opportunities for research in the region of San Cristóbal, the area was relatively unknown. To attract scholars who could use his home as a base of operations, he spread the news in *Teocentli,* a newsletter circulated among anthropologists. He explained that graduate students would find material available "for more than a hundred theses" in the fields of philology, ethnology, folklore, physical anthropology, archaeology, botany, and zoology; later he added the broad subject of Spanish colonial art, life, and thought. He pointed out that Na Bolom was strategically located at the center of "a territory inhabited by more than 200,000 Indians, who speak seven different languages, six of which are of Maya stock. Those Indians, due to their isolation, have retained a surprising amount of their pre-Spanish ways of life and thinking inherited from the highest culture of ancient America." Irked that so much attention was given to the aborigines of the United States, he remarked that the Indians of Chiapas "should, therefore, be much more interesting to study than the Navajo." He concluded his call with " 'Come and get it.' "

Eventually scholars began to appear, and within a few years Blom's dream of making his home a center for research began to take shape. As early as 1953 he had been commissioned by Ray Smith of the Department of Entomology and Parasitology at the University of California, Berkeley, to find specimens of amber containing petrified insects. Frans made three expeditions into the mountains for that purpose and secured sufficient specimens to arouse interest. Beginning in 1956, J. Wyatt Durham and Paul Hurd, from the same university, began the first of numerous field seasons at Na Bolom; in the following years Durham also brought students to help in the search for amber. Dr. McSwain, sociologist from the same university, showed up with a boa constrictor, and "scared visitors away by giving snake-charmer performances in our patio," Blom explained. McSwain's scientific work was not explained.

Scholars from other universities also came for research. Sol Tax, anthropologist from the University of Chicago, appeared with students, who worked on projects in a number of different fields. Later on Robert Adams, from the same institution, also came with students to investigate the archaeology of the region. Evon Vogt, anthropologist from Harvard, spent numerous seasons at Na Bolom, directing students in mastering native languages and in studying local Indians. He and Norman McQuown, anthropologist from the University of Chicago, held a round table for anthropologists in 1958 with thirty-four persons in attendance. For a season or so Stanford University was represented by visiting ethnologists.

Other fields of study attracted still other scholars. A husband and wife team studied plants. Another botanist investigated the origin of the tomato; in order to dry the seeds he spread the patio with newspapers covered with mashed tomatoes; a sudden rainstorm ended that display with a flood of red juice, "streaming toward the central drain of the courtyard." One season some researchers appeared from South Carolina to look for Indian tobacco which might have a low moisture content. Edward Weyer, from the American Museum of Natural History, recorded Indian songs, and Albert Mattson, director of the Minneapolis Blood Bank, sought samples of blood from the Indians. To add variety, Nat Burwash, an American sculptor Frans had known in the Tulane days, "filled the patio with splinters, while he was carving monkeys." Georgia O'Keeffe appeared in 1960, though it is not clear whether she was a casual visitor or a guest. As late as 1962 Blom noted that one group of scientists "was catching rabies-carrying vampire bats" and "another group was chasing butterflies."

Scholars also came from Europe. Guy Stresser-Péan from the Sorbonne collected Indian costumes for the Musée de l'Homme in Paris. Roger Heim, director of the natural history museum in the same city, spent several seasons in search of hallucinogenic mushrooms; he, too, found it convenient to dry the specimens in the patio. Although he failed to find the intoxicating variety, "he settled down in our kitchen and produced one of the most delicious mushroom stews I have ever tasted," Blom observed. Helmut Wagner, director of the Overseas Museum in Bremen, collected exhibits for his institution. At one time or other, Frans Termer from Germany, Jacques Soustelle from France, Sigvald Linné from Sweden, and J. Eric Thompson from England paid longer or shorter visits to Na Bolom. Frans boasted in 1956 that "more and more scientists turn up, including Toynbee" and "a professor of oriental art from the imperial university of Tokyo to spend his sabbatical among the Maya ruins."

Blom enjoyed the company of those professionals. "In front of the big fireplace in the library of Na Bolom, as the logs are crackling and flaming," he remarked, "many and varied subjects are discussed." He reveled in "getting lectures on a variety of subjects from a variety of experts." Perhaps he was happiest with the meeting of the Eighth Round Table of the Sociedad Mexicana de Antropología, which took place in San Cristóbal in 1959. If he could not induce a university to take over his home for field headquarters, he was satisfied with the next best arrangement, the presence of numerous scholars pursuing their research.

Three guests who showed up in 1960 did not fit into the circle of university people Frans was accustomed to entertain. He was amused as he described "the lady who had 1) a truck, 2) a husband, 3) a fourteen year old daughter, 4) an upright piano on the truck, and finally eight choice milking goats. . . . The lady wants a ranch where they can produce their own food, and also she knows how to save the Lacandóns."

Organizing and conducting expeditions into the jungle provided one more way for the Bloms to earn money. Individuals with specific projects wrote to Frans for guidance in finding the best location for their research. "If they want pack teams and guides," he explained, "we arrange for them. So when they arrive here, they stay at our house, and the next day, if they so desire, they can proceed to the field." He made all of the arrangements, from hiring pack animals and muleteers to securing provisions and reservations. Among the early field trips he conducted were those of scientists looking for amber with petrified insects. "These seven or eight hours a day on horseback keep me in good trim," he told a friend. In reply to an inquiry in 1954, he itemized the expenses of an expedition with six persons, twelve animals, two mule drivers, and other helpers at $40 a day plus $10 a day for Blom as organizer and director of the project. Three years later he was charging $12 a day.

When a scientist proposed an agenda for a trip in 1955,

he showed complete ignorance of roads and trails. Blom replied, "Are you nuts or have you got a helicopter?" Then Frans drew up a realistic route. He added the advice: "It's tough on suitcases to be strapped on cargo mules. Sacks are preferable. No revolver, please. It only makes the Indians suspicious that we are there to make trouble."

Frans and Trudi conducted expeditions individually, depending on the interest of the visitor. Trudi escorted a Canadian and his mother through the jungle to photograph wildlife; on her return Frans led an expedition of men in search of amber. In the early part of 1956, however, when Frans was ill, Trudi headed an expedition for amber on a twelve-day trip.

The pay was so attractive and the visits to archaeological sites so congenial that he sometimes conducted tourists on such expeditions. Dr. Winifred Pitkin, a physician in her late seventies, commissioned several airplane jaunts to Maya sites and also a trip through the jungle. When a representative of a Paris picture magazine showed up, Trudi took him on a two-week trip to the Lacandones, and later she led Albert Mattson to the same natives for blood samples.

Although Blom needed the income from such expeditions, he turned down a tempting offer at least once. The head of Pemex, the Mexican national oil concern, proposed a jaunt with twenty-one friends. The prospect of managing a train of sixty to seventy animals was bad enough, but in addition, said Blom, the men would want special comforts and several cases of whiskey taken along; moreover, those prominent persons would ask "a million silly questions." " . . . I declined the honor."

He insisted that Na Bolom must be preserved as a permanent research center in that part of Mexico. Some months before he bought the building, he had already decided on its eventual disposition. He would will it to the state of Chiapas, "as I to my knowledge have no children, and my family in Denmark are doing well. . . ."

Two years later he decided upon the School of Archaeology at the University of Mexico as the eventual recipient. Still later, after he had made considerable headway in accumulating the library, he completely excluded the state of Chiapas from consideration on the grounds that the politicians would get their hands on his home.

He hoped that some university in the United States would take over Na Bolom as a permanent research center while he and Trudi continued to live in it. He approached the Department of Anthropology of the University of California with a proposal that it should use the building for research and pay him $250 a month for life, with the provision that he would will the place to that organization. A little later he made a similar bid to the Department of Anthropology at the University of Chicago. He valued the property and its contents at $25,000.[3] Neither institution showed interest. As far as is known, his last thought on the matter was to give the place to the University of Mexico, with the stipulation that the library must not be moved from Chiapas.

After Blom died in 1963, Trudi appointed a small group of trustees to administer Na Bolom after her death. Unless there is some change in that arrangement, it appears that Frans's plans for a permanent institution are assured.

Blom's interest in the Lacandón Indians, strongly seconded by Trudi's deep concern, appeared in two remarkable actions. During the expedition of 1950, when the Bloms camped at San Quintín, they learned that the Lacandones of the Rio Jataté region were starving. After a difficult journey through the jungle, they arrived at their goal and learned the full facts. "Then we found," Frans wrote a little later from San Quintín, "that for several years their crops had failed—too much rain when burning the clearings and scorching sun when the maize grew up. They are emaciated, weak, with hungry bellies. Their small children are skeletons in a sack of skin." At

San Quintín a small plane that came to collect alligator skins provided contact with the civilized world. "At once I sent a message out for aid, hoping that something would be done. . . ."

"And, by God, something was done!" he exclaimed with satisfaction. Gamboa, minister of health, and Caso, director of the National Institute for Indian Affairs, and other governmental agencies as well as some individuals acted with amazing speed. Medicine, clothing, and three and a half tons of maize, beans, and rice came to San Quintín by plane. "The Lacandón men came up the river in their long (30 foot) canoes, and at first they were silently amazed, but quickly they understood the wonder—food for them, their women and children. They remained with me until the last plane came in. . . . Then with loaded canoes, they went down the river to their 'caribals' [clusters of huts]. Meanwhile our pack mules have been hauling maize, etc., overland, and now we are joining them. . . ." In view of the usual red tape and delay in governmental offices, Frans scored a remarkable achievement in securing supplies to save the Indians before it was too late.

Another crisis of a different kind occurred two years later. Vicente Bor, whom the Bloms had known during earlier expeditions, returned from tilling his milpa one day in September 1952 and found that alligator hunters had raided his home. They had abducted one of his wives and three of his children, stolen his machete and tools, which he needed to earn a living, and burned his house and corn. After the calamity his pregnant younger wife gave birth to a baby, but both mother and child died. Bor and his two remaining sons, Kin and Kayum, made their way to the settlement of El Real. As soon as the Bloms learned of the tragedy, Trudi hastened to El Real and brought the refugees to Na Bolom.

Bor and his sons remained eight months with the Bloms. Physically ill and almost demented over the tragedy which had befallen him, Bor needed time and patience to recover. The sons gradually began to learn some of the customs of civilization and a few words of Spanish. Eight-year-old Kin helped his father to recover and to understand the generous actions of the Bloms. Frans had no intention of turning the natives away from their culture; as soon as they were ready, he would return them to the forest. After three months at Na Bolom, they showed marked improvement. In December Frans explained that "these last evenings we have made recordings of their songs."

When Bor began to think of going back to the forest, he realized that he had no woman to make tortillas. So he stood on the street corners of San Cristóbal, asking every Indian woman who passed by to accompany him. "It was pathetic," Frans remarked.

The return to the forest was expensive. The Bloms bought corn, seeds, tools, and an ox to enable Bor to set up a new home, and they provided pack mules for the journey. Frans had little spare cash at the time, so he sold duplicate artifacts to finance Trudi's trip to El Real and from there Bor's return to the jungle. Some weeks later news arrived that all was well with the former refugees. Frans was frank enough to admit that having the three Lacandones at Na Bolom "for about eight months became somewhat trying."

That was not the end of Bor. When any Lacandón became sick and could not be cured in his home, he was brought to Na Bolom for medical treatment. As a result, one or more natives were usually living with the Bloms. In 1958 Trudi brought Bor and his family to her home for the purpose of educating one of the sons. The entire party consisted of the father, his two sons, and the daughter of Bor's deceased brother. Frans tells the story:

> Bor is an amazing extrovert and loves nothing better than to tell dramatic stories, and sing his ancient and sacred songs to one and all who turn up with tape recorder. He is the last living Lacandón

who has had his nose perforated for a nose
ornament, and when he feels extra good he will turn
up with flowers stuck in his nose. He is most
dramatic. In short: he is a circus.

Kin, Bor's eldest son, has long wanted to go to
school. Now, the ritual of the Lacandón says that
their gods become very angry if the Lacandón men
cut their long hair. It was, therefore, a most drastic
step for Kin to take, when he asked to have his hair
cut short, and to be dressed in ladino (mestizo)
clothes. He is now in school, as he wished, and is
learning our way of living, which by no means can
be easy for him, he being a free young man who
never had to be exposed to all our taboos as to what
one can and cannot do.

Little Kayum also had to have his hair cut short
when he saw big brother with short hair. He is a
cheerful and lively child, and bright as can be.

So one morning Bor disappeared and returned
with *his* hair cut short, boasting that he was a ladino.
It took him a few pegs down when I told him that
all ladinos worked hard to earn their food. Work is
certainly not Bor's favorite occupation.

Little Rita, who never had been outside the jungle
before she came to us, took only two days to manage
fork and spoon like a perfect lady. Her poise is
extraordinary, and she takes everything in stride. In
no time she learned to sew and to iron her own
clothes. She insisted on making up her own bed.
She has an extraordinary dignity.

Bor became a problem for Frans, because the Lacandón seemed to be spending a considerable time at Na
Bolom. Amusing as he was, he could also be tiresome. At
least once Frans described him as a scheming liar,
though Trudi refused to accept that evaluation. In a fit of
annoyance Frans declared in 1958, "I'll be damned if
I'm going to have him living around Na Bolom for the
rest of my life." In this instance Blom lost. Trudi had a

great fondness for the Lacandones and took them in on every occasion. As late as 1974 Bor, with a young wife and relatives, spent some weeks at Na Bolom, while two of his group received medical attention. By that time both of Bor's sons had entered useful professions; one was a teacher and the other a medical assistant among their own people.

Frans also had a strong interest in other natives. In 1953, when Dr. Clarence Weiant, a chiropractor-archaeologist friend, worked with Blom, he had firsthand evidence of Frans's concern. Weiant reports:

> He was particularly fond of the Indians of Chamula, with whom he kept up close friendly relations year after year. He knew many of them by name and took an active interest in all their problems. On our way to the site [Moxviquil] each day we had to pass through one Indian village. If we met any of the people, there were always profuse salutations, and often brief friendly conversations. If somebody was ill, he always showed concern and several times insisted upon my being invited into their huts to render chiropractic service to the sufferer. I enjoyed such opportunities, and was usually quite successful in solving the problem.

Blom continued to carry on archaeological expeditions into his sixties. The Viking Fund provided money for a three-year search of Maya ruins in the jungles of Chiapas. In 1950, the first year of the project, Trudi accompanied him to study the Lacandones; Frederick Peterson, a recent graduate in archaeology, three helpers, and a number of trail cutters completed the party. By this time Frans had also become increasingly interested in the early accounts of Spanish travelers in the forests of Chiapas, and he attempted to follow the route of the sixteenth-century explorers. He set up headquarters at San Quintín, an abandoned chicle camp at the junction of the Perlas and Jataté rivers. Then he explored Lake

Lacandón with a collapsible rubber boat fitted with an outboard motor. On the shores of the lake he found Maya ruins and burial caves and on the island of El Peñol he examined retention walls, terraces, and mounds of crude construction. From the burial caves he collected some skulls and sent them to the anthropological museum in Mexico City.

When he attempted to visit the Lacandones in the Río Jataté area, he ran into difficulties. "The forest in these parts," he wrote from San Quintín, "is the damnedest I have yet found. It took us six days to cut twenty kilometers to the Lacandóns." On reaching his goal, he rescued those natives from famine.

The expedition of 1951 pitted Blom directly against the forces of nature in the jungles of Chiapas. The party, consisting of Frans, Trudi, and some helpers, left Ocosingo and reached Laguna Ocotal without incident. He explored the cluster of lakes with his inflated raft with outboard motor, and found ruins on the islands. "Then we ran into trouble. Along the east side of the lake region runs a barrier mountain chain. Slowly we searched for a way through. It took us about a month to chop our way out to the abandoned chicle camp of El Cedro, one of the approaches to Bonampak, and at that we only covered about eighty kilometers." After receiving supplies by plane, he examined ruins north of El Cedro. "It became quite evident that we had to stick quite close to the Cedro and Lacanjá rivers, and doing so, we located a total of 14 minor sites. . . ."

Finally, he and Trudi arrived at Bonampak, where he took notes on the temple with the paintings. But "it got drier and drier and our animals got thinner and thinner, and so we retraced our steps over the trails we had opened from El Real to Ocosingo . . . adding a couple of caves to our finds." Lack of water drove him from the jungle, and exhaustion and scant fodder killed three of his pack animals. Careful not to exaggerate his trials, he described the journey as "a somewhat tough trip."

Frans had ambitious plans for the third expedition, to

be undertaken with money from the Viking Fund. He intended to study the basins of the Usumacinta, Chixoy, and Lacantún rivers. The plans called for headquarters at Agua Azul on the Usumacinta, and the use of large dugouts with motors. "If half of what my guides tell me is true, then we should come home with a good harvest."

The third expedition, however, never took place, because the Viking Fund canceled his grant early in 1952.[4] He never received a satisfactory reason for the sudden termination, but he attributed it to the personal pique of the agent in the New York office of the foundation. Frans rewrote his report in order to explain why he lacked conclusions. The report, it should be noted, was never published.

Blom had good luck late in 1952, when he secured funds from another source for an excavation near his home. William P. Taylor of San Antonio, Texas, who headed an organization called the Mayan Order, advanced money to excavate Moxviquil, a site which was only half an hour from San Cristóbal. Although the Mayan Order apparently sold horoscopes based on the Maya calendar, Blom was happy to have the money. It is not clear what use Taylor planned to make of Frans's work.

It happened that Blom teamed up with another man for the excavation. Dr. Clarence W. Weiant, dean of the Chiropractic Institute, Peekskill, N.Y., secured a grant from the Explorers Club in New York City to help in the excavation. Dr. Weiant had a curious past. Trained in chiropractic and interested in Spanish, he set up an office in Mexico on two different occasions in the 1920s, but internal political disturbances drove him back to the States. While practicing his profession, he developed a serious interest in archaeology. Graduate courses in that subject led to fieldwork with Matthew Stirling at Tres Zapotes, which provided the ceramic data for Weiant's doctoral dissertation. One summer he also worked with Alfonso Caso at Monte Albán. Weiant managed to carry on two careers simultaneously, chiropractic and archaeology. As a part-time faculty member in archaeology at Hunter College, he represented that institution at the Congress of Anthropology and History at Jalapa in 1952, where he met Blom.

Weiant found Frans agreeable and engaging. He recalls:

> I was immediately impressed by his naturalness. There was nothing stuffy about him, no trace of intellectual snobbery. He was rugged, intense, filled with enthusiasm, friendly, outgoing, happy to answer questions, ready to listen to others.
>
> He told me of his discovery of the Moxviquil site, of his eagerness to dig there, and said, "Why don't you come down and look at it?" And that is exactly what we did. As soon as the Congreso was over, we [Weiant and his wife] went down to San Cristóbal by bus, stayed at Na Bolom, and made plans to return the following summer and get to work. I went alone in 1953 and spent the month of August working under his direction, while living at Na Bolom.
>
> During the rest periods he would reminisce. He spoke of his first encounters with the Maya..., of his training at Harvard (he had a special fondness for Tozzer), and of his unhappiness at Tulane.... He was happy only when in the field.

The men made progress at the ruins of Moxviquil. In the winter of 1952 Blom cleared the site of vegetation, exposed the walls, and excavated a small temple. In the following year after the rainy season, he and Weiant continued the work. "I cut a trench through a large mound...," Frans explained, "thinking that it might contain a buried building. It contained nothing." Weiant worked on another low mound, found burial vaults, figurines, and various pottery vessels.

Blom believed that he had found an ancient "arms factory" nearby:

The pottery vessels and sherds found at Moxviquil show that merchants from far away came to trade at this ancient center. Why did we find objects from Monte Albán as well as from the Maya of the hot lowlands along the Usumacinta River and even from more distant places? The answer was revealed when Weiant cleared one of the widest of the terraces. Here large chert slivers and [a] complete javelin and arrow points came to light. On the advice of the workmen, a few days later we rode only 20 minutes away to a small open valley strewn with worked stone. Another deposit lies the same distance from the ruin in a northeasterly direction.

He concluded that "evidently here was the arms factory of the region, and traders brought their wares from the hot country to trade them for weapons." He considered the find unusual.

The work at Moxviquil came to a sudden halt. About the time Blom made his discovery, he wrote to Taylor an excited report of the find. Later Frans learned that Taylor had died without learning of the successful work at Moxviquil. Taylor's widow had no interest in the project, and with the end of the subsidy Blom halted the excavation.

Aside from Moxviquil, Frans gave only casual attention to ruins in the neighborhood of his home. Five sites existed on the edge of the valley of San Cristóbal, but he never reported on any of them except Moxviquil. In 1956 he wrote to a friend that "we visited a large group of ruins right smack on the Pan American Highway. But nobody ever took the trouble to inspect them." On another occasion he found that a walk of an hour and a half brought him to a cave, where Indians worshiped stalactites and stalagmites, which looked like saints; he found no ancient remains there.

As the years passed and Frans grew older, he gave up the hardships of the trail and the struggle with excavation in favor of visiting Maya sites as the guide on chartered plane trips for well-to-do patrons. In that capacity he went to Yaxchilán, Palenque, Tikal, and Bonampak. At Palenque, which he visited twice in 1955, he stood amazed before the tomb found in the depths of the Temple of the Inscriptions. Dr. Pitkin commissioned a trip to Yaxchilán, Blom's favorite site. "It is such a magnificent place," he exclaimed after returning from the journey. He brought back part of a lintel with a low-relief carving of a Maya profile and twenty-one pottery figurines for the Chiapas State Museum. Tikal struck him differently. A visit there in 1959 made him "realize the near brutal strength of this largest of Maya sites. It is overwhelming." At that time the University of Pennsylvania team was already excavating parts of the site. In the last year of his life he visited those major sites again, and early in 1963 Matthew Stirling accompanied him on a final trip to Bonampak, only a few months before his death.

Frans put forth more ideas during this period than he had previously. He found old legends among con-temporary natives, criticized the care of Bonampak, looked into the Maya's control of erosion, deplored the rising price of artifacts, exposed fake codices, and passed judgment on some professional associates.

He believed that anthropologists could still gain valuable information by collecting stories from the Indians, which often showed vestiges of the *Popul Vuh*. He explained to Alfred Tozzer how he elicited that kind of information. When Frans was in Comitán, sitting in a store, he learned that the natives met once a year when their elders related the traditions. "I used my old trick of telling a scene from the *Popul Vuh* in the wrong way, and was immediately corrected." Where are the anthropologists? asked Blom, and he answered his own question with a smile, "among the Navajo, I suppose."

On returning from a visit to Bonampak in 1951, he complained to Alfredo Caso about the lack of proper

measures to preserve the temple with the murals.
Someone had had all of the trees cut down around the
building, and Blom pointed out that the blazing sun
would dry the walls and eventually cause the mortar and
stucco surface of the paintings to deteriorate and
crumble. When he wrote the same complaint to Tozzer,
the Harvard teacher reminded him that Herbert J.
Spinden years before had called for retaining trees over
ruins in order to prevent sudden changes in temperature
on a building. Caso took Blom's advice and instituted
measures to protect the famous structure at Bonampak.

Incidentally, the fame of those murals inspired the
performance of the Ballet Bonampak at Tuxtla Gutiérrez
in 1951. The Ateneo de Chiapas sponsored the
production. Although Frans was called on for advice, it is
not clear how much help he gave. He was dubious about
the artistic project; despite his fears, however, he
considered the performance "amazingly impressive."[5]

Evidence that the ancient Maya had methods to
control erosion of the soil, Frans pointed out, appeared
on the Pan American Highway in the valley of Comitán.
"Fields were planted in many places as a defense against
drought," he explained. With the appearance of the
white man, however, the system disappeared. "Then the
Spaniards came and established private property,
erecting boundary markers. The agricultural methods of
the Indians broke down. They were forced to plant
wherever they could, and the peonage labor system
introduced by the Spaniards did not leave time for the
Indians to maintain their stone walls built against
erosion."

In regard to the sale of artifacts, Blom feared that their
rising value would have disastrous results for research.
He wrote directly to a dealer in Mitla, taking him to task
for paying high prices for those objects from the past.
With that enticement, he told the man, "you have started
a wave of pot hunting, which is highly destructive to
serious investigation" by professional archaeologists.
"Can you state exactly where each piece comes from?"

he asked. "Do you have records of the conditions under which each piece was found?" "There is hardly a mound that does not show pock marks," Blom continued. Until recently only non-Indians engaged in treasure hunting, but "now, because of the high prices paid, even the Indians are beginning to pot hunt, thus destroying data of great value." Frans died before the mania for wholesale pillage of Maya monuments took hold in Mexico.

Fake codices intrigued him, and he enjoyed detecting and exposing them. In the 1930s he denounced the Gomesta manuscript, and also published a short article on fake codices. In the 1940s he exposed the lienzo of Tlascala, and from 1949 to 1952 he was consulted on three other spurious documents. The Narstkovo Museum in Prague sent him photographs of a codex in 1956; Blom had to reply that the record was a fabrication by the notorious Género López, who had manufactured numerous fakes.

Thereupon, Blom wrote a brief, unpublished paper with some facts about López. In the late nineteenth century Francisco del Paso y Troncoso, Mexican historian, found the manuscripts of Fray Bernardino de Sahagún, the sixteenth-century ethnographer, in a library in Florence, Italy. He hired López to copy the illustrations. With that background, López began to compose fake codices, but with his limited knowledge he concocted transparent frauds. He mixed Maya and Aztec signs and portrayed a Maya warrior driving a Roman chariot followed by a plumed serpent. In the Prague manuscript there was a column of bars and dots which made no sense. López drew upon the Dresden Codex for many of the illustrations in his fake productions. When Blom was at Tulane he bought a López concoction for $50 partly to keep it off the market.

On one occasion Frans participated in an attempt to buy a "valuable" codex. He described the event:

I clearly remember that with much secrecy, much whispering and much mystery, I was led into a women's hairdresser [establishment] and parked behind a curtain in a booth. More whispering and stealthy glances, and at last a man sneaked in, and from under his coat he took the "treasure"—the codex—worth a million dollars; but then they, as a special concession to me, would let it go for $10,000. The whole performance was a huge joke, and ended up as I expected. That codex was a fake done probably by a pair of brothers—their name escapes me now—who were also manufacturing fake painted pottery.

In the last years he retained his tendency to criticize. On reading a book or magazine article, sometimes he sent a letter to the publisher, pointing out minor factual errors. Had he passed on his comments directly to the author, one could understand the motive as that of helpful criticism. Nor had age softened his criticism of certain persons. Now he called Morley "a frustrated Egyptologist," a characterization difficult to interpret, and condemned his popular book, *The Ancient Maya*, as misleading to the innocent reader. By 1954 Oliver La Farge had fallen from grace, for Blom referred to one of his volumes as "the silly La Farge book," and exclaimed, "what a conceited ass he has turned out to be!"[6]

Frans also turned against Frederick Peterson. After that man aided Blom in 1950, there was trouble between them. Peterson later condemned the way Frans handled the expedition of that year, and Blom considered Peterson as an unsatisfactory assistant. A few years later, when Peterson and Juan Leonard explored Chiapas, Blom laughed at the "discoveries" they relayed to the news services. Once Frans asserted that Peterson knew nothing more than what Blom had shown him in 1950.

The relations between Blom and Wolfgang Cordan have not been completely clarified. Although Cordan visited Na Bolom on one occasion, the two men soon became hostile. Frans considered the German "a brilliant . . . journalist, who wrote fine German prose." He added, however, that Cordan was "completely unreliable," that he exaggerated and told lies to make his stories interesting. He remarked that "that is the way to make lots of money. Sometimes I wish I could do the same thing." Cordan in his *Secret of the Forests* made claims to archaeological discoveries in Chiapas. He regarded Frans as a desperate enemy, who drove him out of San Cristóbal in the late 1950s. In fact Cordan would not even mention Blom by name in his book.[7]

It is surprising that Frans responded negatively to Tatiana Proskouriakoff's striking *Album of Maya Architecture*,[8] a book of superb drawings of major Maya sites. The artist had visited each place and taken into account all of the latest archaeological data in order to prepare "reconstructionary" views of the sites as they appeared during the high tide of Maya civilization. Frans considered the book unreal, reeking "of library dust and photographs, which is probably an unfair judgment on my part." It appears that he did not fully comprehend how Proskouriakoff had proceeded with her research. Soon he revealed that the joy of exploration meant more to him than the view of a site in its prime:

> *But* the emotion of standing in the middle of the great plaza of Tikal, of mapping Uaxactún, of having to destroy that glorious carpet of wild pink begonias that covered the roofs and temples of Palenque, of going up the exquisite forest park that embraces Yaxchilán is something that makes all those buildings and stelae alive and speaking to you. May that [and] the ticks and other discomforts add to the joy. That Maudslays and others were at Yaxchilán before you does not really matter. When you step ashore and climb the steep bank to stumble upon the first building, then you have the sensation of being the first to step upon such marvelous places.

On other archaeological matters he was cautious. Although he asked Yuri V. Knorosov for copies of his publications for the library at Na Bolom, Frans could not accept the Russian's interpretation of glyphs. Earlier,

Blom considered Matthew Stirling's work on the Olmecs in Mexico interesting, but he wanted to see results of more digging before he was willing to accept Stirling's claims.

After moving to Na Bolom, Frans continued to write. Still in need of money, he followed the habit of turning out popular articles for newspapers. He credited himself with some twenty-seven items in Mexican papers in the early 1950s; thereafter he almost ceased that form of activity, probably because he began to gain an income from his home. Sometime in the mid 1950s he agreed to become a stringer for *Life* magazine, that is, to supply information or background material for stories about the region. He accepted the arrangement on condition that his name would never be used; there is no evidence that he made any contributions in that capacity. At least a half-dozen unpublished items from this period remain in manuscript. He wrote on Tikal, on hunting amber, on the discovery of some Maya ruins in Chiapas, and he edited several old accounts of travelers in the region.

As the quantity of his popular writing declined, he increased his production of scholarly articles. He did a brief study of a polychrome plate for the *Notes of the Carnegie Institution of Washington* and an account of a retablo in a sixteenth-century church in Chiapas for the Institute of Aesthetic Investigations at the University of Mexico. In addition to other minor articles, he wrote on Cortés and the costumes of Cristoph Weiditz and edited the diary of Juan Ballinas, a late nineteenth-century traveler in the jungles of Chiapas. Papers on burial customs and on pre-Cortesian life among the Indians of Chiapas are two of his better monographic works. In his last contribution he joined with Trudi to provide a brief description of the Lacandón Indians for the *Handbook of Middle American Indians*. In that instance he insisted that Trudi's name precede his in the attribution of authorship. An interesting rumor has it that the chapter was originally written in a mélange of several languages because of the multilingual attainments of the authors. It required serious editorial work to make the contribution conform to the format of the volume.

He failed to secure publication of a number of items with commercial houses. The request that Houghton Mifflin issue another edition of 1,500 copies of *The Conquest of Yucatan*, to sell at $2.50 a copy, was rejected. The same fate befell his proposal to submit five hundred typewritten pages of his book on the work of the mountain men in Chiapas. When he proposed an English translation of the de la Torre account, which he had edited in a Spanish version a few years earlier, Alfred A. Knopf told him that it was not designed for a commercial house and referred him to the University of Texas Press; the volume never appeared. After he had made an English translation of the writings of Bartolomé de las Casas, the publisher refused to accept it.

The map of eastern Chiapas, on which he had labored many years, appeared in 1954. The Mexican government bore the expense of printing it. Although generally receiving little notice, it was one of his proudest achievements.

There is no doubt that the major publication of the last period of his life was the two-volume *La selva lacandona*, written jointly by Frans and Trudi. When the manuscript was completed about 1950, the authors sent it to President Alemán of Mexico, who promised to have the work published and to establish a fund from the sale of the volumes to forward the work of the Bloms. After waiting four years, they heard nothing, and rescued the manuscript from the president's office just before he left his post. At that point Hans Lens, a friend of Frans, donated the paper and Editorial Cultura ran off 1,000 copies. The authors received nothing from the publication except some copies for their own disposal.

The first volume, written by Trudi, gives a personal account of the expedition of 1948 and flashbacks to the 1943 expedition, with emphasis on travel, adventure, and Lacandón Indians. The story appears in full detail, with numerous interesting passages and many photographs.

Frans wrote the second volume, which appeared two years later, on archaeological sites he examined in the jungle. Photographs, plans, and sketches supplement the description of the text. A unique feature is a large copy of his map of eastern Chiapas at the end of the volume. He made no effort to be complete or thorough, as he explained in the opening pages, for he considered himself but an explorer, pointing the way for future investigators.

La selva lacandona received little attention. Perhaps the relatively small edition had something to do with it. It is more likely, however, that the volume appeared at a time when Maya archaeology was already moving toward other approaches.

Even in his sixties Blom continued to be physically impressive. People still described him as tall, though it was his bearing rather than his height that they actually noticed. The shock of white hair gave him a distinctive appearance; sharp blue eyes and shaggy brows suggested alertness; and the recital of what he was doing at the moment was always enthusiastic. Generally he dressed in a native cotton shirt of blue, pink, and red with a scarf about his neck; old jeans and sandals completed the attire. In appearance he remained the gringo. It is said that in Mexico City cabdrivers attempted to charge him tourist rates until he asserted that he was Mexican and began to haggle over the fare.

At Na Bolom his favorite seat was a small throne chair at the left side of the fireplace in the library. On special occasions Trudi sat facing him on the right side. When guests were present, some observers felt that they "paid court" to the Bloms. Frans uttered compliments, carried on felicitous small talk, and attracted women of all ages.

His conversation could flow from one topic to another with ease and usually with liveliness. Anything pertaining to Chiapas stirred him to speak. When there was no pressing topic for discussion, he reminisced about his travels and experiences. Neither religion nor politics, however, ever entered the conversation. With close friends he might grumble about some recent disappointment, but his eternal optimism moved him to devise project after project to support Na Bolom, though many of those plans failed.

He generally enjoyed good health. In the early days of the expedition of 1950, he suffered briefly from sinus trouble. Late in 1956 he became ill, apparently from pneumonia; six months later, however, he learned that the illness had been a heart attack, and he went to Mexico City for examination and treatment. He believed that the medication he received put him into good shape. Then in 1963 he came down with liver trouble; that affliction, complicated by pneumonia, caused his death on June 24.

Four years after the Bloms moved to San Cristóbal, Frans received a notable local honor. He was awarded the prize for contributing to the cultural advancement of the state of Chiapas. He received it with becoming grace, and did not boast about it. To a friend abroad, he defined it as "a sort of baby Nobel prize." Perhaps the happiest part of the award was the money—5,000 pesos—which accompanied it. Although the governor of the state forgot to sign the diploma, Frans was grateful that he did sign the check, which "cleared up some debts. I surely fell in a dry spot."

Although he enjoyed the simple comforts of modern civilization, he condemned the shoddy practices that the natives learned from western culture. After an Indian attempted to sell him a piece of amber which was actually only plastic, Frans held his head in his hands and exclaimed, "Sometimes how I hate this civilization of ours; it destroys so many values, so much beauty."

In the last years he slipped a bit in strength and in personal habits. He attended the meeting of the International Congress of Americanists in Mexico City in 1962. With fifteen hundred Americanists and eight lecture halls, he declared, "it was impossible to attend the many papers, which were of personal interest. Even a flea jumping on a hot brick could not keep up. I know, because I was one of those jumping fleas. On top of the formal Congress, there were receptions, some official and others private. When I returned to Na Bolom, I spent two days in bed to recuperate." Some former associates thought that he had become careless about his appearance; one archaeologist who had known him in earlier years described him as looking seedy.

Trudi had established a strict rule at Na Bolom to keep Frans from reverting to alcohol. She banned all forms of intoxicating liquor from the premises. Today the house rules, displayed in each guest room, allow visitors to use liquor only in their own quarters, emphasizing her hatred of the "poison." Despite her care, in the last year or so of his life Frans slipped over the traces occasionally when she was absent on expeditions.

There was always an air of liveliness around Na Bolom. Various kinds of visitors, curious, serious, and nondescript, appeared. Frans had great respect for Trudi, who managed the growing household, specialized in photography, had an independent mind, and was a live wire who could emit a shower of sparks. "Trudi thrives with the extra people in the house," he remarked, "and flies off the handle a dozen times a day. She is a small riot and a hurricane all in one." Christmas became an elaborate celebration; in addition to decorations and a festive air, there were presents for all the servants on Christmas morning. Although that celebration has survived, at the present time Trudi's birthday on July 7 has become the dramatic event.

Frans continued to dislike Protestant missionaries. On the expedition of 1951, when he stopped at El Real, a missionary invited him to dinner. "Singing, Bible reading, and prayer—ugh!" he exclaimed. After talking with missionaries at a nearby camp, he characterized them as "a nice and dumb lot who carry Jesus Christ and the Lord on their coat sleeves. A nice lot of hypocrites!" Later he declared sarcastically that anthropologists should collect the tales of contemporary Indians "before the Protestant missionaries here fill them up with B'rer Rabbit and Aesop's fables or Beowulf. . . ."

His reply to a letter from a pious girl in Detroit more fully revealed his views on the subject. "You are very young and very sincere," he began, "and you have a dream of going out among the non-Christians to work as a missionary. The Lacandóns are deeply devoted to their beliefs," he continued, and "it is their kind of religion which is preserving their integrity, and which may help them to survive." Christian missionaries, however, come along with their preaching, condemn evangelicals of other denominations, and confuse the Indians. The natives' "ancient gods have given them rain for their cornfields, sun to give growth to their corn, and then some outsider turns up to tell them about Christ, who, to their way of thinking, knows nothing about growing corn." The girl's work in Chiapas would only add to the confusion of the Lacandones. He concluded by asking her if she were able to separate herself from the ways of civilization, endure a primitive mode of living, and perhaps suffer from malaria. If she could not undergo those hardships, what good would she do? This is one of Blom's best letters—simple, persuasive, and carefully worded so as not to hurt the recipient's feelings, and at the same time designed to teach her something of the complex nature of the problem.

He disclaimed any desire for publicity. When a Danish travel writer visited Na Bolom "to write a book about my checkered career, which he thinks is full of adventure," Frans dubbed him a "poor boob." In 1956 Mrs. Jessie K. Brown, a librarian in Texas, began to collect reminiscences and anecdotes from persons who knew Blom for a projected book. After receiving only a few responses, she died. Frans showed no interest in the project, and hoped that the volume would never be published. "I frankly hate publicity about myself, and always have," he declared. "I much prefer [Giles] Healey. He has a pathological hatred for me, because he thinks that I have been scheming to take the credit for

Bonampak away from him. So in letters to people he calls me 'the old bastard Blom' and more like that. You definitely know where you stand with a guy like that." Occasionally some persons speculated that Frans was the mysterious author B. Traven, a rumor he considered more annoying than amusing.

He was helpful in giving the benefit of his knowledge to persons known and unknown to him. When Ross Parmenter stopped at Na Bolom for information about Yanhuitlán, Blom reminded him of the Codex of Yanhuitlán, which he must read, advised him to visit the town's parish priest, and suggested that he take a present of some liquor for the cleric. Serious inquiries by mail also received Blom's attention. Authorities at a museum in Antwerp believed that they possessed an inscribed stone from Palenque. They sent a photograph to him; the figures appeared to be Zapotec, and he forwarded the inquiry to Alfonso Caso. On the other hand, he could not waste time with foolish ideas. In his files is a letter from an author in Guatemala who wrote books on archaeology, with the terse notation at the top, "told the nut off."

Even in his later years he continued to think of ways to educate the public at large. After the Pan American Highway came through San Cristóbal, he sensed a new urge among the young people of that community to learn. Na Bolom could provide a small response to the need. "I am a godforsaken idealist and dreamer," he remarked in 1961, "but the dream of spending the last years of my life in this lovely country came true, so why should my dream of creating a lasting place of educational values not come true also?"

For a time, he regularly invited students and their parents to see motion pictures at his home. They were not used to movies, and he counted on the novelty of the performance to attract large numbers. With a projector and films on loan from the United States Information Service in Mexico City, he chose educational subjects, like soil erosion, sanitation, and other practical, everyday topics. When he invited students, he told them to bring their parents, because he believed that the adults needed the information as much as the youngsters.

At first the attendance was small, and Frans could not understand the reason. Then he began to understand. Protestant missionaries had already invaded San Cristóbal and crusaded against saints in that "fanatically Catholic" community. Because the Bloms looked like gringos, they were considered Protestants and therefore evil. This was ironic, for they had no sympathy with missionaries and never attacked Catholicism. So Frans went to the leading Catholic official in the town and explained the situation. The official informed all the young men training for the priesthood how the Bloms differed from the missionaries. "That did it, and the attendance grew," Frans remarked with satisfaction. He also had mechanical troubles with his movie plan, for the electrical power burned out too many bulbs in the projector, so after a time he discontinued the program.

A few years later he resumed movies at Na Bolom, this time with a new procedure. Because the children could not understand the voice from the loudspeaker, he had the teachers come in first to view the film and listen to the narration. When the students arrived, he showed the picture without sound, and the teachers supplied the information. Then he showed the complete sight-and-sound record. On the first showing, he observed, the children enjoyed it only as fun and failed to grasp the meaning. With a second and third showing, they began to understand.

On another occasion, he used motion pictures for a different educational purpose. In Mexico City he presented movies of the expedition of 1950 in the Chiapas jungles to inform the general public. The overflow crowd was so great that he had to repeat the showing.

He also devised ways to improve the general knowledge of the better educated citizens of Chiapas, who were largely isolated from outside contact. Once he importuned the United States Embassy in Mexico City to send someone to San Cristóbal to teach English, but the embassy did not respond. More elaborate was his optimistic proposal to the governor of Chiapas to create fifteen $200 fellowships. Five would go to foreign investigators, five to Mexicans, and five to individuals from Chiapas. Apparently, the local grantees would be expected to study outside of the state, while the foreign and Mexican grantees would come to Chiapas, where local students could learn from them. Nothing came of the plan.

In 1952 another inspiration bore more directly on his archaeological interest. Blom explained:

> We have just acquired a new governor here, a man of culture who is going to do quite a lot towards forwarding all kinds of research and giving special facilities to such groups of investigators who turn up. . . . He has asked me to start a quarterly relating to Chiapas. I plan something like *Maya Research,* though such good paper costs too much. Anyway, the quarterly will deal with all kinds of research in Chiapas. Papers will be accepted in any language and translated into Spanish. . . . Financing will come from rich Chipanecos and the state.

The fine plan bore no fruit.

Acting on his own impulses, Frans had moved toward larger, more comprehensive concerns. He took an interest in the people of the community. He tried to increase the knowledge of the educated class and to impart better methods of living to the general masses. He had broadened his consciousness to include concern for the people about him. If he had been an "artist" much of his life, he also became an "idealist" in the later years. He developed a new outlook, and it made him happy and contented.

At Na Bolom Frans created his utopia, or at least conditions as near utopian as he could expect. He had a home of his own in a country he loved. The research library grew in size and usefulness. Serious visitors came in increasing numbers. And he found ways to solve the financial problems. Uninterested in enhancing his professional reputation, he traveled in the highlands he loved and wrote on topics that appealed to him. If articles and books failed to get into print, he did not care. The visitors who came to Na Bolom and the Indians about the town and out in the jungle meant more to him than kudos from the archaeological establishment. At last he could carry out his inmost desires of discovering unknown Maya ruins, enjoying the beauties of the highlands, and helping simple people. Regardless of what others thought of him, he had learned to enjoy life in his own way.

Epilogue

The story of Frans Blom is the strange odyssey of a man who sought the solace and beauty of the forest, though he was forced to live within the confines of western culture for many years. The first indication of his revolt against modern life occurred when he rejected his father's wish that he enter a business career. During his early Mexican venture Frans found a response to his inner desires. As he traveled through the forests and enjoyed adventure, new experiences, and the beauty of nature, he felt the fulfillment of his emotional yearnings. He entered the profession of archaeology, perhaps scarcely understanding the reason for the choice, because archaeology would constantly take him back to the hinterland of Mexico. The profession, however, involved him in the intricacies of modern civilization; he was expected to aspire to professional success, administer a department, seek funds for special projects, and even engage in a building campaign. He, or at least his inner nature, had not bargained for those mundane details.

The years at Tulane University brought his downfall. Although he renewed contact with the forest in 1925, 1928, and 1930, thereafter he did not return periodically to Mexico. In a sense he also became a victim of the depression, for money was not forthcoming for expeditions. His spirits began to slump, his professional research fell off, his marriage dissolved, and finally the Tulane building campaign proved too much for him. Unable to solve his problems and with no prospect of returning to Chiapas, he took refuge in alcoholism. After several years of personal defeat, he returned to Mexico.

Finally, at the age of fifty, he was able to spend time in the forest every year. He also found an ideal companion in Trudi. He extended his interest to the Lacandones, who lived in a simple relation to nature, and by extension he took an interest in the plight of all Mexican Indians. Frans did not scorn the advantages of

237

civilization; he enjoyed modern conveniences in his home, and he knew how to entertain guests with good food and social amenities. At Na Bolom, however, the forest was always at his back door, the mules and horses waiting for a journey into the jungle.

Although archaeology and map making appeared to be important interests in the latter period of his life, perhaps he did not fully comprehend that he valued those activities primarily because they provided him with an excuse to travel through the forest. As we look back on Blom, it is evident that he instinctively chose tasks that would bring him into direct contact with the jungle. His map making dealt with Chiapas; moreover, in archaeology he explored rather than excavated, for exploration allowed him to travel over large areas of the country. Also his interest in Indians grew out of his love of the unsettled lands where the natives lived, little touched by civilization.

Just as he loved the forest, so he instinctively disliked civilization, or at least certain aspects of it. Although he was fully at ease in the pleasantries of social intercourse, he came to dislike the inanity of many social gatherings, the strict regulation in dress, and the stilted formalities of polite society. The ugly aspects of urban civilization also annoyed him, from noisy traffic to deceit and fakery and the driving ambition to succeed.

He sought a modestly comfortable life which avoided the pressures of civilized living. He wanted to be able to go into the jungle for long trips, to commune with nature, and to associate with the simple Lacandones. At Na Bolom he created the ideal environment. He achieved the goal, of course, at a price—loss of connection with a learned institution, lack of a regular income, and the decline of his reputation—and he had to engage in dreary labor to support the kind of life he had chosen. It appears that the price was worth the result, for he lived at peace with himself in the last two decades of his life.

Blom's story is that of a man who ultimately found

himself. Most of the friends he had left in the United States lost interest in his career in Mexico. They failed to realize the inner nature of the man; most of them remembered only that he had failed at Tulane and had slipped into alcoholism. They never realized that eventually he fulfilled his ambition and enjoyed life in his own way.

He cannot be fairly judged on his professional record alone, though there are bright spots in that record. He must be judged as a man who came to terms with himself, an ideal which many men fail to achieve.

Appendixes

APPENDIX 1
Tata, a Prince of an Indian
by Frans Blom

Somewhere in Tabasco, Mexico many years ago, to be exact, 1925, we were headed from the coastal plains of Tabasco up into the mountains of Chiapas. There were no broad roads in front of us, only mule trails. So we needed a batch of saddle and pack mules, and with them a first-rate muleteer to handle the packs and the other muleteers.

A friend who formerly had worked in Tabasco recommended an Indian, Lázaro Hernández. He lived outside of the town where we were stopping, and we sent for him. Early next morning we were looking over mules presented for sale and making other preparations for our long ride. Somebody said, "Here comes your man." I looked down the wide and sun-dried main street and saw an elderly Indian. He wore an old palm-leaf sombrero, under which was a furrowed old face. A white shirt, blue trousers, and he wore sandals on his bare feet. As he came along in the street, each step in the deep dust kicked up a smokelike cloud.

He came up to me and said simply: "Señor, you are a friend of my friend Mister Gerald Jones. You say that he says that I should work for you. I will do so. You say that you have a letter from my friend to me. I cannot read. Will you read it to me?" As I read the letter to him, his face lighted up, his eyes sparkled with memories and his thousand wrinkles gathered into a big smile.

"When do I go to work—tomorrow?" He never asked what kind of work nor how long we would be gone. He just said, "I will be here tomorrow."

During the rest of the day we bought mules, and hired an engaging rascal, who knew his mules but also knew his "Americanos," one of those lazy ones who had worked too long in an oil camp.

Anyway, the mules were O.K., and we fired him some

weeks later. He had, though, acquired several lowland mules, i.e., unshod mules who had never climbed rocks before. So a blacksmith had to be found. That evening our delightful rascal spread himself out over town to find a watchmaker to repair one of my watches and a blacksmith to appear at dawn to shoe our mules.

Sometime after dark Señor Rascality returned full of stories about the handsome señoritas, and advising that we should stay in town a couple of weeks. There would be a fiesta and many dances, and we would have a wonderful time.

Eventually, I got around to his errand. "Oh, si, señor. The blacksmith can repair your watch, but is not so sure he can shoe a mule!" I said to myself, "Hell, I can shoe a mule, but it is hard work and I would rather let someone else do it." "No hay remedio." There was no remedy for it. I learned that the next morning I had to shoe the darned mules, and went to it.

Sweating in the morning sun, and thinking that it might be a beneficial idea to let the newly acquired mules understand that I spoke the profane Spanish that they were used to, I cut hoofs, warmed shoes, and nailed them. While doing so, I noticed a benevolent-looking gentleman who was watching me with a twinkle in his eye, a rotund little man with an "I know better" smile.

Wiping gallons of sweat off my face, I turned to him and handed him the tools. As he went to work, I thought that I heard a murmur go throughout the crowd of spectators. After all, we were like a circus in town, far more unusual than the bimonthly river boat; so wherever we went we were sure of an audience. "Little Sun Face" turned his rear against the rear of the mule, grabbed one of its hind legs between his knees, and went to work with hammer and nails, looking very professional with a handful of nails in his mouth. For a moment I felt like Tom Sawyer, when he got the kids to paint the fence.

But alas, our expert friend rammed a nail into the soft and tender part of the hoof. A swift kick from the mule, and our "expert" lay sprawling on the ground with the imprint of a mule's hoof on his cherubic seat. And what cursing, what magnificent profanity; even the mule paid attention by turning around and cocking its ears.

A roar of laughter went up from the crowd, and everybody scrambled to restore the dignity of our friend. Then I saw Lázaro standing next to me. He smiled, but his smile was not quite approving.

"Señor, you did not know that the señor who helped you is the priest of our town."

Lázaro followed us to our quarters, when we had the job finished. "Are you coming with us?" "Si, señor." "We are going up into the mountains of Chiapas and as far as Guatemala, and maybe we will take you all the way to the United States. We will send you back from there to your home." "Muy bien, señor. I have my clothing with me." He had been carrying a bundle about the size of a small suitcase, wrapped in a small mat. As far as he was concerned, he was ready to follow us to the end of the earth.

Finally, we started. The mules had been shod, the saddles inspected. Our specially constructed boxes were filled with our gear, such as camp cots, blankets, mosquito bars, cooking utensils, cameras, films, machetes, arms and ammunition (not because we expected trouble with the natives, but we expected to live off the land). . . .

The morning we started it rained. Not just rained, but really it came down from the clouds; it came down as thick as a Hollywood tropical downpour multiplied by five. We had to load at our quarters, unload at the river bank nearby, leave the packs in dugouts, swim the animals across. Sloshing down one muddy bank and up the other bank. Imagine a snowman made of mud. Well, that is what we looked like when we at last had saddled and packed again.

Afternoon the sun came out. The mud dried and began to peel off as we jogged along. After a while we were free of mud, and when we made camp that night, I knew several things: one, that life was hell; two, that hot tea with lemon and a double slug of rum was heaven; three, that Lázaro was a treasure.

Day by day, Lázaro became more valuable to us, more precious. I do not remember when we began to call him *Tata*. Tata is an Indian expression of respect towards an elder. It is used with a father, a beloved uncle or as a respected address to an old man, respected for his wisdom and kindness. Soon Lázaro was Tata to us. He was old. His wrinkled old face smiled over. Be the day bright and trail easy, or be it fast rivers to cross, bad mountain passes to climb, or rain and mud, Tata was always hard at work. Very soon he treated us as if we were his sons, and quickly our devotion for him grew. He was our Tata.

Day upon day we traveled the trails, sometimes over huge savannas that were so hot under the scorching sun of the day that we could only travel by night to spare both men and mules. Well do I remember one long ride. We mounted about eight-thirty one night after a long day's work. It was pitch dark and the tropical night felt like touching black velvet.

Rule one: when riding mules, let them alone. They will pick out the trail. Tata could be heard behind us, urging on the mules with endearing words: "Come on, pretty Maria; step lightly, big strong Pedro." When one of the animals would get stuck in a mudhole, his intonation changed from caressing to caustic: "Get going, you damned fool . . . ." etc., etc., unprintable.

After a while we got out of the forest and before us lay the savanna under the eerie light of a full moon. Pretty soon we came to a telephone line, which we had been told to follow. Crooked poles or trees along which was strung a single wire, a ridiculously thin thread that is the modern life-line between isolated communities.

The moon climbed higher, and its light helped us to grope our way, winding in and out among clusters of trees and big patches of elephant ears that took the most fantastic forms and shapes; really, it was spooky. It is always a joy to travel by moonlight. The surroundings are merged into a vague, olive-green obscurity, in which the outline of things is beautifully blurred.

On and on we went through the night. Tata's urging kept our animals going. Now and then, small night-hunting animals flashed by and at times they followed the trail for a little while, then suddenly became scared by us as a danger and vanished into the darkness. The trail lay before us like a white ribbon in the dark grass. Our guide was supposed to know the trail, but soon we came to a place where many white trail ribbons were going hither and yon. He took the wrong ribbon. To our right was a long range of mountains, and all I knew was that we should go east, and keep those mountains on our right.

Upon a small hill was a native house. Tata and I rode up to it and called. No answer. We called again, and suddenly the door opened. Out came three spooky looking figures dressed all in white, three frightened women who thought that we were bandits or worse. Soon assured that our intentions were honorable, they guided us. They seemed to glide before us, white robed, in the moonlight. Again we found the white ribbon of the main trail. From Tata, "Muy asustadas, las viejas"; "Very scared, the old girls."

We were getting very tired. Often we dozed in the saddle, to wake up with a jerk when our animals suddenly stopped to nibble on some grass. We were really tired. We began to see things. The bushes took strange shapes in our minds. At times we dismounted and grabbed the tail of our mule, letting it drag us along so that we would stay awake.

A faint light of dawn showed to the east. That damned Tata was still talking to his mules. If he just would shut up. Moonlight paled into short darkness, and then slowly dawn painted the mountains to our right with millions of colors. The golden glow of sunrise seemed to infuse our bodies with a fresh desire to live. Hours more and ahead of us lay our destination, a small village. The mere sight of our destination seemed to un-tense us. Suddenly we

felt more tired than ever. "Only give me a deep drink of
water, maybe a bite to eat, and then sleep, sleep for
ages."

But Tata trotted his mule by and ahead of us. The old
boy was full of life, and yelling to us and the mules. He
was cheering us with the news that soon we all would
find rest. With work and the night ride we had no sleep
for 28 hours, under gruelling conditions. Sleep for us,
but Tata, twice our age, was all full of pep, and
proceeded to get himself a huge drink of rum. That
somehow established a schedule. Tata never took a drink
while we were on the trail, but he soon got himself
comfortably mellowed when we reached a village where
we expected to rest for a few days. He was twice our
age, and on the trail he was harder on the work than we.
No punishment from trails could down Tata.

Now we rode into country new to Tata. We began to
climb mountains. This was new to him, as all his life had
been spent in the lowlands. Gradually we climbed
through the tropical forests of north Chiapas, and then
we came into the pine country.

By that time he had become very dear to us. He had
become a part of us. We shared all with him. Now and
then we would get to a ranch, and to us it was only
natural that Tata was one with us. Not quite so with the
ranch owners, where we stopped at great intervals.
Native servants have their meals in the kitchen. But Tata
was no native servant; he was ours; he was our Tata.
Frankly, if it had not been for Tata, I wonder how we
would have accomplished our aim. And then some few
stuck-ups considered him a servant. That would make
me mad as Hell.

One day up there in the pine forests of the highlands,
I smelled something familiar—strawberries. Then I
remembered that the mother country of all strawberries
is America. I got off my mule and picked a handful of
"fraises du bois," and gave some of them to Tata. He
tasted them first, and with a smile of contentment got off
his mule and gathered more of them.

Then we spent a week of rest in a highland town, a place conquered in the early days by the Spaniards, and to which they had brought many of their own fruits, such as pears and cherries. One day, returning to our quarters, I found Tata seated on the sidewalk, with his hat full of cherries. He was having a wonderful time, sucking cherries and spitting the seeds into the street. As I approached, his dear old face wrinkled into his fascinating smile. He held his hat towards me. "I am in my own country, Mexico, and you strangers know more about it than I do. You must like my country! Will you have some?" So we settled down on the edge of the sidewalk, and we ate all the cherries in his hat, and spat the seeds into the street.

Naturally, Tata had his fling when we got to that town, and he deserved it. He also had a carousal the night before we left. And the only time I ever saw Tata get really mad was when we left that charming place. He got darned impatient with the mules, so drunkenly mad that he messed up the team for a short while. He swung the long loop of the lariat and whipped them. He was feeling devilish and on top of the world. We, who were riding ahead, stopped and wondered. He saw us, stopped his magnificent mule-cursing, the swirling end of his lariat dropped, and he rode up to me. "Don Pancho, I should not do that!" The rest of the day his head was hanging low. By evening he sensed that he was a little in disgrace, but not disgraced.

APPENDIX 2
Louis Bristow, Jr., to His Mother

From "Tulane Research Party Vanquishes Yucatan Jungle"
New Orleans *Picayune*, May 6, 1928

It's pretty bad, but there's no use of you and Dad worrying, because I can't mail this letter till we get to civilization; so if you get this letter at all, it will prove we're all right.

Dear Mother—Excuse this pencilled letter. but we're out of ink and almost everything else for that matter. We have sugar, coffee, and beans enough to last about five more days, but our rice and bread gave out long ago, and we are sixteen or eighteen days from the nearest town. However, there are lots of game and other edible stuff in the forest, and as long as our ammunition holds out, we'll not starve. We eat only two meals a day, anyhow.

We are coming through territory that is unmapped and unexplored, and we couldn't get Indian guides; so if we can get out at all it will be because we just happened not to go around in circles. Of course, there are no trails, so every day we go out and cut trails through the bush with machetes.

There are seven of us now—Mr. Blom, McBryde and me; then Kantor, a boy of German parents who speaks an Indian dialect, and a good, hard-working kid, and Ciriaco, the Mexican cook, 28 years old, who has lived in the woods all his life and knows more about them than all of us put together. He's a great cook, can make a meal out of green bananas or stewed palm leaves or what have you. Every morning when I wake up, he has coffee ready for me, and he keeps coffee hot all day long; so when we come in, he has it ready. Then there are a couple of muleteers, Joseph and Epifanio, both mighty good men, who work hard and know mules. Both Kantor and Ciriaco

Reprinted by permission of the Times-Picayune Publishing Corp.

mean to come back to the United States with us and work, and are trying to learn English from us.

Mr. Blom has just come in from scouting for the best way to go. He says he found a blank wall at least a thousand feet high we've got to go down, and has been trying to find a way all day and has failed. It is the most serious obstacle we have met yet, and may delay us several days more. . . .

. . . I told you we were living largely off the forest. There are two kinds of big, turkey-like birds, and one is good for a meal for the seven of us. I've done my share of food supplying—shot four of the birds and caught fish enough for several meals. It takes two men to get an armadillo, and Kantor and I have killed the only two gotten so far. I'm beginning to feel like a professional scout. . . .

We had no meat yesterday, but toward evening I shot a big howler monkey, and we had monkey steak for supper. The boys won't eat it, and Kantor wouldn't even come up and look; they say it makes them feel like cannibals, but I'd rather eat like a cannibal than not eat; so we had the monkey last night and will finish him tonight. These monkeys are hard to kill. . . .

. . . I'm getting along swimmingly when you consider what a little I know about medicine. All these Indians want pills. While we were going through the towns before we got lost out here, I had some mighty curious requests for medicine. One man came to me and told me his sister had been married two years and had no children, and wouldn't I please give her a pill, too.

They were glad to pay for the pills; would bring me vegetables, fruit, and so forth. All the Indians wanted pills, any pills would do; they just wanted a pill. I usually gave them a soda pill. If they returned several times and I thought nothing was the matter except the novelty of taking medicine, I gave them some powdered quinine with instructions to dissolve it in water and drink it slowly. They never came back. . . .

. . . A couple of days have passed. Everything seems

against us. The mountain cliff is terrible; we can't get down, because the river has cut a deep gorge and is filled with rapids. The cliff is broken up with limestone projections, making it impossible to make a trail for the mules. We left the last Indian town almost a month ago, but have advanced very slowly because of the heavy jungles. We have to cut every foot of the way. Yesterday morning we sent back Kantor and Joseph to find an Indian town somewhere around here and get food. They ought to manage to cut a trail and get back in seven days.

. . . Even the weather is against us. This is supposed to be the dry season, and it rains, rains. We came back on our own trail today. The river makes a big bend, so we figure if we come back and go directly north we may miss the wall and strike the river again. I hope so, because we're in a hole now, especially as Mr. Blom told me last night that we have only forty shots left for the shotgun, and very few fish hooks. . . .

. . . I've had my first experience with a cougar, the American lion, the other day. Ciriaco, Mr. Blom and I killed one sixty-four inches long. . . . Mr. Blom wants to put it in the museum at Tulane. . . .

March 26. Gee, I'm happy. Kantor and Joseph came in a minute ago, and just in time. We were eating supper, and had a pot of chocolate and no sugar, a lot of palms we had cut in the forest and boiled, and a can of army emergency rations, and with appetites we'd been trying to keep down for several days because of short rations. We had one pot of beans left and were saving that. Then appeared Kantor and Joseph, and they had six big birds with them, and I mean to tell you that night of starvation turned out to be a feast of celebration.

They also brought news of a rebel general who had passed somewhere near here, hot-footing it to Guatemala four years ago, and told us they had been told he went along the opposite bank of the river; so we will probably pick up his old trail. That means we should be into some kind of civilization in fifteen days, if we don't find ruins to hold us up. Mr. Blom has been worried about our home folk, thinking you'll be sure we are dead or something, because we haven't been able to communicate with you in so long.

We are fixed up fine now, like Christmas—beans, coffee and sugar for eighteen days, tortillas (Mexican hard tack) for seven or eight days, lard for ten days, and information of a trail, which if correct should put us to habitation again in fifteen days more.

March 28. We crossed the river yesterday. The raft we built was only big enough for one man and two boxes or saddles; so we had to make about twenty trips. Dad would have enjoyed seeing me half naked, standing on the front end of a homemade raft, using a homemade paddle to fight the current in the middle of a broad river, and taking care of a load of cargo at the same time.

April 7 or 8. I've lost track of time. . . . We got to San Quentin yesterday. That means we've accomplished what they all said was impossible and what no other expedition has been able to do. . . .

About four days ago we saw six Lacandon Indians. Mr. Blom says they are probably the wildest of these tribes, which means there are few, few people in the world more primitive. . . .

San Quentin, by the way, isn't a place; it's a deserted camp. There's nobody here but those crazy Indians. . . . Our food has been low again, so we've fallen back on the forest. The temperature was 113 degrees yesterday on the savannas. Yesterday we found some green bananas, and by experimentation found several ways to eat them. We are only about six days from the outposts of civilization now, so we are all right. I sure do miss home dinners. Ciriaco is the best camp cook in the world and can make more different dishes from one thing than anybody else, but camp grub is just grub. . . .

Love,

Louis.

APPENDIX 3

Don Carlos B.

Don Carlos B., representative of the Mexican government assigned to accompany the expedition of 1928, never did fit into the team. When he joined the party at Comitán, he arranged for quarters for the group at what turned out to be a hotel. Blom, disgusted with this maneuver, considered it a device entirely for Don Carlos's own convenience. At the same time Frans already suspected the man of laziness, noting that he talked much of making ethnological studies, but had done nothing. "I am pretty sure that he is here to spy on us, and the poor brute is going to get a hard deal," remarked Blom. One of the college boys revealed that when they learned that Don Carlos suffered from bladder trouble, Frans wished that he would become sick enough to return home.

Don Carlos found it convenient to avoid all of the hard traveling through the jungle, and turned up at towns along the route. In the field letters Blom wrote during the journey and forwarded to Tulane, he mentioned the government official only twice, saying that he was making ethnological collections. At Anaïte in the middle of May, Blom gave the following sketch of the man. Two weeks later Don Carlos left the team at Flores, much to the relief of everyone.

Blom's Diary, May 16, 1928:

> Without knowing it, our fat friend Don Carlos is rapidly becoming the nuisance and the joke of the expedition. The first days in the forest it was all new to him, and he enjoyed it, but now that the novelty is wearing off and the mosquitoes and other insects are getting their share of his blood, he likes it less every day. Yesterday evening he gave me a lecture on my way of organizing the expedition. The Americans were so rich, and from a rich university,

so we ought to travel with more comfort and luxury. We should have a servant per man to put up our cots, etc., etc.

He is full of theories, and his clumsiness and laziness are causing much amusement. My, he is lazy. All the time he invents reasons for cutting the little work he does down to less or makes excuses for not doing things. He can't do this because now it is too late; he should have started from the beginning of the trip; or he can't do that because somebody else did something in the same line. He never investigates, but picks up stray information that comes his way. Some fine investigator!

In Comitán and Ocosingo he strutted around like a rooster on a dung heap, with all the small schoolteachers cackling at him. There he was, the big man from the Department of Education in Mexico City, and he enjoyed it. But out here in the forests, where men are mostly concerned with men, mules, and lumber, he makes a sorry sight.

After he had gone to bed last night, his fancy patent steel contraption, which he calls a camp cot, collapsed under him, and I confess that it gave me a lot of fun to see him trying to extract himself from an entanglement of blankets, mosquito nets, and cot.

He does naturally not know how to curl up in a cot under a net, so the mosquitoes get him. This morning they chased up about four, and then he paced wildly up and down for a while. He may stand it until Flores, but how he will stand the trip up through the Petén and Quintana Roo, I wonder.

There is a sequel to the story. Blom invited the Mexican to visit Tulane and to make use of the facilities of the Middle American Research Department. Don Carlos arrived in New Orleans in September, and soon several articles about him appeared in local newspapers. Frans, who was absent from Tulane at the time, warned President Dinwiddie how to treat the visitor. "He is a man who can be both useful and also dangerous to our future work, and should, therefore, be treated with abundant courtesy and complete distrust." Frans instructed his secretary to keep the man out of his office. "He should not know that we have taken out things . . ."; and he should be kept from the rare books and manuscripts "till we have sized him up." The Mexican, on the other hand, could make profitable use of the library.

Seven years later Blom recommended the man for a Guggenheim grant for study.

Notes

Chapter 1

1. His friend McBryde remembered his dress as even more informal: "baggy woolen trousers supported by an Indian sash that he wound around his waist, tucking the loose ends under. His shirt was always white and rumpled, open at the neck and sleeves rolled up."

2. William Spratling and William Faulkner, *Sherwood Anderson and Other Famous Creoles* (New Orleans: Pelican Bookshop Press, 1926), appeared in an edition of 250 copies and sold for $1.50. The edition was exhausted in one week, and the following January a printing of 150 copies was issued. The volume became scarce in the ensuing decades. In the 1960s the *Texas Quarterly* republished the pictures, and the University of Texas Press issued a hardbound reprint in 1966, with an essay by Spratling.

3. In 1924, when Frans had only a small income, he esteemed Alfred M. Tozzer and Sylvanus Morley so highly for their encouragement and help that he ordered as a gift for each man a fine piece of pottery to be made in Denmark. It is likely that his mother paid the bill.

4. Frans offered all kinds of advice to the young man. He explained how he could save fifty dollars on transportation from New Orleans to New York; told him to secure from Hermann Beyer a list of museums and letters of introduction to European scholars; and warned him that, although all his expenses would be paid, "you will need cash to buy cigarettes (those German cigarettes are punk, but the American are darned expensive over there), wine, women and song."

Chapter 2

1. In later years he told a friend that he had also served as interpreter on the Danish royal yacht, which probably provided the basis for the rumor that he became friendly with a member of the royal family.

2. A story that he was in Russia during the revolution is not supported by family tradition. Years later Frans told an associate that while serving in the navy, his boat visited a Russian port, which is a likely basis for the story.

3. Perhaps it is more than coincidence that he devoted so much space to this expedition, which included Maya sites, Tabasco, and the route straight through Chiapas. In *I de Skore Stove* he apportioned 36 percent of the pages of the volume to that journey, which represented only one tenth of the time covered by the book.

4. The next year, however, in "Notes on the Maya Area," *American Anthropologist* 26 (1924): 408, 409, he referred to Garrido's "rather fantastic article" and his "fanciful statements."

Chapter 3

1. Childs Frick, son of Henry Clay Frick, who later became interested in collecting prehistoric bones.

2. Soon after the Tulane party returned to Villahermosa, a brief notice, "Las ruinas de Comalcalco" appeared in the Villahermosa periodical *Rendención*, April 29, 1925. If it was not written by Blom, he supplied the information for the article. He dismissed the earlier work of Charnay as inefficient, estimated that it would require five months to examine the site thoroughly, and praised the perfection of the stucco figures.

A reproduction of the interior of the tomb and the stucco reliefs is on exhibit in the museum of the Institute of Middle American Research, Tulane University. Robert Wauchope reports that the reproduction and Blom's photographs are the only records of the figures, which are now almost wholly destroyed.

3. For an affectionate description of the man, see Blom's "Tata, a Prince of an Indian," printed for the first time as Appendix 1 of this volume. It is interesting to note that this later version does not agree in every detail with the passages about Tata in *Tribes and Temples*.

4. Although Blom appears as a first-class villain in the Gates pamphlet, only one statement made Frans uneasy. Gates asserted that Blom had written a book attacking the Mexican government. His only book was *I de Skore Stove;* as we have noted, when Gamio read the manuscript before publication he offered no objections. If the Mexican government had anything against Blom, however, it could hamper his plans to work in that country in the future. So he wrote to the head of Antropología at the National Museum and inquired into the matter. He was relieved to learn that there were no accusations against him.

5. In the years following Gates's departure from Tulane, Frans considered him with contempt. At times he affected pity for the old man, especially when Gates faced bankruptcy in 1928. After Gates left the Johns Hopkins University and condemned the policies of President Isaiah Bowman, Frans wrote facetiously to Bowman, congratulating him on becoming a member of the "billy goat" society, composed of people whom Gates hated. Years after the death of Gates, Blom simply referred to him as "the old nut."

Chapter 4

1. Although Blom's major interest was archaeology, the department fostered some work in ethnology, physical anthropology, linguistics, and early history.

2. I have stated the aim as it evolved in the work of Blom and in the development of the department. On one occasion he expressed a far more ambitious aim, but surprisingly omitted mention of expeditions, the museum, and publications (Blom quoted in "Mayan Symposium and Exhibits at New Orleans," *Science* 74 [December 4, 1931]: 570).

3. In the Latin American Library at Tulane one can consult the Gates catalog today and note the items which are missing from those offered for sale in New York.

4. In a report prepared in 1937 Arthur Gropp noted the following items: "Cortes' 'Ordenanzas' . . . ; the Chronicles of the Indies by Ovieda y Valdes

printed in Salamanca, 1547; the Mani documents, manuscript, being the oldest known writing in the Maya language with Latin characters, dated 1557; the Tabi documents, 1569 . . . ; the Nuremberg imprint, 1524, of the second Cortes letter; the Mesquiaguala maguey fibre manuscript, 1569; the Starr codex on maguey paper, before 1550; the hieroglyphic census of Tepozlan, before 1550; the Novus Obris Regionum by Grynaeus, printed in Basil, 1532; the Vargas Machua work, 'Milicia y Descripcion de las Indias, printed in Madrid, 1599 . . . ; Beltran de Santa Rosa's 'Arte de el Idioma Maya,' a rare item printed in Mexico, 1746; . . . the original manuscript of the Libro del Judio in 17th century hand, a medical and botanical work of the Maya; two imprints, a vocabulary and a Christian doctrine in the Tarascan Indian language, both 1559 . . . ."

5. These figures are from *Linking Past and Present Americas,* a brochure for the building campaign of 1939-40. Arthur Gropp's report on the library at the end of 1937 estimated 41,389 items, including 3,000 clippings; by that time 25,000 books and pamphlets had been cataloged.

6. There is probably a connection between an anecdote and a news report about a shrunken head in the museum. In the 1950s one of Blom's friends told of a trick played on the archaeologist. When Frans wanted a shrunken head of an Indian from South America for display, his artist friends fashioned one from a turnip, put hair on it, and placed it in a bell jar. Blom was delighted until it began to sprout in a few days. A local newspaper reported in 1931 that workmen had found a shrunken head of a South American Indian as they excavated for a new high school in New Orleans. The foreman sold the object to Blom for $30 for display in his museum, and Frans reportedly constructed a theory to explain how the object had found its way to the city.

7. When a New Orleans newspaper noted La Farge's story "No More Bohemia" in *Harper's Bazaar* in 1935 about life in the French Quarter a decade earlier, the writer exclaimed, "Who will ever forget Oliver's Indian dances!"

Chapter 5

1. In Mexico City Frans bought twenty-eight Totonac and Maya plaster casts from the National Museum.

2. For Bristow's version of the preceeding weeks, see Appendix 2.

3. Don Carlos B., the agent the Mexican Government designated to accompany the expedition, left the party at Flores. Blom's opinion of and relations with the man appear in Appendix 3.

4. It was on this expedition that Frans determined that the masonry built into the river at Yaxchilán was a breakwater. He came to the conclusion by watching the course of pieces of wood thrown into the river upstream by his assistants.

Chapter 6

1. I have not encountered any contemporary appreciation of Blom's multidisciplinary approach. Sylvanus Morley and later Alfred V. Kidder announced the use of specialists from various disciplines in the project

centered at Chichén Itzá under the Carnegie Institution of Washington; the approach, however, never produced the anticipated results. Edward T. Hinderliter, "The 1930 World's Fair Expedition to Uxmal, Yucatán," (M.A. thesis, Temple University, 1972), emphasizes Blom's use of the multidisciplinary approach.

2. Despite the former close friendship between the two men, Frans became critical of Morley, who continued to be kindly toward his protégé. Blom envied the money that the Carnegie Institution of Washington placed at Morley's disposal for the project at Chichén Itzá. Frans believed that with the same resources he could have excavated many unknown Maya sites. In addition, he believed that Morley introduced too many refinements of civilization at Chichén. After visiting the place in the late 1920s, he snorted that "Morley buzzed around guests, attended by four Chinese servants.... I am wondering. whether they are going to put in roulette tables." Tozzer also disapproved of the elaborate expenditures, but on the ground that the C.I.W. paid too small allowances to its retired professionals and their wives.

3. Peter Keenagh, *The Mosquito Coast: An Account of a Journey through the Jungles of Honduras* (London: Chatto & Windus, 1938). For Mitchell-Hedges, see R.L. Brunhouse, *Pursuit of the Ancient Maya* (Albuquerque: University of New Mexico Press, 1975), chap. 4. Captain Stuart Murray wrote numerous books of travel. For Gregory Mason, see Brunhouse, *Pursuit*, pp. 105-8. Richard Byrd explored Arctic and Antarctic regions.

4. J. Leslie Mitchell, *The Conquest of the Maya* (New York: E.P. Dutton & Co., 1935). The newspaper article failed to note that Mitchell also said that much of Maya culture had been imported from Asia and Oceania.

5. A few comparisons of the extant diary, dating from the end of 1921, with the version in *I de Skore Stove*, suggest that he did little more than condense and copy the diary, with an occasional excision of remarks reflecting unfavorably on Mexico.

6. The plan to reproduce the Castillo, exotic as the structure would have appeared in New Orleans, was not as harebrained as some critics thought. The building, slated to cost $1,050,000, was to be operated with an endowment of $1,250,000. On the first floor, the plans called for an entrance hall, where the visitor would find an explanation of archaeology and "a cross-section of a modern heap"; an auditorium to seat 500 persons, a special exhibition gallery, and Stela Hall, which would rise through the second floor to display casts of Maya monuments from Middle America. The library, offices, and classrooms would occupy the third and fourth floors, study collections the fifth and seventh floors, and a children's division the sixth floor. Quarters for photography and historical collections would occupy the remainder of the structure.

Chapter 7

1. Several factors might have a bearing on the diaries of 1943 and 1948. They were not composed with the thought of publication, and hence he felt no inhibitions when he wrote. Moreover, internal evidence suggests that he considered the diaries a source of information for future articles, which could explain the details he included. It is also possible that Trudi, who accompanied him on these travels, heightened his sensitivity.

2. In *La selva lacandona* he devoted ten pages of fine print to list and explain the items needed for an expedition.

3. For an account of Frey, see chapter 8, where he appears in connection with the discovery of the murals at Bonampak.

Chapter 8

1. In Frans Blom and Gertrude Duby, *La selva lacandona*, 2:130, he gives the date as 9-8-15-0-0.

2. Blom retained that view in later years; see *La selva lacandona*, 2:23-24, where he cites Cook's works, *Vegetation Affected by Agriculture in Central America*, (Washington, D.C.: U.S. Bureau of Plant Industry, 1909), and "Milpa Agriculture, a Primitive Tropical System," in *Smithsonian Institution Annual Report for 1919* (Washington, D.C., 1921), pp. 307-26, and quoted from one of his articles.

3. Salvador Toscano, *Arte precolombino de México y de la América Central* (Mexico City: Universidad Nacional Autónoma de México, 1944).

Chapter 9

1. Robert Wauchope, Blom's successor at Tulane, reports that he sent two sets of the institution's publications to Frans.

2. His announcement also called for the same instruction for students from Mexico sor the period from December 1 to January 15. Apparently, he put little faith in the midwinter session, for he never mentioned it, and there is no evidence that it ever took place.

3. The proposal was hardly attractive from a financial point of view. One assumes that Frans included his wife in the proposition for life tenure. An institution would be paying him 12 percent a year on his valuation of the property for an undetermined number of years of life remaining to the Bloms. Actually, Frans died ten years after he made his first proposal, and Trudi is still very active in her seventies.

4. The Viking Foundation changed its name to the Wenner-Grenn Foundation for Anthropological Research.

5. *Ballet Bonampak: argumento y texto literario* [por] *Pedro Alvarado Lang . . . Música: Luis Sandi, coreografía: Carlos Mérida* (Tuxtla Gutiérrez, Chiapas, 1951; another edition, 1951).

6. It is not clear which book Frans referred to. La Farge published *Cochise of Arizona* in 1953 and *The Mother Ditch*, a juvenile, in 1954; perhaps he was referring to *Raw Material* (Boston: Houghton Mifflin Co., 1945), an autobiographical volume by La Farge.

7. Wolfgang Cordan, *Secret of the Forests* (Garden City, N.Y.: Doubleday & Co., 1954).

8. Tatiana Proskouriakoff, *An Album of Maya Architecture* (Washington, D.C.: Carnegie Institution of Washington, 1946).

Sources

The following abbreviations are used in describing my sources in the bibliography of Blom:

Archives	Department of Archives, Tulane University Library
LAL	Latin American Library, Tulane University
MARI	Middle American Research Institute, Tulane University
N.O.	New Orleans
Na Bolom	Na Bolom, Blom's home in San Cristóbal, Chiapas, Mexico
Peabody	Peabody Museum Library, Harvard University

Chapter 1

Descriptions of the man and of his apartment are gleaned from letters of the following contemporaries of Blom to the author, 1973-75: Arthur Gropp, Dr. Clarence Wolsey Weiant, F. Webster McBryde, Maurice Ries, and Vera Morrell, and from the following articles: Charles Richard, "He Likes His Job," N.O. *Item-Tribune*, November 9, 1929; Rose Howell, "Mayas Possessed High State of Civilization . . . ." Greensborough *Daily News*, July 16, 1930; "Blom to Explore Honduras . . . ." N.O. *Times Picayune*, September 26, 1935; Harley Perkins, "New Expeditions Prepare to Solve the Mystery of the Mayans," *Boston Evening Transcript*, October 18, 1924; and Gertrude Duby Blom, "Frans Blom," *Siempre!* (Mexico City), supplement, November 13, 1963, p. viii.

All quotations of Blom come from his letters, Na Bolom and MARI. His "Personal Diary, 1926," LAL, gives clues about his social life during that year. Joseph Blotner, *William Faulkner: A Biography* (New York: Random House, 1974), 2 vols., has a few references to Frans; the excursion on Lake Pontchartrain, however, seems to be misdated. The volume by Spratling and Faulkner is mentioned in Chapter 1, note 1.

Some of the anecdotes from the recollections of Blom's friends compiled by Mrs. Jessie Brown, MS, Na Bolom. Material about Zelia Nuttall appears in the Nuttall files, MARI and Na Bolom, and from notes generously made available to me by Ross Parmenter, who is writing the biography of Mrs. Nuttall.

Newspaper items, LAL and Archives, provide information on the Harvard Club, speaking engagements, the sports car, and the excursion to Mexico in 1932. Frans's engagement, wedding, and divorce can be traced in *The New York Times*.

Blom's encouragement of certain young men comes from letters to the author from F. Webster McBryde, Gerhardt Kramer, and Arthur Gropp. Mr. Kramer also kindly loaned me his correspondence with Blom on this subject.

Chapter 2

There is no satisfactory account of Blom during his years in Denmark. Printed biographical sketches give little information on the period, and some of the statements are conflicting. The sketches of his life are the following: Douglas S. Byers in *American Antiquity* 31 (1966):406-7; J. Eric S. Thompson in *Estudios de Cultura Maya* (Mexico City) 3 (1963):307-14; *Library Journal* 3 (1933):4; manuscript account in Archives; Franz Termer in *Anales de Sociedad de Geografía y Historia de Guatemala* 36 (1963):577-83; Alberto Ruz Lhuillier in *Revista Mexicana de Estudios Antropológicos* 19 (1963):127-30; Jens Yde in *Ethnos* 28 (1963):250-51; there is some biographical material in Blom, "Report Requested by the General Education Board, New York, December 28, 1927, MARI; *Who Was Who* 4, p. 95; Jorgen Kiaer to the author, August 1974, gives recollections of Mrs. Kiaer, Blom's sister. Paula Alegría in *Homenaje a Frans Blom . . .*, 2d ed. (San Cristóbal, 1967), pp. 20-21, mentions the meetings in the Hotel d'Angleterre.

Ross Parmenter, who is preparing an extensive biography of Zelia Nuttall, kindly loaned me his notes of several interviews with Blom.

The period in Mexico, 1919-22, is covered in part in Blom's diary, 1921, 1922, in Danish, MARI, and more fully in *I de Skore Stove*. The sources for the season at Palenque, 1923-24, are his report to the Dirección, part of which he translated and printed in *Tribes and Temples*, and several letters at Na Bolom. Morley's MS diary, American Philosophical Society, and Blom-Morley correspondence, Na Bolom, provide the story of the early relations of the two men.

For Blom's work at Uaxactún, see his brief report of 1924 (see Blom bibliography). The description of his work at the site comes from a letter by Blom, Na Bolom. Karl Ruppert in *The Maya and Their Neighbors* (New York: Appleton-Century Co., 1940), pp. 223-31, later showed that other ceremonial sites contained similar groups of structures arranged for astronomical purposes.

Chapter 3

Blom correspondence, Na Bolom, especially Morley and Tozzer folders, is the major source; some newspaper articles, LAL and Archives, contribute details.

For Gates, see Blom and Gates folders, Archives, which give important material. Much information also appears in Gates, *A Gage of Honor: The Development and Disruption of the Department of Middle American Research . . .* (n.p., March 1926), a selection of letters to and from Gates; unfortunately, the editing was hasty; in at least two instances the text of letters is mingled with Gates's narrative of events. In addition, one must remember that Gates selected the material to justify himself. For Gates at Tulane, see "Clippings," LAL and Archives. The newspaper article referred to in the text is Harley Perkins, "New Expeditions Prepare to Solve the Mystery of the Mayans," *Boston Evening Transcript*, October 18, 1924. Gareth W. Lowe, "William E. Gates, a Biography" (typescript, Provo, Utah, 1954), is based on Gates's correspondence; this biography is scheduled for publication in the future. A general account of the man can be found in R.L. Brunhouse, *Pursuit of the Ancient Maya* (Albuquerque: University of New Mexico Press, 1975), and in the same author's *Sylvanus G. Morley and the World of the Ancient Maya* (Norman: University of Oklahoma Press, 1971).

Blom's manuscript diary, original notebook with sketches and maps, and a typed copy, LAL, provide the firsthand material for the expedition of 1925. Blom and La Farge, *Tribes and Temples* is the official report. A few letters by Blom, Na Bolom, are helpful; and *The New York Times* (see Index of 1925) contains a few items. Matthew W. Stirling explained his use of Blom's finds in his "Great Stone Faces," *National Geographic Magazine* 78 (September 1940):310, 312, and 328.

Chapter 4

Much of the material comes from Blom's correspondence, Na Bolom, Archives, and LAL, and in letters from some of his friends to the author. Arthur Gropp kindly provided information about grants and acquisitions of the library. *Bulletin of Tulane University of Louisiana. Report of the President,* 1925-41, lists the members of the department, their titles, and the honorary associates; the data were kindly supplied to me by Archives and by the President's Office, Tulane. J. E. S. Thompson relates the story of loading books on cinder blocks, as told to him by Blom. *Linking Past and Present Americas* (n.p., n.d.) gives some history of the department and provides maps to show the expansion of the department over the entire fourth floor of the Science Building (now Dinwiddie Hall). Newspaper clippings, LAL and Archives, throw light on some of Blom's activities.

For La Farge, see D'Arcy McNickle, *Indian Man: A Life of Oliver La Farge* (Bloomington and London, Indiana University Press, 1971), which is based on the La Farge correspondence; it offers interesting material on the Tulane period, but it must be supplemented by La Farge's diary of 1925 and his sketches, LAL; Blom's diary of 1925, LAL; La Farge folders in Blom correspondence, MARI; and *Tribes and Temples*. A brief account of the man by D. S. Byers is in *American Antiquity* 3 (1966):408-9. Joseph Blotner, *William Faulkner: A Biography* (New York: Random House, 1974), offers the anecdote about dropping the glasses. Blom correspondence, Na Bolom, is useful. Oliver La Farge, *Raw Material* (Boston: Houghton Mifflin Co., 1942), pp. 166-167, deals with the expedition of 1927. "The Land of Gog and Magog: Exploring the Last Maya Civilization and Their Wild Descendants," *Scribner's*, June 1926, gives La Farge's reactions to the expedition of 1925. The journey of 1927 received notice in *The New York Times*, May 27, 1927, 9:1. La Farge, "Doomsday Book of Jacaltenango. Third Tulane Expedition, 1927," MS, MARI, presents the information by topics.

Hermann Beyer receives notice in *El México Antiguo* 9 (1959):13-38, with tributes written by J. E. S. Thompson, Alfredo Caso, Carlos P. Linga, Robert Wauchope, and Arthur E. Gropp. Beyer folder, Archives, and Beyer folders, MARI, provide helpful information. Arthur Gropp to the author, February 1975, relates numerous personal recollections of the man and includes documents showing the failure to have Beyer's last work published. Blom's estimate comes from his correspondence, Na Bolom. Blom's letter to Morley about Beyer's vandalism is in Morley file, Carnegie Institution of Washington, and in Blom correspondence, MARI. See also two articles about Beyer's work in N.O. *Item-Tribune*, December 3, 1929; references to his pro-Nazi views are in N.O. *Item*, November 1, 1938 and in N.O. *Tribune*, November 2, 1938. "Clippings," Archives, contains an index for each volume, which aids in tracing articles about the man in local newspapers.

The material about Thomas Gann comes from Blom correspondence, MARI; for an account of Gann, see Elizabeth Carmichael, *The British and the Maya* (London: British Museum, 1973), pp. 34-37.

On the recent revival of interest in the casts stored away for forty years, see Alberta Collier, "From beneath Tulane's Stadium, Mayan Casts Emerge at Last," N.O. *Times-Picayune*, October 12, 1975.

Chapter 5

Blom "rode us hard to keep our diaries current," Webster McBryde remarks in a letter to the author. It was a fortunate habit, for the manuscript diaries of Blom, McBryde, and Bristow provide an excellent personal record of the expedition. Original and typed copies are in MARI and LAL, together with scientific notebooks by Blom and Bristow. Dr. Bristow kindly loaned me a copy of his diary and a collection of newpaper clippings relating to the expedition. Dr. McBryde supplied excellent details in letters to the author, and Dr. Bristow gave similar information in several interviews. A few of the quotations in the text come from Blom's "Field Reports," mimeographed, and from the N.O. *Item*, August 17 and 19, 1925. Blom correspondence, MARI, adds a few details. Accounts of the expedition in print include two by Blom, "Preliminary Report . . . ," and "Trails and No Trails . . . ," which is the most extensive published report of the journey; and "F. Webster McBryde, Beta Phi (Tulane) . . . ," *The Delta of Sigma Nu*, May 1929, pp. 545-50; and Harnett T. Kane, "Fourth Expedition Achieves Outstanding Success," *The Tulane Hullaballoo*, clipped, n.d., LAL.

Chapter 6

The material about the Uxmal expedition comes from newspaper articles; see "Clippings," LAL and Archives; Gerhardt T. Kramer kindly loaned me his collection of newspaper notices. Kramer's correspondence with Blom contains a mimeographed copy of Field Letter No. 1, March 10, 1930, printed in "The Uxmal Expedition," *The Tulane News Bulletin* 10, no. 7 (April 1930):111-14. A copy of Field Letter No. 2 is in Archives, Blom folder. *The New York Times*, April 16, May 6, 18, 20, 1930 informed the public of the progress of the work. The quotation on camp routine comes from a Blom letter, MARI, and Morley's opinion is in the Morley files, Carnegie Institution of Washington. Blom's remarks on the building at the Fair come from his letters of January 31 and September 1, 1933, MARI. One should also use "Clippings" for 1933 and 1934, LAL and Archives. Among articles on the subject are the following: "Tulane's 'Maya Temple,'" *The Tulane News Bulletin* 14, no. 2 (November 1933):19-25; "Glorious City of the Past," *The Tulane Hullabaloo*, clipping, n.d., in Kramer collection; Wladimiro Rosada y Ojeda, "La expedición de la Universidad de Tulane en Uxmal," *Revista de Revistas*, September 28, 1930, pp. 20-21; *Century of Progress. Official Pictures . . .* (Chicago: Neely Printing

Co., 1934). Gerhardt T. Kramer, "Among the Maya," *Walther League Messenger* 42 (February-June 1934), gives his personal experiences in Yucatán.

For the trip to Honduras, see Blom's MS Diary, MARI, and the official reports by Jens Yde, "A Preliminary Report on the Tulane-Danish National Museum Expedition to Central America, 1935," *Maya Research* 3 (1936):25-37, and *Archaeological Reconnaissance of Northwestern Honduras,* Tulane University Department of Middle American Research, American Research Series no. 9; also offprint from *Acta Archaeologia* (Copenhagen) 2 (1938).

The professional activities of Blom are noted in "Clippings," LAL and Archives. Completed manuscripts of pamphlets and plans for others, Na Bolom, provide the only evidence of his first attempt to write literature for tourists; the endeavor of 1937 is described by Maurice Ries in letters to the author and in a few newspaper articles. Newspaper "Clippings," Archives, also mention the various exhibitions and Blom's views on contemporary civilization.

For reviews of *The Conquest of Yucatan,* see *Book Review Digest, 1936* (New York: H.W. Wilson Co., 1937), pp. 98-99. Miss Marjorie LeDoux provided the information about the Midameres Press. Blom's reaction to the Stacy-Judd proposal is in MARI.

The gradually evolving plans for the projected building for the department are in scattered documents in MARI, LAL, and Archives. For the campaign, see "Clippings," LAL and Archives. Frans's bout with alcoholism is described in letters from his friends to the author. His correspondence, Na Bolom, describes his literary endeavors during this period, the seizure of his personal possessions, and the partial recovery of some of them.

Frans's views on Europe and on education come from N.O. *Item,* September 24, 1935 and from N.O. *Tribune-Picayune,* September 26, 1935 and May 12, 1938. The editorials referred to are in *Item-Tribune,* November 10, 1935 and in the *Item,* May 14, 1938. The *Item,* April 21, 1938, announced that the department had become an institute and would offer graduate courses; Blom's reaction is in N.O. *States,* April 21. "Radio Program ... 6th March, 1936 ...," MS, LAL, provides the script of the performance.

Chapters 7 and 8

Much of the factual material comes from Blom correspondence, Na Bolom and LAL.

On Gertrude Duby, see an autobiographical sketch in her book, *Hay Razas Inferiores?* (Mexico City: Secretaria de Educación Pública, 1944), pp. 7-11; Alberto Barranco Chaverría, "Gertrude Duby habla de sus lacandones," *Señal* (Mexico City), August 1971, pp. 16-18; and numerous clippings from newspapers (often unidentified), Na Bolom, about her.

For the expeditions of 1943 and 1948, Blom's manuscript diaries are the major source; Blom and Duby, *La selva lacandona,* vol. 1, treats the expedition of 1948 in great detail, with occasional passages about the trip of 1943. The journey of 1948 is the subject of José Pérez Moreno, "El Maravillo Mundo de la Selva," *Todo* (Mexico City), February 17, 1949, pp. 30-31, 66 (disappointing), and Antonio Rodríguez, "Importantes descubrimientos...," *El Nacional* (Mexico City), December 7, 1948.

Blom and Duby, "Darkness to All Who Dwell There," *Natural History* 55

(May 1946):231-32, 237, 239, describes the trip to Unión Fronteriza. Manuel Gamio, "Exploración Económica-Cultura en la Región Oncocerosa de Chiapas, México," *América Indígena* (Mexico City) 6, no. 3 (July 1946), gives the background of the problem of onchocerciasis, with only a brief mention of the Bloms. Gertrude Duby, *Los Lacandones* . . . (Mexico City: Secretaría de Educación Pública, 1944), was based on the trip of 1943.

Blom's archaeological notes, "Selva Lacandona. Notas Topográficas," Na Bolom, provides the basis for much of the material in Blom and Duby, *La selva lacandona*, vol. 2.

The literature about Carlos Frey includes the following: Carlos Margáin, *Los Lacandones de Bonampak* (Mexico City: Educaciones Mexicanas, 1951), which contains some material about him; Arturo Sotomayer, *Dos sepulchros de Bonampak* (Mexico City: Librería del Prado, 1949), gives a full description of the expedition on which Frey died; William B. Huie, "The Misfit Who Became a Hero," *Cosmopolitan*, October 1950, pp. 70-71, 131-37, is the best account of the man, with data on his background in the United States: a brother, Gilbert J. Frey, in a letter to the editor, *Américas* 2, no. 12 (December 1950), p. 42, championed Carlos as the discoverer of the murals at Bonampak.

Mabel Knight, "Frans Blom, Archaeologist and Explorer, *Christian Science Monitor*, January 21, 1950, p. 12 briefly describes the Bloms in the field and in Mexico City.

Among miscellaneous items are Antonio Vera Guillén, "Lo que no dijo Mr. Blom," *Chiapas* 1, no. 4, July 1, 1949, who accuses Frans of not mentioning certain sites; and "Se exhibio una película a colores, de los Lacandones," *Excelsior* (Mexico City), January 13, 1951, which notes Blom's performance in Mexico City. Na Bolom has numerous other articles about Blom, including notices of the Chiapas prize, which he received in 1954.

Chapter 9

Blom's correspondence, Na Bolom and LAL, continues to be the major source of information. The running commentary in *Teocentli* also provides interesting information on certain incidents, like the story of Bor's sons.

The account of aid to the Lacandones in 1950 comes from from Blom's letters; see also "Former Tulanian Aids Mexico [*sic*] Natives," N.O. *Item*, June 7, 1950. For the exploration of 1951, see Blom's MS Diary, 1951, and comment in *Teocentli*. Letters from Dr. Clarence W. Weiant to the author give details of the excavations at Moxviquil; see also C.W. Weiant, "Digging in Chiapas," *The Explorers Journal*, Fall 1954, pp. 30-35, and the account in *Teocentli* on the same subject.

Several descriptions of the Bloms and Na Bolom during this period can be found in Julia Hernández, "El Paraiso de los Blom," *El Libro y el Pueblo* (México City) 19 (January-February 1957):61-66; William Hagney, "From the House of the Jaguar," *Science of Man* (Garden Grove, California), no. 9 (April 1962), pp. 88-95; and "Entrevistamos a Pancho Blom al cumplir 65 Años," *Icach*, no. 14 (January-June 1965), pp. 43-48 (written 1958).

Items of a miscellaneous nature include folders on Blom's naturalization and on his death, Na Bolom. His qualifications for the Chiapas Prize are in Alberto M. Barreiro and Eliseo N. Palacios, *Cartas sobre Frans Blom como candidato al Premio Chiapas* (Tuxtla Gutiérrez and San Cristóbal, 1954).

For obituaries of Blom, see items cited in Sources, Chapter 2, first paragraph, and the following: Gertrude Duby Blom, *Siempre!* (México City), supplement, November 13, 1963, p. viii (an excellent description and appreciation); an unsigned article, *Icach,* no. 11 (July-December 1963), p. 506; Guy Stresser-Péan, *Journal de la Société des Américanistes de Paris,* 52 (1963):312-13. *Homenaje a Frans Blom, 31 Julio de 1966* (San Cristóbal: Impresora del Centro, 1966; 2d ed., 1967), is a small volume of tributes.

Chronological Bibliography of Frans Blom

The bibliography is complete as far as possible. Blom indicated that he published numerous articles in periodicals in Mexico and in Europe, though he did not give sufficient detail to identify them.

I have included a few items not directly attributed to Blom, but which appear to have been written by him; I have noted that fact in each instance. I have also included some newspaper articles in which Blom is quoted, which I also note at the appropriate places.

Chronological List of Works by Blom

Blom Correspondence. MARI, Na Bolom, LAL, Archives, and in possession of Gerhardt Kramer.

"Diary, 1921, 1922." MS in Danish, MARI. Also contains some drawings and photographs.

"Las ruinas de Tortuguero." *Ethnos* (Mexico City) 2 época, 1, No. 1 (1923):77-78

"Las ruinas de Palenque, Xupé y Finca Encanto." 1923. MS, with drawings and photographs, Dirección de Antropología, Mexico. A portion was translated into English and quoted in Frans Blom and Oliver La Farge, *Tribes and Temples*, 1:169-89.

I de Skore de Stove; Breve ta fra Meksiko. Copenhagen: Andr. Fred. Høst & Søns Forlag, 1923. Diary-letters, February 3, 1919-July 4, 1922.

"Las Chanecas de Tecuanapa." *Journal of American Folk-Lore* 36 (1923):200-203.

"Report on the Preliminary Work at Uaxactun, Guatemala." In *Carnegie Institution of Washington Year Book,* no. 23. Washington, D.C., 1924, pp. 217-19

"Report on the Ruins of Uaxactun and Other Ruins in the Department of the Peten, Guatemala." 1924. MSS, Carnegie Institution of Washington, Peabody. MS in Danish, with six dated entries, Na Bolom.

"Notes from the Maya Area." *American Anthropologist* 26 (1924):403-13.

"Archaeological Surveying in the Maya Area." 1924. MS, Peabody.

"Chiapas a la llegada de los españoles en el año de 1524. Apuntes." 1924. MS, Na Bolom.

"Rafael de la Cerda, Letters to and from Frans Blom, Reporting on Ruins and Artifacts Discovered in the Vera Cruz, Tuxtla and Oaxaca Regions." 1924-25. MS, LAL.

(With Oliver La Farge) *Archaeological and Ethnological Expedition to Middle America. A Preliminary Report.* Tulane University, N.O., 1925. Reprinted from the *Tulane News Bulletin* 6, no. 1 (October 1925):3-9.

"Diary of Frans Blom on the First Tulane Expedition to Middle America." 1925. MS, LAL. Second half of the original diary and typed copies of the complete diary.

(With Oliver Ricketson, Jr.) *Index to Ruins in the Maya Area* . . . . [Boston, 1925.] Mimeographed; 35 copies issued.

"The Report of the Tulane Archaeological and Ethnographical Expedition to Middle America." *New Orleans Life*, December 1925, pp. 25-26. Although no author is given, the majority of the article was obviously written by Blom.

"Field Letters." From 1925 expedition, mimeographed, five letters.

"Correspondence between E.E. Vater and Frans Blom." 1925. MS, LAL.

"'It Is the City of Stars!' Murmers Awe-Struck Indian Brought Home with Blom." Unidentified N.O. newspaper, August 20, 1925, Archives. Includes quotations by Blom.

"El observatorio más antiguo del Continente Americano . . . ." *Anales de Sociedad de Geografía e Historia de Guatemala* 2 (1926):335-38.

"Personal Diary, 1926." MS notebook, LAL.

"Louisiana Notes." 1926. MS, MARI. Archaeological data.

"Archaeological Objects from Morehouse Parish, Louisiana, Collected by Frans Blom, October 29-31, 1926." MS, MARI.

(With Oliver La Farge.) *Tribes and Temples. A Record of the Expedition to Middle America by the Tulane University of Louisiana in 1925.* 2 vols. N.O.: Tulane University of Louisiana, 1926-27. No authors' names are given on the title page.

"The John Geddings Gray Memorial Expedition, Its Route and Its Aims." [1927.] N.p., mimeographed. Plans for the expedition.

"Masterpieces of Maya Art. The Tomb at Comalcalco . . . ." *Art and Archaeology* 24 (1927):222-27; also as an offprint.

"Report Requested by the General Education Board, New York . . . ." December 28, 1927. MS, MARI. Application for a grant.

"Extracts from Letters between Ralph Roys and Frans Blom regarding Early Toltec Influence in the Maya Old Empire for the Use of O. G. Ricketson, Jr.." 1927. MS, Peabody.

"The Urgent Need of Anthropological and Sociological Research among the Inhabitants of the State of Louisiana." [1927?] MS, MARI. Probably by Blom.

"San Clemente Ruins, Peten, Guatemala (Chichantun)." *Journal de Société des Américanistes de Paris* 20 (1928):93-101; also as an offprint.

"Gaspar Antonio Chi, Interpreter." *American Anthropologist* 30 (1928):250-62; in Spanish, *Tribuna Israelita* (México City), February 20, 1946, pp. 9-11; and in *Icach* (Institución de ciencias y artes de Chiapas, Tuxtla Gutiérrez), no. 11 (1963):17-20.

"Index to Maya Ruins. . . ." 1928. MS, Peabody.

"Archaeological Notes." 1928. MS, MARI. Scientific data on the Gray Memorial Expedition.

"John Geddings Gray Expedition Field Letters." [1928.] Mimeographed; five letters.

"John Geddings Gray Memorial Expedition." [1928.] MS, 2 vols., LAL, MARI.

"Diary." 1928. MS, original and typed copy, MARI. His personal record of the Gray Memorial Expedition.

Department of Middle American Research . . . September 1928. N.O.

"Fourth Tulane Expedition Discovers Temples." Unidentified N.O. newspaper, March 1, 1928. The first field letter of the expedition.

Ruins in the Maya Area. After Blom and Ricketson, with Some Additions by Herbert J. Spinden, 1928, and Revised by Blom, 1928. N.O., 1929. A map. Several copies printed but not published.

Preliminary Report of the John Geddings Gray Memorial Expedition . . . , N.O., January 1928. N.O., 1929, pp. 3-23.

"Exploraciones en el departamento del Petén, Guatemala." *Anales de Sociedad de Geografía e Historia de Guatemala* 6 (1929):182-88.

"Remarks on the Classics of Middle American Research." MS, LAL. Address before Louisiana Library Association, April 19, 1929.

"La importancia de las investigaciones arqueológicas en el América Latina." *Nueva Patria* (New Orleans) 1, no. 2 (February 1929):7-8; also as an offprint.

"Foreword." For Phillips Russell, *Red Tiger* (New York: Brentano, 1929). MS, MARI. (The publisher refused to use it.)

"Preliminary Notes on Two Important Maya Finds." In *23d International Congress of Americanists, 1928.* New York, 1930, pp.165-71; also as an offprint.

"Uxmal, Great Capital of the Xiu Dynasty of the Maya." *Art and Archaeology* 30 (1930):199-209.

"Uxmal Notes." MS, LAL. Archaeological notes on buildings at Uxmal.

"Trails and No Trails. Concerning the John Geddings Gray Memorial Expedition, 1928, Conducted by Tulane University, through the Jungles of Central America." *Holland's: The Magazine of the South* (Dallas) 49 (February 1930):10-11, 29-30, 33, 35.

"Temple Used by Mayan Vestal Virgins 2,000 Years Ago Will Be Reconstructed." Knoxville *News-Standard,* May 25, 1930. Written for the Associated Press.

"The Uxmal Expedition." *The Tulane News Bulletin* 10, no. 7 (April 1930):111-14; also as an offprint. Reprints Field Letter no. 1, March 10, 1930.

"Index to Maya Ruins." *American Anthropologist* 32 (1930):572-74.

"A Maya 'Nunnery' as Model for a Chicago 'Fair' Building." *Illustrated London News,* August 23, 1930, pp. 338-40. No author is given, but Blom is credited for the photographs.

"Plan for the Founding of a Middle American Research Institute at the Tulane University of Louisiana." [1930.] MS, LAL, N.O.

"Review of Emma Lindsay Squier, *The Bride of the Sacred Well.*" *Art and Archaeology* 30 (December 1930):236.

"Blom Declares Maya Expedition Reached Goal." N.O. *Times-Picayune,* May 20, 1939. Quotes Blom.

"Field Letter, No. 2, Uxmal." April 14, 1930, mimeographed. Copy in Archives, Blom folder, and also in Edward T. Hinderliter, "The 1930 World's Fair Expedition to Uxmal, Yucatán, Mexico," M.A. thesis, Temple University, 1972.

"World's Fair to Portray Man's Advance." *Chicago Visitor,* September 1930, pp. 14-15, 25. Quotes Blom.

Ladd, Ada Mae. "Blom and Helpers to Bring Civilization to Maya Temple . . . ." *The Tulane Hullabaloo,* n.d. [1930];clipping in Kramer collection. Quotes Blom.

Campbell, Charles H. "Blom Expedition Sets Back Mayan City's Birth 500 Years." N.O. *Item,* n.d. [May 1930]; clipping in Kramer collection. Quotes Blom.

(With other authors.) "Summary of Archaeological Work . . . 1929 and 1930." *Pan American Bulletin* 65 (1931):400-414; also in *Pan American Union, American Archaeology, No. 5,* pp. 1-15; also in a Spanish translation.

"The Department of Middle American Research of the Tulane University of Louisiana." *Journal of the Louisiana Teachers' Association* 8, no. 8 (April 1931):20-21.

"Reconstructing a City of Ancient America." *Discovery* (London) 12 (May 1931):149-51.

"Ancient Skyscrapers and the World's Fair." *Commerce* (Chicago), March 21, 1931, pp. 14, 27-28.

"Tulane Mid-American Research Department Great Asset to the City." *Action* (N.O.), October 14, 1931, p. 17.

"Tulane University." *American Anthropologist* 33 (1931):300-301. Blom not identified as author; on his work at Uxmal.

"Mayan Symposium and Exhibits at New Orleans." *Science* 74 (December 4, 1931):570-71 contains a lengthy quotation by Blom on the history and collections of the Department of Middle American Research.

"Archaeological and Other Maps of Middle America." *Ibero-Amerikanische Archiv* (Berlin) 6, no. 3 (1932):1-5; also in *Ibero-American Review* 6 (1932):288-92; also as an offprint.

"The Maya Ball Game Pok-ta-pok (Called Tlatchli by the Aztecs)." In *Tulane University, Department of Middle American Research. Publication No. 4*, pp. 488-530. 1932.

"Maya Numbers." *Proceedings of the Louisiana Academy of Sciences* 1, no. 1 (August 1932):7-13.

"Commerce, Trade and Monetary Units of the Maya." In *Tulane University, Department of Middle American Research. Publication No. 4*, pp. 531-56. 1932. Also in *Smithsonian Institution Annual Report for 1934*. Washington, D.C., 1935, pp. 423-40. MS in Spanish, Na Bolom.

"The 'Negative Batter' at Uxmal." *Tulane University Department of Middle American Research, Publication No. 4, Middle American Papers*, pp. 557-66. 1932.

"The Ruins of Sayil in Yucatán." MS, LAL; also in Edward T. Hinderliter, "The 1930 World's Fair Expedition to Uxmal, Yucatán, Mexico," M.A. thesis, Temple University, 1972.

"Tomb Beats Tut's Says Blom." N.O. *Item-Tribune*, April 4, 1932. Quotes Blom on significance of Caso's discovery at Monte Albán.

"Review of Henry Rose Carter, *Yellow Fever. An Epidemiological and Historical Study of Its Place of Origin*." *American Anthropologist* 34 (1932):537-38.

"Review of Miles Poindexter, *The Ayer-Inca*." *Art and Archaeology* 33 (1932):164.

"Maya Books and Sciences." *Library Journal* 3 (1933):408-20; also MS, LAL.

"Short Summary of Recent Exploration in the Ruins of Uxmal, Yucatan." In *24th International Congress of Americanists, 1930*. Hamburg: Selbstverlag der Staats and Universitats Bibliotek, 1933, pp. 55-59.

"L'Art Maya." *Gazette des Beaux Arts* 10 (December 1933):321-40.

(With S.S. Grosjean and H. Cummins.) "Historical Background." In *A Maya Skull from the Uloa Valley. Tulane University Department of Middle American Research Publication* No. 5, pp. 7-14. 1933. Also in *Revista Conservadora del Pensamiento Centroamericano* (Managua), March 8-11, 1968, and in *Anales de Sociedad de Geografía e Historia de Guatemala* 10 (1933):32-36.

"Copies of Maya Documents." MS, LAL. Annotations by Blom and Ralph Roys.

"From Tropic Jungles Comes World's Fair Temple." World's Fair press release for Sunday papers, June 4, 1933.

"Proposed Museum and Library of the Department of Middle American Research of the Tulane University of Louisiana." N.O., 1933. MS, LAL.

"Bringing Home the Maya Temple." *Official World's Fair Weekly*, May 13, 1933, pp. 31-32.

"Finding a Civilization in the Jungle." *Official World's Fair Weekly*, June 10, 1933, pp. 40-45.

(With other authors.) "Summary of Archaeological Work in Middle America, 1931, 1932, 1933." *Pan American Bulletin* 67 (1934):861-82; also in *Pan American Union, American Archaeology*, no. 7, 1935.

"New Exhibits for the Maya Temple in Chicago." *Tulane News Bulletin* 14 (1934):91-92. No author indicated.

(Editor.) *Maya Research*, 3 vols. July 1934-October 1936

"Diego de Landa. Relación de las Cosas de Yucatán." *Maya Research* 1 (1934):53-54.

"The First International Congress of Anthropological and Ethnological Sciences, London, July 30 to August 4." *American Anthropologist* 36 (1934):636-37.

"Department of Middle American Research, Tulane." [1935?] MS, Archives.

"Notes: A Hitherto Unrecovered Building at Labná, Yucatán." *Maya Research* 2 (1935):189-90.

"The Pestac Stela . . . ." *Maya Research* 2 (1935):190-91.

"History below the Surface; Talk . . . ." Tulane University Chapter of Sigma Xi, [N.O.], November 6, 1935. Mimeographed; 50 copies.

"Clark's Tours. Historical Pamphlets on Guatemala. Frans Blom, Editor." MS, Na Bolom.

"Department of Middle American Research . . . ." [1935?] Mimeographed.

"History in the Garbage Can." [1935?] MS, LAL.

"The 'Gomesta Manuscript,' a Falsification." *Maya Research* 2 (1935):233-48.

"More Fakes." *Maya Research* 2 (1935):249-50.

"Airminded Honduras." *Pan American Union Bulletin* 69 (September 1935):687-93; also as a separate in Spanish translation.

"Blom Diary, Honduras, 1935." MS, MARI. The reverse of the early pages contains a long letter to his wife.

"A Checklist of Falsified Maya Codices." *Maya Research* 2 (1935):251-52.

"Maya Calculation and Construction." *The Military Engineer* 27 (1935):1-5; also as an offprint.

"The Ruins of Copán and the Earthquake." *Maya Research* 2 (1935):290-91.

"Note on 'The Temple of the Warriors at Chichen Itza, Yucatan,' by Earl Morris, Jean Charlot and Anne Axtel Morris . . . ." *Maya Research* 2 (1935):203-15.

"Letter to the Editor." N.O. *Tribune*, February 8, 1935.

"A Visit to Quirigua . . . (after 1852) from the Original Manuscript of Dr. Carl Scherzer . . . ." *Maya Research* 3 (1936):92-101; Spanish translation, *Anales de Sociedad de Geografía e Historia de Quatemala* 13 (1937):447-57; also as an offprint.

"Codex Tulane the Most Complete Original Mixtec Pictorial Manuscript in the U.S.A.." *Anthropos* (St. Gabriel-Möoling) 31 (1936):238-39. No author given. Also as a leaflet, n.p., n.d.

"Blom Sees Orleans Dump Heap as Archaeological Treasure Trove . . . ." N.O. *Item-Tribune*, August 30, 1936. Quotes Blom.

(With Hermann Beyer.) "Fine Clay Flasks from the Southern Maya Area." 1936. MS, LAL.

The Conquest of Yucatan. Boston and New York: Houghton Mifflin Co., 1936. Reprinted New York: Cooper Square Publishers, 1971. Spanish translation of chapters 21-30, 32: *La vida de los Maya,* Mexico City: La Biblioteca Enciclopedia Popular, 1944. Idem., Guatemala; Biblioteca de cultura popular, no. 2, 195- and 1967. Danish translation by Jens Yde, *Mayalandets Erobring,* Copenhagen: J. Gjellerup, 1945. For reviews, see *Book Review Digest, 1936* (New York: H.W. Wilson Co., 1937), pp. 98-99.

A Museum and Library for the Department of Middle American Research. . . . 1936. A brochure.

"Editor's Note." *Maya Research* 3 (1936): 1, 229-30.

"An Exhibit Arranged by the Department of Middle American Research of Tulane University Entitled 'The Maya—Past and Present.' " [N.O.] 1937.

"Past Meets Present in America's Fair." *Southwest Business: Official Pan American Exposition Magazine* (Dallas), June 1937, pp. 10-11, 30-31.

"The Maya of Central America." In *The Art of the Maya, November 15th to December 15th 1937.* Baltimore: Baltimore Museum of Art, 1937.

"The Mayas." *Mexican Life* (Mexico City), September 1937, pp. 25-27, 52-57.

(With Maurice Ries and F. Webster McBryde.) "In the Shadow of Volcanos." MS, copy in Mr. Ries's possession.

"A Selective Guide to the Material Published in 1938 . . . ." In *Handbook of Latin American Studies, 1938.* Cambridge, Mass.: Harvard University Press, 1939, pp. 10-19. MS, MARI.

"Middle America." In *Golden Gate International Exposition, San Francisco. Department of Fine Arts. Division of Pacific Cultures.* San Francisco: Golden Gate International Exposition, 1939, pp. 146-48. Followed by photographs and catalog of the exposition.

"Foreword." In Addison Burbank, *Guatemalan Profile.* New York: Coward-McCann, 1939, p. vii.

"Cherchez la femme Maya, or Women's Place among the Ancient Maya." MS in English and also in Spanish translation, Na Bolom.

"Blom Tells How Columbus Made Greatest Error." N.O. *Times-Picayune,* October 8, 1939. Quotes Blom.

"Coronel Modesto Méndez, Explorador del Petén, Guatemala, 1848 y 1852—Tikal, Ixkún y Yxtutz." *Anales de Sociedad de Geografía e Historia de Guatemala* 16 (1940):167-79; also in *Antropología e Historia de Guatemala* 7, no. 2 (June 1955):3-10.

Archaeological Sites in the Maya Area, 1940 Edition for Use with "Index to Maya Sites" (1940) in Middle American Research Institute. Revision of the Frans Blom–O.G. Ricketson, Jr., Map "Ruins in the Maya Area" (1924) . . . Middle American Research Institute, Prepared under a Grant from the Carnegie Institution of Washington. Map in 8 sections.

"Yucatan." *New Horizons* 9, no. 10 (July 1941):2-3.

"Notes on Some Lacandón Arrows Collected in 1928 by Frans Blom." 1942. MS, Na Bolom.

(Translator.) "The Sacred Books of the Quiché Indians: Popul Vuh." 1942. MS, Na Bolom.

"Review of Francisco Hernández Córdoba, *The Diary of Yucatán,* translated by Henry Wagner." *Hispanic American Historical Review* 22 (1942):745-47.

"Diary, 1943-44." MS, Na Bolom.

"Lista de ruinas arqueológicas en la parte este del estado de Chiapas." 1943-44. MS, Na Bolom.

"Report on Zona Romano, Selva Lacandona, Chiapas . . . ." 1943-44. MS, Na Bolom.

"El Desierto de Zendala, Estado de Chiapas. Notas para una mapa preliminar." 1944. MS, Na Bolom.

"Terra Zoque, Chiapas . . . ." 1944. MS, Na Bolom.

"Chiapas y el turismo." *Chiapas Nuevo* (Tuxtla Gutiérrez), August 3, 10, 1944.

Mapa de selva lacandona . . . . 1944.

"Palabras preliminares." In Gertrude Duby, *Los Lacandones* . . . . Mexico: Biblioteca Enciclopedia Popular, 1944, no. 30, pp. ix-x.

"Miguel Angel Fernández." *El Nacional* (Mexico City), December 2, 1945.

"Cacao." 1945. MS, Na Bolom.

"El indio se vuelve cuidadano." *Asi* (Mexico City), November 24, 1945, pp. 14-15.

"Treasures in the Jungle." *Mexican American Review* (Mexico City), February 1945, pp. 32-33.

"El lienzo de Analco, Oaxaca." *Cuadernos Americanos* (Mexico City) 4 (November-December 1945):125-36. Also as an offprint. MS, Na Bolom.

"You Have No Idea How Much Work It Takes—Chicle from Mexico." *Mexican American Review* (Mexico City), February 1945, pp. 32-33.

"El enigma de la arqueología de Chiapas. Una nota." 1945. MS, Na Bolom.

"The Lienzo of Tlascala." 1945. MS, Na Bolom.

"La estrella de David en Chiapas . . . la sal de la tierra'. . . ." *Tribuna Israelita* (Mexico City), July 15, 1945. MSS of English and Spanish versions, Na Bolom.

"Proyecto para estudios arqueológicos en el estado de Chiapas." 1945. MS, Na Bolom.

R.P. Fray Tomás de la Torre–Desde Salamanca, España, hasta Ciudad Real, Chiapas. Diario de viaje, 1544-45. Mexico City: Editora Central [1945]. Prologue and notes by Blom. MS of English translation, Na Bolom.

"Indio Sagaz." *Tribuna Israelita* (Mexico City), November 15, 1945.

"El gran camino de America." *Asi* (Mexico City), December 8, 15, 22, 1945; also in *Nuevo Mundo*, September-November 1949.

"El turista descubre bellos pueblos y ricas zonas, en el route hácia las tierras del cacao. Lo que es una fiesta nupcial en el istmo Tehuano." *Asi* (Mexico City), December 15, 1945.

"The Fairest of Maya Cities." *Mexican American Review* (Mexico City), March 1945.

"John Lloyd Stephens en Mexico." 1945. MS, Na Bolom. Blom's translation of Stephens's text.

"Apuntas sobre los ingenieros Mayas." *Irrigación en México* (Mexico City) 27, no. 3 (July-September 1946):5-16. Also as an offprint. MS, Na Bolom.

(With Gertrude Duby.) "Darkness to All Who Dwell There." *Natural History* 55 (1946):231-32, 237, 239. MS, Na Bolom, bears the original title, "Orchids and Onchocerciasis."

"Mil años de olvido: Yaxchilán, la ciudad sagrada de los Mayas." *Mañana* (Mexico City), no. 157, August 31, 1946.

"All-American Dinner Cooked by Frans Blom." *México Habla* (Mexico City), March-April 1946. MS, Na Bolom.

"An All-American Dinner Served by Frans Blom." 1946. MS, Na Bolom. This is a different version from the published article, noted above.
"Plan for Photographic Record of the Principal Maya Ruined Cities." January 1947. MS, Na Bolom.
"Las Maravillas de Malinalco." *Esta Semana* (Mexico City), February 15-21, 1947.
"La riquesa arqueológica en Mexico." *Novedades* (Mexico City), January 1, 1947.
"Ruinas, Ojos de Agua. Cedro. Miscellaneous Notes, Drawings, Etc....." MS, Na Bolom.
"Informe sobre la región de los Lacandones." *Excelsior* (Mexico City), December 15, 1948. A letter to the editor by the Bloms.
"Turismo a Bonampak." 1948. MS, Na Bolom.
"Diaries, 1948." MS, Na Bolom. Record of three expeditions that year.
"Antes y ahora. F.C. Interoceánico México-Veracruz." *Ferronales* (Mexico City) 19, no. 5 (May 1948):11-12.
"Viaje a Chiapas (Antología por Fray Alonzo Ponce)." *Cuadernos de Chiapas* (Chiapas, Depto. de biblioteca), no. 14 (1948). Copy with interleaved notes by Blom, Na Bolom.
(Report on his activities.) *Teocentli* (Rochester, N.Y.), June 1948, p. 1.
"Expedición a las ruinas de Bonampak, Chiapas." [1948?] MS, Na Bolom.
"Notas sobre Bonampak: The Murals at the Maya Ruin of Bonampak, Lacandon Forests? . . . or What Not Preserved the Murals of Bonampak." MS in Spanish, followed by "Frescoes or Not" in English, Na Bolom. Binder's title gives 1948.
"Informe sobre las ruinas de Bonampak y Yaxchilán." April 7, 1948. MS, Na Bolom.
"Indice geográfico de mapa de la Selva Lacandona." 1948. MS, Na Bolom.
"La ciudad perdida de los Mayas." *Nuevo Mundo* 5 (August 1949):10-15.
"Noches en la selva lacandona (extracto del Diario de F.B.)." *Prometheus* (Mexico City) 1, no. 3 (1949):203-6.
"Ciudades misteriosas en la Selva Lacandona." *El Nacional* (Mexico City), supplement, May 8, 1949, p. 6. Also MS, Na Bolom.
(With Gertrude Duby.) "Entre los indios lacandones de Mexico." *América Indígena* (Institute Indigenista Interamericana, Mexico City) 9, no. 2 (April 1949):155-64. Includes a summary in English.
(With Gertrude Duby.) "Mañana en la selva Chiapaneca." *Revista Manana* (Mexico City), February-March 1949, pp. 36-44, 34-41, 36-43, 28-35.
(With Gertrude Duby.) "Preliminary Explorations in the Lacandon Zone." *Boletín Indigenista* (Mexico City) 9 (1949):80-83. Spanish and English texts.
"Alonso Dávila Cruz a la selva Lacandona en 1529 . . . Anotaciones de Frans Blom." *Chiapas* (Tuxtla Gutiérrez), December 1, 1949, pp. 24-29; with English summary.
"Lacanjá, Chis. La posible ciudad perdida del Imperio Maya." *Novedades* (Mexico City), August 12, 1949. Blom quoted.
"Tausand Jahre Vergessenheit, Yaxchilan, die heilige Stadt der Mayas." *Demokratische Post* (Mexico City), February 1, 1949.
"A Polychrome Maya Plate from Quintana Roo." *Carnegie Institution of Washington, Notes on Middle American Archaeology and Ethnology*, no. 98 (Cambridge, Mass., 1950), pp. 81-84.
"Diary." 1950-51. MS, Na Bolom. 3 vols. Expeditions to Selva Lacandona.

(With Gertrude Duby.) "Los Tuxtlos Fracción del Eden dentro de México." *Esta Semana* (Mexico City), January 7-13, 1950, pp. 35-36; January 14-20, 1950, pp. 37-40.

(With Gertrude Duby.) "Sendas en la jungla." *Voz*, September 14, 1950, pp. 9-12.

"Bonampak. Note on Carnegie Institution of Washington Publication 602 and mapa de Bonampak." [1950?] MS, Na Bolom.

Juan Ballinas–el Desierto de los Lacandes. Memorias, 1876-1877. Tuxtla Gutiérrez: Ateneo de Chiapas, 1951. Introduction and notes by Frans Blom; photographs by Gertrude Duby.

"Diary." 1951. MS, Na Bolom. Record of expeditions.

(Account of his activities.) *Teocentli* (Rochester, N.Y.), June 1951, pp. 2-3; also December 1951, pp. 1-2.

"Tikal, esplendor de los Mayas." [1951?] MS, Na Bolom.

School of Anthropological Field Work . . . 1 July to 15 August 1950 . . . . n.p., n.d.

Summer School on Field Methods . . . July 1 to August 15, 1952. n.p., n.d.

"Apuntas Bonampak 1951." MS, Na Bolom. Account of his three visits to the site.

"Bonampaquitis." *Novedades* (Mexico City), September 21, 1952, p. 4.

(Account of his activities.) *Teocentli* (Rochester, N.Y.), December 1952, pp. 1-2.

First Chiapas Expedition of the Maya Order . . . . [1952.] N.p. Account of his excavation of Moxviquil.

Correspondence with Edith R. Bayles. 1952-56. MS, LAL.

"Chiapas Indígena." *Novedades* (Mexico City), September 21, 1952, p. 1.

"San Cristóbal las Casas." *Novedades* (Mexico City), September 21, 1952, p. 3.

"Correspondence con Charles Upson Clark. Reports and Letters from Investigations of European Archives, 1952-54. MS, Na Bolom.

"Datos sobre las zonas históricas del Sureste, y futuro en la Selva Lacandona." January 1952. MS, Na Bolom.

"Early Colonial Buildings in San Cristobal . . . ." [1952?] MS, Na Bolom.

"Paa Skovtur: Paa jagt efter Maya Ruin byer i Staten Chiapas Urskove, Mexico." 1952. MS, Na Bolom.

La selva lacandona y tierres colindantes. San Cristóbal las Casas, Chiapas, 1953. A map.

" 'Forever Amber,' Being the Story of the Search for Amber Containing Insects in the Region of Simojovel, State of Chiapas, Mexico. On Behalf of the University of California . . . ." 1953. MS, Na Bolom.

(Account of his activities.) *Teocentli* (Rochester, N.Y.), December 1953, pp. 2-3.

"Notes on Bonampak for Rowland Goodman. " MS, Na Bolom.

"Ossuaries, Cremation and Secondary Burials among the Maya of Chiapas, Mexico." *Journal de la Société des Américanistes de Paris* 43 (1954): 123-35. Also MS, Na Bolom.

"La lápida de Chiapas." *Ateneo* (Chiapas) 5 (January-April 1954):41-44. Also MS, Na Bolom.

(With Gertrude Duby.) "Amber, Tobacco, Earthquakes and Coffee. Record of a Twenty-Five Days' Ride among the Central Mountains of the State of Chiapas, Mexico." 1954. MS, Na Bolom.

(Account of his activities.) *Teocentli* (Rochester, N.Y.), June 1954, p.2.

"El retablo de Teopisca en Chiapas." *Anales del Instituto de Investigaciones Estéticas* (Mexico City) 23 (1955):39-42.

(With Gertrude Duby.) *La selva lacandona*. 2 vols. Mexico City: Editorial Cultura, 1955-57.

(Account of his activities.) *Teocentli* (Rochester, N.Y.), December 1955, pp. 2-3.

"Bonampak." [1955?] MS, Na Bolom.

"How Long is a 'una legua'?" April 1955. MS, Na Bolom.

"Relación de los pueblos que comprende el obispado de Chiapas...." 1955. MS, Na Bolom. Notes by Blom.

"On Slotkin's 'Fermented Drinks in Mexico.'" *American Anthropologist* 58 (1956):185-86.

"A Letter from Frans Blom." *New World Antiquity* (London) 3 (1956):133-34. Also MS, Na Bolom.

"Vida precortesiana del indio Chiapaneco de hoy." In *Estudios Antropológicos en Homenaje al Doctor Manuel Gamio*. Mexico City: Universidad Nacional Autónoma de México, Sociedad Mexicana de Antropología, 1956, pp. 277-85. Also in *Revista de Ciencias Sociales* (San Cristóbal), February 1962, pp. 13-17. MSS in Spanish and English, Na Bolom.

(Account of his activities.) *Teocentli* (Rochester, N.Y.), November 1956, pp. 4-5.

(With Gertrude Duby.) "Paths through the Jungles: Senderos en la jungla." *Welcome, Bienvenidos a Mexico*, December 1956, pp. 89, 91-97.

"Notes on the Falsified Codex of Prague. Nov. 10, 1956...." MS, Na Bolom.

"La gran laguna de los Lacandones." *Tlatoani* (Mexico City), segunda epoca, no. 10 (June 1956):4-9.

"Notas sobre la selva. Compaña contra Paludismo." December 1956. MS, Na Bolom.

(With Gertrude Duby de Blom.) "Chilón, Chiapas, El Cerro de Nah-Ten-Tzum." October 7-8, 1956. MS, Na Bolom.

"Bibliográfia selectiva de los Lacandones." *Revista de Ciencias Sociales* (San Cristóbal, Chiapas), April 1957, pp. 25-29.

"Remarks on 'Working Bibliography: Tzeltal Tzotzil,' for E.Z. Vogt, *Revised Tzotzil-Tzeltal Bibliography*. December 1957. MS, Na Bolom.

(Account of his activities.) *Teocentli* (Rochester, NY.), November 1957, pp. 2-3.

"La biblioteca de San Cristóbal de las Casas." *Boletín Bibliográfico* (México City), March 15, 1958. p.3.

(Account of his activities.) *Teocentli* (Rochester, N.Y.), November 1958, pp. 2-3.

"Ruinas de Natezum, Muctana y otras cerca de Chilón, Chiapas." 1958. MS, Na Bolom.

"Historical Notes on the Amber Trade." August 1958. MS, Na Bolom.

"La vida de los Maya." *Nicaragua Indígena* (Managua) epoca 6, 3 (July-August 1958):14-20.

"Historical Notes relating to the pre-Columbian Amber Trade from Chiapas." *Amerikanische Miszellen (Mitteilungen aus dem Museum für Volkerkunde im Hamburg*, XXV) (1959):24-27. MS, Na Bolom.

"Tres Radio, causerier, tilsendt Dansk States Radio, Kobenhavn, Danmark." 1959. MS, Na Bolom. Speech in Danish Embassy, Mexico, June 10, 1959.

"Review of Jorgen Bitsch, *Jivaro*." *Hispanic American Historical Review* 39 (1959): 483.

"Chiapas Adventure." *Mexico This Month*, February 1960, pp. 13, 19-20. MS, Na Bolom.

"Notas sobre algunas ruinas todavía sin explorar." In *Sociedad Mexicana de Antropología. Mesa Redonda VIII*. México City: 1961, pp. 115-25. MS, Na Bolom.

"Dos filologos en Chiapas (Charles Etienne Brasseur de Bourbourg and Carl Hermann Berendt)." 1961. MS, Na Bolom.

(Account of his activities.) *Teocentli* (Rochester, N.Y.), November 1961, pp. 6-7.

(Account of his activities.) *Teocentli*, (Rochester, N.Y.), November 1962, p. 6.

(With Gertrude Duby.) "Proyecto para declarar 'Parque Nacional' al territorio en que se encuentran las ruinas Mayas de Yaxchilán." *Icach* (Instituto de ciencias y artes de Chiapas, Tuxtla Gutiérrez), no. 11, (1963):15-16. MS, Na Bolom. Written 1959.

Selection from "Monteador." *Siempre!* (Mexico City), supplement no. 91, November 13, 1963, pp. ii-vi.

"Hernán Cortés e el libro de trajes de Cristoph Weiditz." *Icach*, no. 11 (July-December 1963):7-14. MS, Na Bolom. Written 1945.

(With Gertrude Duby.) "The Lacandons." In *Handbook of Middle American Indians*, ed. Robert Wauchope and Gordon R. Willey, Vol. 7. Austin: University of Texas Press, 1969, pp. 276-97.

Robert Wauchope, *They Found the Buried Cities* (Chicago: University of Chicago Press, 1965), pp. 295-307, gives a selection from Blom's writings.

For maps by Blom at Tulane, see *An Inventory of the Collections of the Middle American Research Institute, No. 4, Maps in the Library of the Middle American Research Institute...*, N.O. 1941, mimeographed. Lists 38 items by Blom.

Without date

"Archaeology. Miscellaneous Plans, Charts and Drawings." MS, Na Bolom. On Maya ruins in Chiapas; much of this material was used *La selva lacandona*, vol. 2.

"Andanza misteriosa . . . en Chiapas." MS, Na Bolom.

Annotations to the following works: "Alvérez de Miranda Capitán Don Pedro, 1965. Relación escrito por el"; "Crónica de Maya," interleaved with annotations by Frans Blom and Ralph Roys (not found; noted by Arthur Gropp in his list of MSS at MARI); "Relación de Zapotitlán, Gutatmala, 1579," MS, Na Bolom.

"Art in Ancient America. The Art of the Maya." MS, Na Bolom.

"Agua potable para Mexico en tiempo de los Aztecto: Dos cartas según Cortés y Bernal Díaz." MS, Na Bolom.

"Bibliografía Chiapas." MS, Na Bolom; with two supplements.

"Buscando ciudades Maya." MS, Na Bolom.

"La Cabeza 'Saqueda' de las ruinas de Bonampak." MS, Na Bolom.

"Chicle Camps and Archaeological Investigations." MS, Na Bolom.

"Counting Fives Maya Style." MS, Na Bolom.

"Datos geográficos del estado de Chiapas, Mexico." MS, Na Bolom.
"Datos sobre al murciélago Vampire." MS, Na Bolom.
"The Frightful Earthquake of Guatemala, 1541...Notas por Frans Blom." MS, Na Bolom.
"Unos Hallazgos Antiquísimos que son nuevos...." MS, Na Bolom.
"Hallazgos Maya en Chiapas." MS, Na Bolom.
(With Gertrude Duby.) "Index to Archaeological Sites in Various Places in the Chiapas Area." MS, Na Bolom.
"Una magnífica edición nueva de los códices Mexicanos aperce en Dinamarca." MS, Na Bolom.
"Maya Ruins." MS, Na Bolom.
"Ruinas de Toniná; Tenam; Yaxchilán, la ciudad maravillosa de los Maya." MS, Na Bolom.
"Notes on Zapotel, Chiapas, Mexico." MS, not found.
"Tata, a Prince of an Indian." MS, LAL
"Notes by Frans Blom." MS, Na Bolom. About colonial buildings of San Cristóbal, its Indians, and flowers of Comitán.
Interleaved corrections to Carlos E. Castañeda and Jack A. Dobbs, eds., *Guide to the Latin American Manuscripts in the University of Texas Library.* Cambridge, Mass.: Harvard University Press, 1939.
"Tentative Bibliography of Zapotec Texts." Not found. Blom said that this article was accepted for publication in *International Journal of American Linguistics;* it did not appear.

Index

Aalsborg, Denmark, 130
Abreu, Raul Pavón, 189
Adams, Robert, 209
Agua Azul, Mexico, 219
Agua Escondida, Mexico, 48, 81, 157
Aguilar, Ciriaco, 89, 91-103 passim,
  115, 116, 251-54 passim
Aguilar, Francisco de, 198
Album of Maya Architecture
  (Proskouriakoff), 226
Alemán Valdés, Miguel, 228
Alférez, Enrique, 115, 116, 117
Alvírez, Leandro, 49
American Anthropological Society, 33
American Association for the
  Advancement of Science, 122, 123
American Folk-Lore Society, 33
American Geographical Society, 77-78
American Library Association, 75
American Museum of Natural
  History, New York City, 65, 128,
  210
Amram, David, 75
Amsden, A. Monroe, 12, 37
Anaïte, Mexico, 165, 186, 255
Analco, lienzo of, 197-98
Ancient Maya, The (Morley), 225
Anderson, Sherwood, 3
Andrews, Prentiss, 120
Antigüedades Mexicanas, 199
Antwerp, Belgium, 233
Archives of the Indies, 203
Are There Laws? (Blom), 135
Arévalo, Hector, 167
Arriaga, Mexico, 25
Armour, Allison, 33
Art and Archaeology, 136
Ateneo de Chiapas, 223
Ayer-Inca, The (Poindexter), 136

Bacalar, Mexico, 91, 107
Baer, Mary (Mrs. Philip Baer), 179-80
Baer, Philip (Felipe), 178-80
Ballard, Marshall, 41
ball courts, in Chiapas, 109
Ballinas, Juan, 227
Baltimore Museum of Art, 124
Banavil, Mexico, 181, 183-84
Bascán Valley, Mexico, 56
Becal, Mexico, 117
Belize, British Honduras, 35, 37, 38,
  107

Berendt, Karl Hermann, 203
Berne, Switzerland, 147
Beyer, Hermann: account of, 85-87;
  mentioned, 5, 72, 79, 259n
Bibliothèque Nationale, Paris, 203
Biologia Centrali-Americana
  (Maudslay), 33, 131
Blasillo River, Mexico, 46
Blom, Albert (Frans's father), 18-19,
  20-21
Blom, Dora (Frans's mother), 18-19,
  21, 200
Blom, Esther (Frans's sister), 19
Blom, Gertrude Duby (Frans's second
  wife): account of, 147; interest in
  Lacandón Indians, 172-77, 213,
  216-17; meets Blom, 148-49; at Na
  Bolom, 201, 206, 213-17;
  mentioned, x, 4-5, 184, 186, 191,
  197, 218, 227, 228, 229, 231
Blom, Mary (Frans's first wife):
  account of, 7-8; mentioned, 123
Blom, Vera (Frans's sister), 19
Bonampak, Mexico, 153, 188-91,
  192-93, 218, 222
Bonampak Ballet, 223
Bor, Vicente, 214-17
Bosada, David, 48
Bourne, John, 189
Bowman, Isaiah, 260n
Brasseur de Bourbourg, Charles
  Étienne, 203
Brentano's (publishing company), 136
Breton, Adela, 4
Bride of the Sacred Well, The
  (Squier), 136
Bristow, Louis, 89-113 passim; letter
  by, 251-54
British Honduras, 35, 37, 79, 122. *See
  also* Belize
British Museum, London, 33, 35, 78,
  203
Brookhaven, Miss., 14
Brown, Mrs. Jessie K., 232
Bulnes, Enrique, 53
Burwash, Nat, 210
Byers, Douglas, 51, 71, 83, 88
Byrd, Richard, 126

Callejones Valley, Honduras, 121
Cambridge, Mass., 34, 40, 44
Cámera, Ramón, 187

Campeche, Mexico, 117, 189
Carl Schurz Foundation, 12
Carnegie, Andrew, 34
Carnegie Institution of Washington, 11, 26, 33, 34, 35-36, 40-44, 76, 77, 79, 120, 189, 202, 227
Carrillo, Felipe, 35
Caso, Alfonso, 153, 189, 214, 219, 222-23, 233
Centurión, Pepe, 163
Century Club, N.Y., 6
Century Company, 131
chaltunes, in Chiapas, 109
Chamula Indians, 58-59, 201
Charlot, Jean, 136
Charnay, Désiré, 46-47, 260n
"Cherchez la femme Maya" (Blom), 137
Chi, Gaspar Antonio, 134
Chiapas, Mexico: Blom's map of, x, 174, 193-94, 198, 228; mentioned, ix, 4, 15, 16-17, 24, 30-31, 33, 35, 39, 45, 46, 51, 52, 54, 55, 60, 61, 75, 83, 89, 91, 104, 109, 111, 112, 113, 130, 141, 142, 147, 148, 151, 153, 156, 166, 169, 171, 178, 180, 181, 186, 188, 189, 193, 195-98 passim, 199, 200, 202-4 passim, 207, 209, 212-13, 217, 218, 225-29 passim, 232, 234, 235, 237, 238, 243, 245, 248
Chiapas State Museum, Mexico, 199, 222
Chichén Itzá, Mexico, 4, 11, 26, 31, 35-38 passim, 44, 76, 86, 91, 107, 113, 116, 118, 126, 138, 188
Chimila, Guatemala, 107
Chinkultic, Mexico, 48, 110
Chixoy River, Mexico, 219
Chontol language, 52
Clark, Charles Upson, 203
Cline, H. C., 204
Coatzacoalcos River, Mexico, 23
Columbia University, 26
Columbus, Christopher, 128
Comalcalco, Mexico: Blom discovers stucco figures, 47-48; mentioned, 54, 55, 57, 63, 76, 80
Comitán, Mexico, 50, 91, 93, 109, 222, 223, 255, 256
Concordia, Mexico, 196
Congress of Anthropology and History, 220
Conquest of Yucatan (Blom), 127, 133-34, 197, 228
Convici Friede (publishers), 133
Cook, James, 136

Cook, Orator S., 192
Coon, Carleton, 151
Copán, Honduras, 78, 120, 121, 187-88
Copenhagen, Denmark, 9, 19, 20, 32, 130, 153
Cordan, Wolfgang, 225-26
Cortés, Fernando: manuscripts of, 74, 75; mentioned, 124, 227
Costa Rica, 123
Coyoacán, Mexico, 4
Cristolino, Mexico, 181, 182
Cristolino River, Mexico, 157
Cruz, Aureo, 52-53, 110
Cruz, Ulises de la, 186-87
Cuilco River, Mexico, 167
Cuyamel Fruit Company, 41, 90

Dallas, Tex., 124
Danish National Museum, 32, 119
"Darkness to All Who Dwell There" (Blom), 196-97
Denmark, ix, 18-21, 32, 44, 130, 200, 212. See also Copenhagen
Department of Middle American Research, Tulane University. See Middle American Research Institute
Detroit Fine Arts Museum, 124
Dial (magazine), 83
Díaz del Castillo, Bernal, 154
Dinwiddie, Albert: and Blom, 43, 67, 69, 73-74, 83, 84, 103-4, 132, 256; mentioned, 40, 44, 62-66 passim, 82
Dirección de Antropología, Mexico, 26, 28
Dix, Dorothy (Mrs. E. M. Gilmor), 7
Dixon, Roland, 151
Don Quixote (Cervantes), 154
Dresden Codex, 4, 43, 86, 224
Duby, Gertrude. See Blom, Gertrude Duby
Durham, J. Wyatt, 209

Eagle Oil Company, 23, 24
Eastman, George, 91
Editorial Cultura, 228
El Cayo, British Honduras, 37, 107
El Cedro, Mexico, 160-61, 162, 164-65, 182, 184-85, 188, 191, 218
El México antiguo, 85
El Peñol, Mexico, 218
El Real, Mexico, 174, 178, 182, 214, 215, 218, 231
El Retiro, Mexico, 48
El Rosario Ranch, Mexico, 108-9
El Zapote, Mexico, 181, 183

Encanto (finca), Mexico, 48, 89
Encyclopaedia Britannica, 202
Ethnos, 26, 27
Excelsior, 190-91
Exploration Society, Tulane
University, 71
Explorers Club, N.Y., 5, 33, 112, 219

Fair, Herndon, 115, 116
Fairfield Aerial Survey, 115
Faulkner, William, 3, 82
Field Museum, Chicago, 76
Flores, Guatemala, 91, 103, 105-6,
255, 256
Frey, Carlos (Charles), 162-64, 189-90
Frick, Childs, 44, 260n
Frontera, Mexico, 24, 46, 57

Gamboa, Rafael, 148, 150, 214
Gamio, Manuel, 26, 27, 31, 32, 35, 47,
131, 166, 168, 260n
Gann, Thomas, 34-35, 78-79
Garrido, Ramírez, 26, 27, 259n
Gates, William: and Blom, 41, 61-64
passim, 90, 260n; head of
Department of Middle American
Research, 42-44 passim, 61-69
passim, 71, 72-73; mentioned, 33,
35, 37, 40, 124, 131, 135, 136
Gazette des Beaux Arts, 135
General Education Board, N.Y., 71
Gilmor, Mrs. E. M. *See* Dix, Dorothy
Golden Gate International
Exposition, San Francisco, 124
Gomesta manuscript, 135, 136, 224
Gonzalez, Epifanio, 90, 92, 99, 251
Gray, Henry, 89
Gray, John Geddings, 89
Gray, Matilda, 7, 70-71, 76, 89, 104,
151
Gray, William, 89
Gray Memorial Expedition, 12, 15,
77, 88-113, 132, 251-56 passim
Greater Texas and Pan American
Exhibition, Dallas, Tex., 124
Grijalva River, Mexico, 54
Gropp, Arthur, 12, 72, 74, 75, 204,
260-61n
Guatemala, 3, 13, 35, 37, 41, 51, 52,
56, 70, 83, 88, 89, 113, 123, 137,
197, 202, 233, 245
Guatemala City, Guatemala, 60

*Handbook of Middle American
Indians*, 227
Hanover, Emil, 19
Harris, Rufus, 125, 139

Harvard Club of Boston, 33
Harvard Club of New Orleans, 5
Harvard University, 26, 31-34 passim,
40, 45, 65, 77, 78, 79, 151, 209, 220,
223
Hay, Clarence, 65
Hayden, William, 115
Healey, Giles, 189-91 passim, 232
Heim, Roger, 210
Hernández Guillermo, Lázaro, 51-52,
60-61, 132, 243-49, 260n
Heye Museum, New York City, 33
"History below the Surface" (Blom),
128
"History in the Garbage Can" (Blom),
128
Hitler, Adolf, 129, 147
Höffding, Harald, 19
Hoffman, Frederick L., 78
Holland's, Magazine of the South,
132
Honduras, 62, 65, 76, 120, 123-24,
136, 141
Hooton, Earnest A., 151
Houghton Mifflin Co., 84, 133, 137,
227-28
Huaca, Mexico, 183
Huehuetenango, Guatemala, 60
Huixtla, Mexico, 167
Hun Chabín, Mexico, 48
Hunter College, 220
Huntington, Archer M., 33
Hurd, Paul, 209
Hyatt Foundation, 135

I de Skore Stove (Blom), 25, 130-31,
259n, 260n, 262n
Institute of Aesthetic Investigations,
University of Mexico, 227
Institute of Middle American
Research. *See* Middle American
Research Institute
Instituto Linguisto de Verano, 179
Inter-American Indian Institute,
Mexico, 166
International Congress of
Americanists, 83, 112, 122, 123,
134, 230-31
International Congress of
Archaeological and Ethnological
Sciences, 123
International Harvester Company, 19
In the Shadow of Volcanoes (Blom),
137
Iowa (finca), Mexico, 48, 57
Ixtinta, Guatemala, 106

Jacaltenango, Guatemala, 51
Jalapa, Mexico, 220
Jataté River, Mexico, 100, 173, 213, 217, 218
Jethá, Mexico, 105-6
Jethá River, Mexico, 155
Jordán, Mexico, 158
Jones, Gerald, 243
Journal of American Folk-Lore, 27
Joyce, Thomas Athol, 22, 33, 122
Judd, Neil, 38

Kabáh, Mexico, 118
Kantor, Gustavo, 89, 97-98, 100, 101, 109, 251-53 passim
Kaua, Mexico, 108, 111
Kaxil Uinic, Guatemala, 111
Keenagh, Peter, 126
Kidder, Alfred V., 120, 202
Knopf, Alfred A., Inc., 228
Knorosov, Yuri V., 226
Kramer, Gerhardt, 12-13, 72, 115, 116-17

Labná, Mexico, 76, 118
Labpak, Mexico, 118
Lacandón Indians, 101-5 passim, 147, 153, 171, 172-80 passim, 185, 188, 189, 190, 192, 194, 201, 211, 213-17, 218, 227, 228, 232, 254
Lacandón, Lake, Mexico, 217-18
Lacanjá, Mexico, 173, 185, 191
Lacanjá River, Mexico, 176, 190, 218
Lacantún River, Mexico, 219
La Crusada, Mexico, 55
ladinos: Blom on, 178
La Farge, John, 79
La Farge, Oliver: account of, 79-85; and Blom, 11-12, 45, 49-56 passim, 60, 61, 62, 66, 104, 131, 132, 225, 263n; mentioned, 71, 88, 90, 261n
La Honradez, Guatemala, 111
La Martinica (finca), Mexico, 103
Lanthrup, Charles, 78
Lapham, Ruth, 203
las Casas, Bartolomé de, 202, 228
La selva lacandona (Blom and Blom), x, 228-29
Las Tasas, Mexico, 157
Laughing Boy (La Farge), 83, 84
La Venta, Mexico, 46
Lens, Hans, 198, 228
Leonard, Juan, 225
Leyrer, Daniel, 115
Life magazine, 227
Lindbergh, Charles, 126
Linné, Sigvald, 210

Literary Guild, 84
López, Género, 224
López, Rogelio, 158, 159-60
Lothrop, Samuel, 151

McBryde, F. Webster: observations on Blom, 6, 9, 14, 16, 17, 92, 140, 259n; on 1928 expedition, 12, 90, 92, 96, 98-99, 102-7 passim, 251
McQuown, Norman, 203, 209
Macuspana, Mexico, 25, 51
Maler, Teobert, ix, 110, 118, 186
Malinche, 198
Martínez, Enrique, 158
Martínez Hernández, Juan. 5
Mason, Gregory, 126
Mattson, Albert, 210, 212
Maudslay, Alfred P.: Blom meets, 32; mentioned, 131, 226
May, Francisco, 107
May, Inez, 117
Maya and Their Neighbors, The, 137
Maya Architecture (Totten), 125
Maya Research, 135, 141, 235
Maya Society, 33, 41
Mayan Order, 219
Mayapán, Mexico, 119
Means, Philip A., 134
Mérida, Mexico, 5, 7
Merriam, John C., 43, 44
Merrill, R. H., 115
Mexico, ix, x, 3, 7, 13, 14, 17, 21, 25, 35, 41, 45, 46-59, 62, 63, 73, 79, 80, 85, 90, 130, 135, 137, 143, 144, 146, 147, 152, 153, 166, 192, 194-98 passim, 202, 207, 219, 224, 227, 237, 249; Department of Health and Public Welfare, 150, 173, 177. *See also individual place names*
Mexico City, Mexico, 7, 25, 26, 27-28, 30, 47, 53, 74, 80, 90, 148, 149, 150-52 passim, 162, 170, 174, 190, 191, 196, 200, 218, 229, 230, 233, 234, 256
Midameres Press, 136
Middle American Papers, 72
Middle American Research Institute, Tulane University: Blom at, 2, 9-11, 40-45, 62-87 passim, 114; Blom dismissed from, 139-41; building proposals, 128-29, 138-39, 262n; founded, 41-42; library, 73-75, 124-25; museum, 75-77; mentioned, 8, 12, 15, 61-67 passim, 142-43, 260n
Minatitlán, Mexico, 23

Mirador Pass, Mexico, 56
Mitchell, J. Leslie, 127
Mitchell-Hedges, Frederick, 126
Mitla, Mexico, 223
Möerner, Magnus, 205
Monte Albán, Mexico, 148, 189, 219, 221
Morley, Sylvanus G.: and Blom, 11, 12, 26-27, 30-31, 34-36, 40-41, 42, 44, 86, 125-26, 225, 259*n*, 262*n;* and Hermann Beyer, 86; mentioned, ix, 13, 38, 43, 118, 261*n*
Motozintla, Mexico, 167
Moxquivil, Mexico: Blom excavates at, 205, 219-21
Mulux, Mexico, 117
Muna, Mexico, 117
Murray, Stuart, 126
Musée de l'Homme, Paris, 210
Museum of Archaeology, Mexico, 174, 191
Museum of Arts and Crafts, Copenhagen, 19

Na Bolom, 200-236 passim
Nacajuca, Mexico, 55
Naranjo River, Mexico, 182
Narstkovo Museum, Prague, 224
National Geographic Society, 39
National Institute for Indian Affairs, Mexico, 153, 214
National Research Council, 115
Natural History, 169, 196
Newberry Library, Chicago, 203
Newcomb College, 121
New Orleans, La., 2-11 passim, 13, 14, 21, 43, 45, 60, 61, 62, 63, 74, 78, 81, 82, 84, 85, 87, 88, 89, 90, 104, 107, 112, 115, 120, 121-24 passim, 126, 128, 140, 144, 150, 151, 152, 196, 200, 203, 256
New Orleans Museum of Art, 76
New York, N.Y., 3, 7, 8, 9, 21, 33, 37, 41, 53, 64, 66, 71, 84, 130, 189, 203, 219
New York Times, The, 81
Nilsen, Nils, 153
Notes of Carnegie Institution of Washington, 227
Noyes, Ernest, 72
Nuevo Amatenango, Mexico, 167
Nuttall, Zelia: Blom and, 4, 22, 27, 31, 63

Oaxaca, Mexico, 110, 140, 148, 150, 152, 169, 201

Oberlaender Trust, 12
Ocosingo, Mexico: Blom visits, 24-25, 30, 55, 56, 91, 103-4, 148-49; mentioned, 35, 189, 218, 256
Ocotol, Laguna, Mexico, 218
Ojo de Agua, Mexico, 184
O'Keeffe, Georgia, 210
Olmec region, 46
onchocerciasis, 152, 166-69, 196-97
Ordenanza of 1524, 73-74
Otomí Indians, 147
Overseas Museum, Bremen, 210

Palenque, Mexico: Blom's visit to in 1922, 25, 130; Blom's visit to in 1925, 48-50; Blom's work at in 1922-23, 28-30, 31; night ride to, 57-58; mentioned, 26, 34, 35, 38, 56, 76, 187, 192, 203, 222, 226, 233
Pan American Highway, 200, 206, 221, 223, 233
Pan American Institute of Geography, 174
Paniagua, Flavio, 60, 75
Pantoja, Pablo, 115
Paricutín Volcano, Mexico, 153
Paris, France, 122, 203, 210
Parmenter, Ross, 233
Parra, José, 167
Paso y Troncoso, Francisco del, 224
Pateras Canyon, Mexico, 93
Peabody Museum of American Archaeology and Ethnology, Harvard University, 34, 42, 68, 76, 111
Perlas River, Mexico, 175, 183, 217
Pestac, Mexico, 110
Petén, the, Guatemala, 26, 35, 38, 39, 50, 91, 111, 256
Petén, Lake, Guatemala, 106, 107
Petersen and Company, H. C., 19
Peterson, Frederick, 217, 225
Piedras Negras, Guatemala, 182
Pitkin, Winifred, 212, 222
Poindexter, Miles, 136
Pontchartrain, Lake, La., 3, 121
Popul Vuh, 143, 144, 222
Porrúa bookstore, Mexico City, 74
Progreso, Mexico, 38
Proskouriakoff, Tatiana, 226
Puebla, Mexico, 150
Pueblo Bonito, New Mexico, 38
Puerto Barrios, Guatemala, 60
Puerto México, Mexico, 25, 80
Pulitzer Prize, 84

Quezaltenango, Guatemala, 60

Quiché language, 144
Quintana Roo, Mexico, 91, 107, 111, 256
Quinteros, Camp, Mexico, 192
Quiriguá, Guatemala, 60

Rare Americana (Gropp), 75
Rateike, Ernest, 58
Recess Club, New Orleans, 11
Red Tiger (Russell), 136
Reduction of Maya Dates, The (Spinden), 125
Reno, Nevada, 9
Ricketson, Oliver, Jr., 12, 34, 35, 37, 193
Ries, Maurice, 72, 124
Río, Antonio del, 203
Rockefeller, John D., Jr., 71
Rockefeller Foundation, 71, 75, 76-77
Roosevelt, Archibald B. ("Archie"), 8, 44, 78
Roosevelt, Mrs. Theodore, 78
Rosenwald Foundation, 71
Royal Geographical Society, Copenhagen, 153
Roys, Ralph, 72
Russell, Phillips, 136
Ruz Lhuillier, Alberto, 29

Sahagún, Bernardino de, 224
San Angel Paper Company, 174
San Antonio, Mexico, 156
San Antonio, Tex., 219
San Clemente, Guatemala, 111
San Cristóbal de las Casas, Mexico, ix, 56, 58-60, 75, 104, 140, 150, 180, 200, 201, 207, 208, 211, 215, 219, 220, 221, 226, 230, 233, 234, 235
San Juan, Mexico, 164
San Pedro, Mexico, 161-63
San Pedro Sula, Honduras, 120
San Quintín, Mexico, 101, 213-14, 217, 218, 254
Santa Clara, Mexico, 165
Santa Margarita Hacienda, Mexico, 24
Santo Domingo River, Mexico, 101-3 passim, 105
Santo Ton, Mexico, 48, 181, 183
Saturday Evening Post, 196
Saville, Marshall H., 33
Saxon, Lyle, 3, 196
Sayil, Mexico, 117, 118
Scribner's magazine, 83
Seville, Spain, 203
Shreveport, La., 14
Simojovel, Mexico, 25
Simulium ochraeum, 166

Sivaca, Mexico, 104
Smith, Ray, 209
Smith, Wilbur, 89
Smithsonian Institution, 38
Sociedad Mexicana de Antropología, 211
Société des Américanistes de Paris, 123
Sorbonne, Paris, 210
Soustelle, Jacques, 203, 210
Spinden, Herbert J., ix, 77, 125, 134, 223
Spratling, William, 3, 82, 152-53
Squier, Emma Lindsay, 136
Stacy-Judd, Robert B., 119
Stanford University, 209
Stephens, John Lloyd, 198
Stirling, Matthew W., 46, 219, 222, 227
Stockholm, Sweden, 205
Stone, Mrs. Doris, 10, 72
Stresser-Péan, Guy, 210
Stromsvik, Gustav, 120
Swedish Latin American Institute, 205

Tabasco, Mexico, 23, 33, 46, 54, 130, 153, 243
TACA (Transportes Aeros Centro-Americanos), 120
Tacaná Volcano, Guatemala, 92
Tampico, Mexico, 90
Tapachula, Mexico, 89, 91, 92, 111
Tapisalá River, Mexico, 167
Tata. *See* Hernández Guillermo, Lázaro
Tax, Sol, 209
Taylor, William P., 219, 221
Tecojá, Mexico, 53, 172, 181
Tecuanapa, Mexico, 23, 27
Tegucigalpa, Honduras, 120
Tehuantepec, Mexico, 152, 169
Tejeda, Antonio, 191
Tenam, Mexico, 48
Tenango, Mexico, 74
Tenejapa, Mexico, 54, 140
Tenosique, Mexico, 24, 160, 162, 165
Teocentli, 208
Teotihuacán, Mexico, 26, 91
Tepancuapán, Lake, Mexico, 110
Termer, Franz, 210
Texcoco, Mexico, 150
Thomas, Mary S. *See* Blom, Mary
Thompson, Edward H., 33, 76
Thompson, J. Eric S., 210
Thompson, J. H., 115
Tierra Zoque, Mexico, 198

Tikal, Guatemala, 106, 110-11, 113, 187, 222, 226, 227
Tila, Mexico, 25
Tlascala, lienzo of, 198-99, 224
Toniná, Mexico, 52, 110, 154, 182
Torre, Tomás de la, 197, 228
Tortuguero, Mexico: Blom on stela at, 26-27; mentioned, 35, 48
Toscano, Salvador, 197
Totten, George O., 125
Toynbee, Arnold, 210
Tozzer, Alfred M., 12, 27, 31, 34, 42, 63, 65, 78-79, 125, 126, 131, 136, 137, 151, 220, 222, 223, 259n, 262n
Trahan, Ray, 76
Traven, B., 233
Tres Zapotes, Mexico, 219
Tribes and Temples (Blom and La Farge), 5, 45, 48, 81-82, 83, 131-32, 260n
Tribuna Israelita, 196
Trifolio Seed Company, 173
Trinidad, Mexico, 181-82
Trocadero Museum, Paris, 122, 123
Trujillo, Gonzalo, 115
Tula, Mexico, 201
Tulane Codex, 74-75
Tulane University. *See* Middle American Research Institute
Tuxtla Gutiérrez, Mexico, 25, 148, 174, 190, 207
Tzajalob, Mexico, 110
Tzeltal Indians, 89, 157, 158, 177, 179

Uaxactún, Guatemala: Blom at, 12, 35, 37-38; mentioned, 31, 34, 38, 40, 41, 111, 188, 226
Ulúa River, Honduras, 120
Unión Fronteriza, Mexico, 167-69, 196
United Fruit Company, 137, 189
United States Government Printing Office, 11
United States Information Service, 233
University of California, 209, 213
University of Chicago, 203, 209, 213
University of Mexico, 213
University of Pennsylvania, 76, 182, 203, 222
University of Texas, 143
University of Texas Press, 228
Uspanapa River, Mexico, 23
Usumacinta River, Mexico-Guatemala, 166, 173, 219, 221
Uxmal, Mexico: Blom at, 11, 114-18, 136; mentioned, 76, 119, 127

Vaillant, George, 128
Vásquez, Alfredo Barrera, 194
Vega, Pedro, 156
Vega, Gregorio de la, 50-51
Veracruz, Mexico, 91
Veracruz State, Mexico, 23, 46, 130
Viking Fund, 217, 218-19
Villagra, Augustín, 191
Villahermosa, Mexico, 6, 55, 57
Vinton, La., 89
Vogt, Evon, 209

Wagner, Helmut, 210
Waldeck, Jean Frédéric, ix, 28-29, 203-4
Washington, D.C., 33, 44
Wauchope, Robert, 260n, 263n
Weiant, Clarence W., 217, 219-21
Weiditz, Cristoph, 227
Weyer, Edward, 210
Willard, T. A., 72, 119
Wissler, Clark, 128
World's Columbian Exposition (1893), Chicago, 76
World's Fair (1933), Chicago, 76, 114-15, 118-19, 128, 136

Yanhuitlán, Mexico, 233
Yanhuitlán, Codex of, 233
Yaxchilán, Guatemala, 91, 110, 149, 153, 165, 186-88, 222, 226, 261n
Yaxhá, Lake, Guatemala, 111
Yde, Jens, 119-20
Year Bearer's People, The (La Farge and Byers), 83
Yocotán language, 52
Yojoa, Lake, Honduras, 120
Yucatán, Mexico, 26, 33, 35, 36, 37, 83, 113, 114-17 passim, 119, 128, 136, 180, 199

Zaculeu, Guatemala, 60
Zamorra, José Domingo, 90, 92, 97-98, 251, 253
Zapaluta, Mexico, 56, 93
Zapata, Emiliano, 147
Zapotal, Mexico, 93-94, 95, 97-98 passim, 103, 112
Zemurray, Samuel, 10, 41, 62, 66, 69-70, 72, 131, 139
Zona Romano, Mexico, 198
Zurich, Switzerland, 147